INFORMATION **C**OMPUTER **C**OMMUNICATIONS
POLICY

19

GW01071975

INFORMATION
TECHNOLOGY
AND
NEW GROWTH
OPPORTUNITIES

ORGANISATION FOR ECONOMIC CO-OPERATION AND DEVELOPMENT

Pursuant to article 1 of the Convention signed in Paris on 14th December, 1960, and which came into force on 30th September, 1961, the Organisation for Economic Co-operation and Development (OECD) shall promote policies designed:

- to achieve the highest sustainable economic growth and employment and a rising standard of living in Member countries, while maintaining financial stability, and thus to contribute to the development of the world economy;
- to contribute to sound economic expansion in Member as well as non-member countries in the process of economic development; and
- to contribute to the expansion of world trade on a multilateral, non-discriminatory basis in accordance with international obligations.

The original Member countries of the OECD are Austria, Belgium, Canada, Denmark, France, the Federal Republic of Germany, Greece, Iceland, Ireland, Italy, Luxembourg, the Netherlands, Norway, Portugal, Spain, Sweden, Switzerland, Turkey, the United Kingdom and the United States. The following countries acceded subsequently through accession at the dates hereafter: Japan (28th April, 1964), Finland (28th January, 1969), Australia (7th June, 1971) and New Zealand (29th May, 1973).

The Socialist Federal Republic of Yugoslavia takes part in some of the work of the OECD (agreement of 28th October, 1961).

Publié en français sous le titre:

TECHNOLOGIES DE L'INFORMATION
ET LES NOUVEAUX DOMAINES DE CROISSANCE

This report was requested by the Information, Computer and Communications Policy Committee in 1986/87 and approved at its meeting on 23rd to 25th March 1988. The projet was directed by Dieter Kimbel of the Secretariat. The report is published under the responsibility of the Secretary General.

Also available

ICCP "INFORMATION, COMPUTER AND COMMUNICATION POLICY" Series

No. 18 – TELECOMMUNICATION NETWORK-BASED SERVICES: Implications for Telecommunication
Policy (May 1989)
(93 89 02 1) ISBN 92-64-13205-8 280 pages   £24.00 US$42.00 FF200.00 DM82.00

No. 17 – INTERNATIONALISATION OF SOFTWARE AN COMPUTER SERVICE (December 1988)
(93 88 06 1) ISBN 92-64-13129-9 210 pages   £14.50 US$26.50 FF120.00 DM52.00

No. 16 – NEW TELECOMMUNICATIONS SERVICES: Videotex Development Strategies (July 1988)
(93 88 03 1) ISBN 92-64-13106-X 80 pages   £9.00   US$16.50 FF75.00   DM33.00

No. 15 – SATELLITES AND FIBRE OPTICS: Competition and Complementary (July 1988)
(93 88 02 1) ISBN 92-64-13107-8 42 pages   £7.50   US$13.50 FF60.00   DM26.00

No. 14 – THE TELECOMMUNICATIONS INDUSTRY: The Challenges of Structural Change (June 1988)
(93 88 01 1) ISBN 92-64-13092-6 114 pages   £9.50   US$18.00 FF80.00   DM35.00

No. 13 – TRENDS OF CHANGE IN TELECOMMUNICATIONS POLICY (April 1987)
(93 87 02 1) ISBN 92-64-12940-5 354 pages   £12.50 US$25.00 FF125.00 DM56.00

No. 12 – INFORMATION TECHNOLOGY AND ECONOMIC PROSPECTS (April 1987)
(93 87 01 1) ISBN 92-64-12927-8 222 pages   £9.50   US$19.00 FF95.00   DM42.00

No. 11 – TRENDS IN THE INFORMATION ECONOMY (September 1986)
(93 86 03 1) ISBN 92-64-12861-1 42 pages   £4.00   US$8.00   FF40.00   DM19.00

No. 10 – COMPUTER-RELATED CRIME: ANALYSIS OF LEGAL POLICY (August 1986)
(93 86 01 1) ISBN 92-64-12852-2 72 pages   £4.00   US$8.00   FF40.00   DM20.00

No. 9 – SOFTWARE: AN EMERGING INDUSTRY (September 1985)
(93 85 04 1) ISBN 92-64-12755-0 204 pages   £12.00 US$24.00 FF120.00 DM53.00

No. 8 – AN EXPLORATION OF LEGAL ISSUES IN INFORMATION AND COMMUNICATION
TECHNOLOGIES (January 1984)
(93 83 03 1) ISBN 92-64-12527-2 136 pages   £7.00   US$14.00 FF70.00   DM31.00

No. 7 – MICRO-ELECTRONICS, ROBOTICS AND JOBS (May 1983)
(93 82 02 1) ISBN 92-64-12384-9 266 pages   £12.50 US$25.00 FF125.00 DM62.00

VENTURE CAPITAL IN INFORMATION TECHNOLOGY (March 1985)
(93 85 02 1) ISBN 92-64-12696-1 54 pages   £5.50   US$11.00 FF55.00   DM25.00

TELECOMMUNICATIONS. Pressures and Policies for Change (April 1983)
(93 83 02 1) ISBN 92-64-12428-4 142 pages   £6.90   US$14.00 FF69.00   DM34.00

GUIDELINES ON THE PROTECTION OF PRIVACY AND TRANSBORDER FLOWS OF PERSONAL
DATA (February 1981)
(93 81 01 1) ISBN 92-64-12155-2 42 pages   £3.00   US$6.00   FF30.00   DM13.00

To be published

No. 20 - SPECIAL PROGRAMMES FOR THE DEVELOPMENT OF INFORMATION TECHNOLOGY
IN R&D

Prices charged at the OECD Bookshop.

THE OECD CATALOGUE OF PUBLICATIONS and supplements will be sent free of charge
on request addressed either to OECD Publications Service,
2, rue André-Pascal, 75775 PARIS CEDEX 16, or to the OECD Distributor in your country.

TABLE OF CONTENTS

Part I

ANALYTICAL REPORT

SUMMARY 8

INTRODUCTION 9
  1. Background Information 9
  2. Objectives and Scope of the Project 9
  3. Methodology and Structure 9

Chapter I. THE PARAMETERS OF INFORMATION TECHNOLOGY (IT) 11
  1. Introduction 11
  2. Technical Definition and Economic Scope of IT 11

Chapter II. THE IT GROWTH POTENTIAL 13
  1. Technological Change and Economic Growth: A Simplified Concept 13
  2. IT-induced Growth Incentives and Growth Generating Mechanisms 14
  3. The Drive Towards Qualitative Growth 16
  4. Quantitative Growth – the Example of Telecommunication Networks and
    Services 17

Chapter III. FORECAST OF IT RELATED GROWTH 19
  1. IT-induced Growth Industries and World Market Forecasts 19
  2. Expected IT-related Growth Areas and their Economic Significance 22
    a) Intermediate and Final Demand of Industry 24
    b) Government Purchases 27
    c) Private Household Demand 28
    d) Infrastructure Investment 30

Chapter IV. IT: THE HIGH TECHNOLOGY SECTOR MYTH AND THE CHANGING
    ROLE OF MANUFACTURING AND SERVICES 34

Chapter V. CONSTRAINTS, BOTTLENECKS AND POLICY IMPLICATIONS . . . 37

Chapter VI. POLICY CONSIDERATIONS 39

Chapter VII. CHANGE IN POLICY FOCUS AND FUTURE WORK 44

BIBLIOGRAPHY 46

Part II

RESEARCH PAPERS

1. POTENTIAL OF INFORMATION TECHNOLOGY AND ECONOMIC
   GROWTH IN JAPAN 49
   (Ken-ichi Imai)

2. NEW INFORMATION TECHNOLOGY AND INDUSTRIAL
   ORGANISATION 81
   (Cristiano Antonelli)

3. ELECTRONIC AND COMPUTER AIDED PUBLISHING:
   OPPORTUNITIES AND CONSTRAINTS 101
   (Richard J. Solomon)

4. POLICY OPTIONS FOR PROMOTING GROWTH THROUGH
   INFORMATION TECHNOLOGY 133
   (Eric Arnold and Ken Guy)

Part I

ANALYTICAL REPORT

SUMMARY

This report investigates the growth propelling forces and the growth areas likely to emerge over the coming 10-15 years from broader production and use of information, information technology (IT) based systems, and supporting services such as software tools.

The aim is to make decision makers aware of the salient medium-term socio-economic potential of broader use of information and IT.

The report confirms the increasing trend towards integration and interconnecting of IT equipment with telecommunications to build networks. More importantly, as IT equipment is physically interconnected to build new electronics based infrastructures, new forms of information flows (allowing instant interaction between consumers, producers, societal needs and public and private response) become economically feasible and attractive, opening new opportunities for customisation in the production and delivery of goods and services.

The characteristics of IT – miniaturisation, improvement of quality and adding of "intelligence" to goods and services, rapidly decreasing costs both in the equipment and in the processing of information and the "network feature" – trigger a number of growth propelling incentives hitherto not available.

These opportunities provide a central role in the transition from quantitative to qualitative growth in the production of goods and services. At the macrolevel, with the possibility to "optimise" factor inputs to meet real customer needs, IT ultimately may lead to a positive technology paradigm, with economic growth predominantly linked to the extended use of human intelligence and creativity and much less to increased consumption of scarce natural resources.

Quantitative growth will occur from increased expenditure and demand for high technology R & D, the production and use of IT-based goods and services, and the expansion of information and knowledge sold in the market place. Future growth areas to be induced by broader IT production and use will be nurtured from demand of industry, government purchases, private households and the investment in new infrastructures.

The report argues that the high technology sector, however defined, produces only a small fraction of total output; on its own it will have only a limited impact on overall performance and standards of living. IT induced growth depends mainly on the capacity to disperse IT capabilities across a broad range of economic activity.

Since there is nothing automatic or inevitable about the response of the market to the opportunities of emerging IT trends, there is a danger that the adjustment to IT will be supplier driven and piecemeal with little integration of IT into the broader social and economic framework. The result may be lost growth opportunities on the manufacturing side and considerable welfare losses to the world economy.

To ease the exploitation of the IT related potential may require more policy attention to the "network" aspects of information and IT usage both within and across organisations.

INTRODUCTION

1. Background Information

In the context of the CICCP project Information Technology and Economic Prospects *(ICCP Report No. 12)*, an analytical framework has been developed to investigate more systematically the relationships between information and communication technologies and IT-based innovations and their importance for output growth, employment and trade in the medium term future, i.e. the next 15 years. Among other findings, the project shows that the fears of mass unemployment through the introduction of "unmanned offices" and computer-robot controlled factories have been unjustified. On the contrary, IT holds great growth potential for OECD countries. IT-based innovations can be expected to generate a new wave of growth in advanced industrialised countries.

2. Objectives and Scope of the Project

This report considers the propelling forces and the growth areas likely to be induced or triggered by the increased production and use of information and information technologies. It therefore focusses on the product and process innovation potential of IT at the firm and sector level, and likely IT-related applications in industry, homes and governments. The study investigates both direct and indirect implications of the expected broader production and use of information and IT-based components, systems and services. It also considers their synergistic effects on the nature of advanced industrial societies.

Given the statistical and conceptual difficulties in measuring IT-based goods and service production, the report is not concerned with forecasting technology determined futures or with spotting future markets. The aim is rather to identify the propelling forces likely to emerge and to help decision makers to be aware of the salient socio-economic potential of emerging broader IT diffusion.

Always, the purpose is to stimulate thought, to provoke discussion and to open up further debate and study.

3. Methodology and Structure

This analytical summary on the growth dynamics, emerging growth areas and the discussion of policies and strategies is based on four background papers issued for this project. Additional material has been used to the extent as it assisted in developing a conclusive common perspective.

The research papers commissioned addressed the following themes:

- Potential of Information Technology and Economic Growth in Japan and Associate Policy Problems by Ken-ichi Imai, Hitotsubashi University, Tokyo, Japan.
- New Information Technology and Industrial Organisation: Experiences and Trends in Italy by Chistiano Antonelli, Politecnico di Milano, Milan, Italy.
- Electronic and Computer-aided Publishing: Opportunities and Constraints by Richard J. Solomon, MIT, Cambridge, Mass., United States.
- Policy Options for Promoting Growth through Information Technology by Eric Arnold and Ken Guy, SPRU, University of Sussex, Brighton, Sussex, United Kingdom.

Chapter I defines IT and tries to show its importance in a broader economic context.

Chapter II points to IT-related growth propelling forces and shows the growth relationships of R&D expenditure, IT inventions and IT diffusion. It also includes an analytical attempt to highlight the quantitative and qualitative nature of growth to be expected from broader IT use.

Chapter III presents results of modelled IT induced growth in selected countries and world market forecasts on IT production and the use of information. This macroeconomic growth is then broken down into likely emerging growth areas.

Chapters IV and V report on the structural changes occurring in OECD economies and point to constraints to broader IT diffusion.

Chapter VI presents some policies and policy tools for facilitating the diffusion of the potential of information resources and information technologies.

Chapter VII proposes directions for future work in this area.

Chapter I

THE PARAMETERS OF INFORMATION TECHNOLOGY

1. Introduction

Information Technology (IT) occupies an important place on the policy agenda of most industrialised countries. Emerging in large part from microelectronics, IT has become a powerful agent for economic development through products and service industries generated directly and indirectly, and through transformations permitted nationally at the firm, industry and branch level and internationally through the changing pattern of comparative cost structures and trade flows.

IT now comprises a major growing branch of economic activity in its own right, which in some countries already outstrips traditional industrial activities in terms of value added and new job opportunities offered. It also generates a flow of product and process innovations in user industries. IT encompasses both productivity enhancing and growth promoting innovations which enable new types of economic activity. This potential is not limited to the production of IT. The innovation potential has a qualitative dimension which rests on the capabilities and functions which can be performed with IT, namely to process, store, manipulate and disseminate large quantities of information at decreasing costs.

2. Technical Definition and Scope of IT

The term "information technology" is used in this paper to cover all technologies used in the collection, storing, processing and transmission of information, including voice, data and images. This includes microelectronics and opto-electronics technologies and other technologies dependent on them.

With the invention of the microprocessor in the early 70s and subsequent progress in miniaturisation, the production and use of IT led to a wide range of new goods and improved existing goods and services by extending their capabilities and adding "intelligence" allowing greater functionality and ease of use. In essence, this development focussed on individual stand alone equipment; for example, personal computers (PCs), word processors, industrial robots and numerically controlled machine tools.

Recent developments show an increasing trend towards integrating and interconnecting IT with telecommunications to build networks. In the office, telephones, facsimile machines, PCs, text and data processing equipment are being integrated into network systems. In the factory, the integration and interconnection of robots, machine tools and computer-aided design (CAD) will gradually allow the smooth interlocking of what are now discrete production phases – design, production planning, machining and assembling, inventory and stock control – and will ultimately allow computer controlled manufacturing.

These developments in the office and the factory are not independent. Information technology advances are leading to the integration of production activities with organisational and management processes which are also being radically changed by IT. Eventually, this tendency may integrate all these activities into a network system.

There are perhaps four dimensions to the unifying capacity of IT:

i) The first dimension emphazises the process innovation potential (particularly in productivity enhancement) of microelectronics and miniaturisation, as is evident in factory and office automation. It is also concerned with embedding IT-based techniques into existing products and processes to create new value added (e.g. microelectronics in automobiles);

ii) The second dimension regards IT industries as major new branches of the economy, leading, through new products, services and activities, to new job and income creating opportunities and thus macro-economic growth;

iii) The third dimension stresses the importance of information as a new resource, leading to profound shifts in production and fundamental restructuring of economic activity (Information Economy);

iv) The fourth dimension focusses on IT and information as a new means of organising and interlinking the production and consumption processes of the economy (techno-economic paradigm shift) and leading to new synergies as IT is blended with other emerging technologies for example advanced materials.

None of these captures as a single concept the IT complex, but together they build a concept broad enough to:

- Perceive the direct growth of IT related goods, services and systems and related industries;
- Capture the multiplier effects (price, income, capacity) and IT knock-on effects across economies.

Chapter II

THE IT GROWTH POTENTIAL

1. Technological Change and Economic Growth: A Simplified Concept

The process of technological change has traditionally been presented as one which starts with invention, proceeds to innovation and then to diffusion of the innovation. Research has been seen as the seminal part of the process; development and commercial activities as of secondary importance. The process has also been viewed as linear in that it is conceived as necessarily starting with research and invention, leading in an orderly manner to widespread adoption of the innovation and consequent economic impact. In fact, the process of technological change is redolent with uncertainty and irregularity; for example, the inadequacy of an invention may become apparent only during diffusion of the innovation, providing essential information for research for Mark II of a product.

What is happening in all parts of the innovative process is that information is being collected and assembled; even research is really an information collecting rather than an information creating procedure. The essence of an innovation is information arranged in a pattern that has not previously existed. Most of the required information tends to come not from research at all, but from the systems which must develop, produce, market and – above all – use the innovation. This is the case with all innovations, but perhaps particularly with those whose applications require extensive interaction with users, innovations which cannot simply be plugged in or tacked on to an existing system. Innovation in information technology is perhaps the sublime example of interaction which must be extensive and intimate if potential widespread economic benefit is to be realised.

The link between R & D and growth is considerably weaker, in as much as it is measurable at all, than the link between diffusion and growth. This does not mean R & D expenditure should be ignored: it is indeed a vital input into the generation of new products embodying advances at a later stage.

To penetrate the complex area of technological change, and its economic implications, it is useful to introduce by means of illustration a further simplification regarding the quantitative impacts of IT and IT diffusion on the economy in terms of orders of magnitude.

The attached graphic, Microelectronics, IT and the Economy, attempts to illustrate the growth relationships involved.

The high technology sector, accordingly, provides only a small contribution to total output, and on its own has limited impact on productivity and competitiveness and standards of living. Its real impact stems from the capacity to deploy technical capabilities across all economic and industrial activities.

Figure 1. **MICROELECTRONICS, IT AND THE ECONOMY**

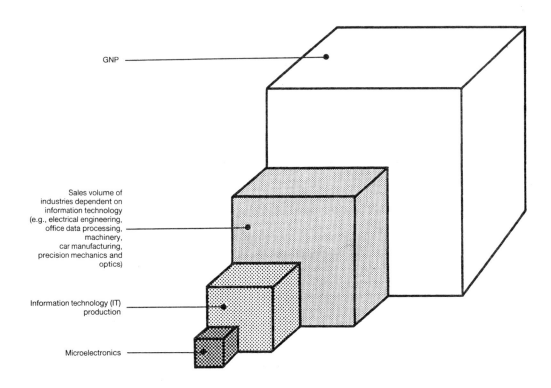

Source: Adapted from "Microelectronics and the Economy" in *World Electronics, Creating the Environment for Growth,* presented by Uwe Thomas at the Financial Times conference, London, 1985.

2. IT-induced Growth Incentives and Growth Generating Mechanisms

The dominant characteristics of IT – miniaturisation, improvement of quality and adding of "intelligence" to goods, services and processes, rapidly decreasing costs and the "network feature" – increasingly promise to trigger a number of growth mechanisms hitherto not available. At least six IT related incentives are operating and can be identified as propelling forces for IT production and use.

i) Physically, IT is becoming smaller, faster and cheaper. Speed enhances the capacity to store and forward information and miniaturisation reduces the size of components. As miniaturisation continues, IT can be more readily incorporated in consumer and investment goods. Fierce competition in IT together with learning economies ensure that prices fall as costs fall. The lowering of the cost/performance ratio of these products is one of the determinants of their broader application;

14

ii)   IT can increase *productivity* (in the classical sense) by making better use of input factors (capital, labour, buildings, location, time, etc);

iii) IT can increase *flexibility* as production lines in factories come to be equipped with programmable machinery so that small batch production and "customised production" become not only technically possible, but economically viable;

iv)   IT incorporated in products can provide higher *quality* and the adding of intelligence increases usefulness and consumer appeal;

v)   IT can *extend the "limits to growth"*, helping to overcome what some believe to be long-term limits imposed by scarcity of natural resources (fossil energy and other extractive materials);

vi)   In addition, as various IT-based equipment is physically interconnected to build networks, information flow between users, manufacturers and equipment makers is improved and extensive exchange of information with other related activities is rendered possible. This networking leads to a wider creation of knowledge and know-how in the economy, encouraging numerous small innovations to be made in a cumulative fashion.

Again, in a simplified manner, Figure 2 attempts to illustrate networking occurring at various levels. This is a new type of intelligent infrastructure built around electronics and telecommunications technologies and interlinking, in real time, consumers and producers.

Figure 2.   **INTEGRATION AND NETWORKING TO BRIDGE SUPPLY AND DEMAND**

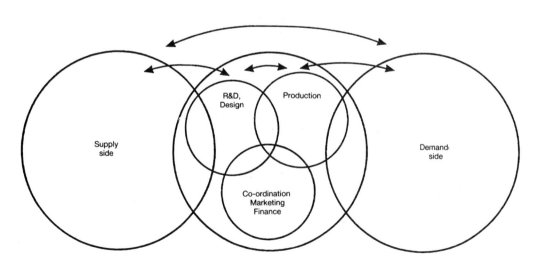

Source: D. Kimbel, "IT-Diffusion, Changing Industrial Structures and Policy Implications", Korean Advanced Institute for Science and Technology (KAIST), Seoul, 1987.

15

3. The Drive towards Qualitative Growth

The characteristics of IT provide a central role in the transition from quantitative to qualitative growth in the production of goods and services. Under the heading of qualitative growth one may include both improvements in quality of the production system (including cost efficiency, quality of work environment) as well as the impact on the external environment and improvements in the price-performance ratio as perceived by the consumer of the IT-based goods and services.

Antonelli's paper, describes in considerable detail how IT has been used in some segments of Italian industry to develop and restructure the procurement, manufacturing and marketing function of individual firms. He concludes that the introduction of new communication intensive techniques in manufacturing in Northern Italy has led to a reduction of the traditional gap between rigid mass production with large economies of scale and flexible craft production characterised by small production units. On the purchasing and marketing side the quality of goods and services received and provided appears to have improved. Higher quality standards perceived by customers have provided a basis for higher sustainable prices and increased purchases.

In addition, Antonelli found that IT has been adopted by firms as a means to cope with growing economic problems caused by slow market growth and increased competition.

It appears that important aspects of these observations from Northern Italy can be generalised to other countries and to other industries and economic sectors. The stagnation of volume growth in many product markets since the mid 1970s has caused overcapacity and intense competition in many industries. In addition to forcing companies to try to rationalise their operation to cut costs, there has been a growing incentive for producers to try to differentiate their products from those of their competitors. Thus there has been a powerful drive among suppliers to customise their products in terms of product design, delivery schedules, financing arrangements etc. Interdependencies among producing firms have tended to propagate the trend towards customisation through the entire production system. The final consumers have in many cases reacted favourably to the growing sensitivity among producers to the needs of individual consumers. Frequently there may have been a latent demand for more differentiated product offerings which was not taken seriously by producers as long as their markets showed sufficient volume growth.

Computer-based production technology has already eliminated dangerous, dirty and monotonous jobs often performed in hot and hazardous environments (e.g. robots used in steel foundries, mining, deep sea exploration, nuclear plants, etc). Similarly, IT has an important role in the monitoring of environmental quality and control of processes, including automobile engines and industrial processes, to reduce pollution.

On the macro-economic level, even more extensive qualitative improvements in standards of living may occur once sophisticated IT networks become more common and widespread. The almost instant interaction between consumers, producers, societal needs and public and private response could lead to a new, more "creative" world. A transition to more customised goods and services, and subsequently, to increased standards of living (in its broadest sense) could emerge. Furthermore, electronics-based flexible production systems may not only encourage small batch, customised production, they may also increase the demand for highly skilled craftsmen. The second industrial revolution, characterised by mass production and mass marketing, largely discarded craftsmanship through standardization and mass marketing of goods and services. With networking to evaluate ultimately the customer's real needs and requirements, and with IT-based reprogrammable production equipment, customisation becomes possible. Smaller production units as a result of

16

reprogrammable machinery (the capital saving potential of IT) producing small batches economically may generate new forms of creativity and customisation.

Since IT networks might link producers and customers more directly (see Figure 2), there is an increasing potential to meet more closely the consumer's true needs. The principle of producing the necessary volume of goods and services just in time (at the firm level a major imperative to increase capital and labour productivity) may lead at the macro-economic level to new forms of dynamic resource allocations and more steady economic development trajectories.

Economies based on real time network infrastructures would probably suffer less from "information deficiencies", generally the cause and consequence of "overproduction", overcapacities, and thus unstable courses of economic development.

Ultimately, with the possibility to "optimise" factor inputs to meet real customer needs, IT may lead to a positive technology paradigm, with economic growth predominately linked to the extended use of human intelligence and creativity, and much less to increased consumption of scarce natural resources.

The potential of IT to stimulate innovation and creativity is a major theme in Imai's paper, but touched upon also in the other papers. The basis for this relation between IT and innovation is the fact that IT networks shorten the lead times in information flows as well as in material flows, with the effect of dramatically shortening the time it takes for a producer to get feedback from customers or suppliers in response to changes he makes in product or production processes. The producer may make further rapid changes in response to this feedback. IT is providing the means for a continuous shortening of the time required to close feedback loops. Each producer is, however, linked with customers and suppliers of goods and services through a large number of such feedback loops, some naturally more important to innovation than others. The economy as a whole may thus be viewed as a myriad of feedback loops made up of flows of material, money and information, intertwined with each other. Changes in one part of the system frequently necessitate adjustments in other parts; sometimes of a purely quantitative nature, in other cases requiring or stimulating qualitative adjustments ranging from incremental to radical innovations, depending on the nature of the adjustments that need to be made. The more rapidly these adjustments can be made, the more innovative the economy will be.

There is thus a close correspondence between widespread diffusion of IT and the innovating capacity of the economy. The generally recognised phenomena of shortening product cycles in most industries gives strong support to this interpretation.

4. Quantitative Growth – the Example of Telecommunications Networks and Services

Quantitative growth will occur from increased expenditures for high technology R&D and production and use of IT-based goods and services. Growth will also occur from the expansion of information and knowledge sold in the market place. This includes the growing use of information and data in research, the production and delivery of goods and services and marketed information (entertainment, leisure, cultural services) in the home.

Another source of quantitative growth will be from investment in new telecommunications networks. As various IT-based goods and services are interconnected through communication networks, all investment in components, including terminals, transmission equipment (e.g. cable, fibre optics and satellite), switching equipment and the software to operate such electronic infrastructures will create direct and indirect long-term growth incentives. Integrated services digital networks (ISDNs), for example, may lead to a broad range of new personal and business services. Some of these emerging services are inputs in the design of the new opto/microelectronics-based networks, others will be delivered on such networks. Such "enhanced" or "value-added services" are becoming technically feasible as advanced computer/telecommunications systems emerge. They allow users to undertake a much broader set of customer data or service activities without significant cost increases through allocating equipment, development and software costs over a broader base of applications (economies of scope). This potential growth category could comprise:

- A wide range of data bank services of a professional and private nature;
- New financial services (electronic funds and 'smart' charge cards in electronic payment systems);
- Entertainment, leisure and cultural services;
- Health care services;
- Educational services.

These expected advanced and less regulated network facilities and services hold a large indirect growth potential for upstream and downstream industries with possibly more significant investment multiplier effects than those to be derived from investments in the networks themselves. The transmission of sports events on Pay-TV, cable and direct satellite broadcasting systems and spill-over effects to the sports equipment industry, including the shoe and textile sector is a good example.

Chapter III

FORECAST OF IT RELATED GROWTH

1. IT-induced Growth Industries and World Market Forecasts

These background observations lead to the second set of questions to be addressed in this project. It is accepted that the IT sector will continue to grow rapidly. This will stimulate growth in other sectors of the economy. Which areas, how much growth and with what implications?

The ICCP report *Information Technology and Economic Prospects* has already revealed the growth in information processing in the activities of the firm and the role of IT-based change in such functions. This suggests that the future pattern of change may be different from that in the past. The firm of the future is prototyped as an information organism, less concerned with materials than with the processing, collection and transmission of information. As goods and services become more custom tailored and international, the role of information in development, design, insurance, transportation and finance grows. As a consequence, production costs and the factor input mix are changing in favour of information based activities and related equipment and services.

The trend towards more custom tailored production is increasing industry's demand for flexible, programmable production equipment. This has a number of basic implications: demand for market and economic information to monitor changes in consumer patterns is increasing; investment expenditure in traditional plant equipment and inventories is tending to decrease; investment in "soft" capital (software, know-how) to operate the computer equipment is increasing. The role of human capital (highly skilled or re-trained manpower, for example) is gaining in importance.

It is extremely difficult to track the significance of these phenomena on the changing character of the world economy and to link them to IT developments revealed in published statistical data.

Recent ICCP work has attempted to surmount these difficulties and the analysis shows that the contribution of the production of IT-related goods and services has grown everywhere over the period 1970-1980 (see Table 1).

Given the difficulties when quantifying the contributions of the IT-complex to current GDP, the estimations of its future contribution to total output and employment growth are obviously to be made with even greater care. The forecasts for the three basic IT segments (IT hardware, software and telecommunications) presented in Table 2 are based on IT industry projections for the period 1985 to 1995.

Similar results have been generated in a quantitative assessment of the growth of the Japanese information industry for the decade to come. The MITI report on IT for the year 2000 is not based on a mere linear projection of current growth in the segments, but uses a

Table 1. **Production of IT-based goods and services as a percentage of gross domestic product in selected OECD countries**

	1970			1980		
	IT-based goods as % of GDP	IT-based services %	Total %	IT-based goods %	IT-based services %	Total %
Belgium[1]	1.8	12.8	14.6	1.8	16.1	17.9
Finland	3.4	12.9	16.4	4.2	16.8	21.0
France	2.7	15.8	18.5	2.7	16.4	19.1
Germany[2]			14.8			16.9
Japan	1.7	6.7	8.4	7.3	14.5	18.8
Sweden	1.8	15.7	16.9	2.4	16.7	19.1
United Kingdom[3]	3.5	19.6	23.1	3.7	22.2	25.9
United States[4]	2.2	17.4	19.6	3.5	20.8	23.8

1. Belgium, 1975,1985.
2. Data for Germany calculated by DIW Berlin.
3. United Kingdom, 1972, 1980.
4. United States, 1972,1980. Data for the United States prepared by M. Rubin, 1987. These data have a different statistical base and are not comparable directly with results for other countries in this table.
Source: Adapted from *OECD/ICCP Report No. 11*, "Trends in the Information Economy", Paris, 1986.

Table 2. **Worldwide growth estimates for marketed production of IT-hardware, software and telecommunications equipment over the period 1985-1995**

Billion US dollars at 1985 exchange rates

	1985	1986	1990	1995	Av. Annual Growth Rate
IT Hardware[1]	200	225	380	730	12 %
Software[2]	70	84	175	400	20 %
Telecommunications[3]	80	85	108	145	6 %
Total	350	394	663	1 275	

1. IT-hardware is defined so as to comprise electronics, all kinds of computers, office automation (including text and data processing machines) and private telecommunication equipment (including telex, telefax, modems, etc.). The figures also include user expenditures associated with the introduction of IT.
2. Software and services include value added networks and services and maintenance.
3. Telecommunications refers to switching and transmission equipment owned and operated by telecommunication administrations and Recognised Private Operating Agencies (RPOA).
Source: OECD Secretariat estimates based on IT industry sources.

complex model including targetted policy objectives for the Japanese economy of the year 2000.

It predicts that while sectors other than the information industry are expected to expand domestic production by 1.8 times, the electronics industry will expand 8.3 times, the telecommunications industry 3.7 times and the information services industry will expand 12.9 times (see Table 3). Yet, the major contribution of IT is not derived from the growth of the IT industry itself, but will be based on the diffusion and use of IT in the other sectors of the economy. Growth will occur as IT is used to revitalise agriculture, manufacture and service

ERRATUM

INFORMATION, COMPUTER, COMMUNICATIONS POLICY
19
INFORMATION TECHNOLOGY AND NEW GROWTH OPPORTUNITIES

(93 88 05 1) ISBN 92-64-13102-7

The following tables cancel and replace Table 3 (page 21) and Table 1 (page 54)

Table 3. **Semi-macro prediction of Japan's information industry,
4 Sectors input-output table of 1984 and 2000[1]**

From \ To	Electronics	Telecommu- nications	Information Service	Other Industries	Sub- Total	Final Demand	Domestic Production
Electronics[2]	8.0	0.6	0.3	1.5	10.5	17.2	27.7
	40.7	3.6	8.5	27.4	80.2	148.7	228.9
	(5.1)	(6.0)	(28.3)	(18.3)	(7.6)	(8.6)	(8.3)
Telecommu- nications[3]	0.2	0.07	0.04	3.1	3.4	1.5	5.0
	1.7	0.4	0.8	4.8	7.6	10.9	18.5
	(8.5)	(5.7)	(20.0)	(1.5)	(2.2)	(7.3)	(3.7)
Information Services[4]	0.2	0.02	0.1	2.7	3.0	0.02	3.0
	3.6	0.2	3.0	11.0	17.7	20.9	38.6
	(18.0)	(10.0)	(30.0)	(4.1)	(5.9)	(1 045.0)	(12.9)
Other Industries	10.6	0.4	0.7	306.7	318.4	288.1	606.5
	132.3	0.7	4.9	461.0	598.8	516.9	1 115.8
	(12.5)	(1.8)	(7.0)	(1.5)	(1.9)	(1.8)	(1.8)
Sub Total	19.0	1.1	1.2	314.0	335.3	306.9	642.2
	178.4	4.8	17.1	504.1	704.4	697.4	1 401.8
	(9.4)	(4.4)	(14.3)	(1.6)	(2.1)	(2.3)	(2.2)
Value Added	8.7	3.8	1.8	292.5	306.9		
	50.5	13.7	21.5	611.7	697.4		
	(5.8)	(3.6)	(11.9)	(2.1)	(2.3)		
Domestic Production	27.7	5.0	3.0	606.5	642.2		
	228.9	18.5	38.6	1 115.8	1 401.8		
	(8.3)	(3.7)	(12.9)	(1.8)	(2.2)		

1. Upper figures: 1984; lower figures: 2000; figures into brackets: 2000/1984.
2. Computer and its ancillary apparatus, other associated electronic equipment, electron tubes, semiconductor devices/IC, communication and related equipment, measuring instruments, radio and television receivers, acoustics.
3. Telecommunications industries of the first kind like NTT and KDD. Services by the second kind are included in Information Service.
4. Information processing, software and information supply service.
Source: The *Report of MITI's Special Committee of the Industrial Structure Council, 1987/6.*

Table 1. **Semi-macro prediction of Japan's information industry,**
4 Sectors input-output table of 1984 and 2000[1]

From \ To	Electronics	Telecommu-nications	Information Service	Other Industries	Sub-Total	Final Demand	Domestic Production
Electronics[2]	8.0	0.6	0.3	1.5	10.5	17.2	27.7
	40.7	3.6	8.5	27.4	80.2	148.7	228.9
	(5.1)	(6.0)	(28.3)	(18.3)	(7.6)	(8.6)	(8.3)
Telecommu-nications[3]	0.2	0.07	0.04	3.1	3.4	1.5	5.0
	1.7	0.4	0.8	4.8	7.6	10.9	18.5
	(8.5)	(5.7)	(20.0)	(1.5)	(2.2)	(7.3)	(3.7)
Information Services[4]	0.2	0.02	0.1	2.7	3.0	0.02	3.0
	3.6	0.2	3.0	11.0	17.7	20.9	38.6
	(18.0)	(10.0)	(30.0)	(4.1)	(5.9)	(1 045.0)	(12.9)
Other Industries	10.6	0.4	0.7	306.7	318.4	288.1	606.5
	132.3	0.7	4.9	461.0	598.8	516.9	1 115.8
	(12.5)	(1.8)	(7.0)	(1.5)	(1.9)	(1.8)	(1.8)
Sub Total	19.0	1.1	1.2	314.0	335.3	306.9	642.2
	178.4	4.8	17.1	504.1	704.1	697.4	1 401.8
	(9.4)	(4.4)	(14.3)	(1.6)	(2.1)	(2.3)	(2.2)
Value Added	8.7	3.8	1.8	292.5	306.9		
	50.5	13.7	21.5	611.7	697.4		
	(5.8)	(3.6)	(11.9)	(2.1)	(2.3)		
Domestic Production	27.7	5.0	3.0	606.5	642.2		
	228.9	18.5	38.6	1 115.8	1 401.8		
	(8.3)	(3.7)	(12.9)	(1.8)	(2.2)		

1. Upper figures: 1984; lower figures: 2000; figures into brackets: 2000/1984.
2. Computer and its ancillary apparatus, other associated electronic equipment, electron tubes, semiconductor devices/IC, communication and related equipment, measuring instruments, radio and television receivers, acoustics.
3. Telecommunications industries of the first kind like NTT and KDD. Services by the second kind are included in Information Service.
4. Information processing, software and information supply service.
Source: The *Report of MITI's Special Committee of the Industrial Structure Council, 1987/6.*

Table 3. **Semi-macro prediction of Japan's information industry, 4 Sectors input-output table of 1984 and 2000[1]**

To \ Firm	Electronics	Telecommu- nications	Information Service	Other Industries	Sub Total	Final Demand	Domestic Production
Electronics[2]	8.0	0.6	0.3	1.5	10.5	17.2	27.7
	40.7	3.6	8.5	27.4	80.2	148.7	228.9
	(5.1)	(6.0)	(28.3)	(18.3)	(7.6)	(8.6)	(8.3)
Telecommun- ications[3]	0.2	0.07	0.04	3.1	3.4	1.5	5.0
	1.7	0.4	0.8	4.8	7.6	10.9	18.5
	(8.5)	(5.7)	(20.0)	(1.5)	(2.2)	(7.3)	(3.7)
Information Services[4]	0.2	0.02	0.1	2.7	3.0	0.02	3.0
	3.6	0.2	3.0	11.0	17.7	20.9	38.6
	(18.0)	(10.0)	(30.0)	(4.1)	(5.9)	(1 045.0)	(12.9)
Other Industries	10.6	0.4	0.7	30.7	31.8	288.1	606.5
	132.3	0.7	4.9	461.0	598.8	516.9	1 115.8
	(12.5)	(1.8)	(7.0)	(15.0)	(18.8)	(1.8)	(1.8)
Sub Total	19.0	1.1	1.2	314.0	335.3	306.9	642.2
	178.4	4.8	17.1	504.1	704.4	697.4	1 401.8
	(9.4)	(4.4)	(14.3)	(1.6)	(2.1)	(2.3)	(2.2)
Value Added	8.7	3.8	1.8	292.5	306.9		
	50.5	13.7	21.5	611.7	697.4		
	(5.8)	(3.6)	(11.9)	(2.1)	(2.3)		
Domestic Production	27.7	5.0	3.0	606.5	642.2		
	228.9	18.5	38.6	1 115.8	1 401.8		
	(8.3)	(3.7)	(12.9)	(1.8)	(2.2)		

1. Upper figures: 1984; lower figures: 2000; figures into brackets: 2000/1984.
2. Computer and its ancillary apparatus, other associated electronic equipment, electron tubes, semiconductor devices/IC, communication and related equipment, measuring instruments, radio and television receivers, acoustics.
3. Telecommunications industries of the first kind like NTT and KDD. Services by the second kind are included in Information Service.
4. Information processing, software and information supply service.
Source: The *Report of MITI's Special Committee of the Industrial Structure Council, 1987/6.*

sector activities and through the new activities and employment opportunities resulting from the "networking" of the Japanese economy.

K. Imai expects that such networking will encourage a continuous stream of further innovations and will lead to the "creation of information" as a new resource for growth. Included in this resource are both the findings of research and science and specialised information about the socio-economic environment as a major tool for decision making and action, and thus the driving force of all economic activities (see Table 4).

This growth in demand for information services is not limited to Japan. Table 5 shows recent growth in demand in other developed countries for information from electronic data bases.

This interaction of various actors and the "creation of information" is not yet obvious as a pronounced market activity. The table on Marketed Information may, however, serve as a proxy to provide a quantitative feel for the emerging importance of this sector of the economy. The specialised information industry in the OECD area is currently composed of approximately 800 scientific and technical and 1 000 economic, on-line databases. They are

Table 4. **Forecast of information service demands in Japan by subsectors**

Billion yen

	1984 (A)	2000 (B)	(B)/(A)
Information Processing	631	4 570	7.2
Software	512	7 867	15.4
Information Supply Services	97	3 386	34.9
Export	5	1 761	352.2
Import	23	3 024	131.5

Source: K. Imai (Background Paper).

estimated to represent some 10 per cent of the total "information market", which still basically operates through printed media.

Information technologies and information as a resource can be expected to generate a number of growth propelling forces for the economy on both the demand and the supply side.

On the supply side, the extended production and use of IT will provide growth of the relevant industries as their components are used extensively within the production and delivery of "information services" and other industries (agriculture, manufacture).

As networking of inventors, users and manufacturers at various levels is advancing, a continuous creation of further innovations, knowledge and know-how may emerge providing the basis for incremental innovations and increased efficiency within all sectors.

Growth is thus likely to emerge through:

   i) The extended production of IT;
   ii) More importantly, through the extended use of IT in other industries and economic sectors;
   iii) Through "networking", that is allowing horizontal and vertical linkages between various sectors which opens new opportunities and synergistic growth effects.

This growth seems likely to be reflected in employment increases in IT areas, as Professor Imai's predictions for Japan suggest. In fact, it would seem that almost half of all employment growth in the whole Japanese economy will be attributable to increased employment in and through IT.

The impact of these developments on employment is shown in Table 6. The "Electronics" and "Information Service" industries create substantial new employment opportunities – 1.45 million positions in the "Electronics" industry and 0.9 million positions in the "Information Service" industry. The information industry as a whole is expected to add 2.5 million new jobs, which will constitute nearly 50 per cent of Japan's total employment growth (5.69 million jobs by the year 2000).

2. Expected IT-related Growth Areas and their Economic Significance

Some emerging applications of new technologies are predictable; others are surprising. Predictable applications often involve replacing one technology or production technique with

Table 5. Marketed electronic specialised information[1]
In millions US dollars

	Scientific & Technical Specialised Information			Economic Information			Total			Total		
	1984	1987	Average Growth p.a.	1984	1987	Average Growth p.a.	1984	1987	Average Growth p.a.	1990	1995	Average Growth p.a.
USA	1 320	2 794	29%	2 125	3 880	22%	3 445	6 674	25%	12 929	38 922	25%
OECD Europe	24	45	24%	430	850	26%	454	895	25%	1 764	5 469	25%
Japan	32	67	28%	280	522	23%	312	589	24%	1 112	3 206	24%
Total	1 376	2 906	28%	2 835	5 252	23%	4 211	8 158	25%	15 805	47 597	24%

1. Using on-line data banks.
Source: Adapted from: *Specialised Information Programme of the Federal Government of Germany for Specialised Information 1985-88*, The Federal Minister for Research and Technology, Bonn, 1985, page 77.

Table 6. **Forecast of employment growth in Japan**[1]

Industry	1984 (A)	2000 (B)	Increase (B)-(A)
Electronics	0.91	2.36	1.45
Telecommunications	0.32	0.47	0.15
Information Services	0.37	1.27	0.90
Sub Total	1.60	4.10	2.50
All Industries	57.66	63.35	5.69

1. Unit: million person.
Source: K. Imai (Background Paper).

another: microprocessor-controlled robots replace paint-sprayers operated by human beings, word-processors replace mechanical typewriters, etc. What is likely to be more important for emerging new IT applications is IT's potential to integrate and/or interconnect functions and activities that old technological production regimes and the division of labour kept apart. Given, however, the fact that there is almost no function or activity not involving the collection, manipulation, monitoring, storing, sensing, counting, actuating and transmission of data and/or information, there are practically no limits to IT applications. It therefore proves extremely difficult to develop categories for indicating likely development trends or even to map emerging growth areas. Available forecasts attempt to catalogue economically viable and feasible applications of IT. Some experts propose classifying micro electronics applications into new and old products and market types in order to differentiate between rationalising and growth promoting applications. Another approach lists likely key IT applications by economic sectors indicating their likely relative importance (see Tables 7 and 8). Figure 3, showing the convergence of communications and computing, even attempts to locate IT innovations in time. Yet, these attempts give a rather static picture and may not totally capture the "trajectories" of likely IT induced diffusion over time.

A more systematic approach suggests that future growth areas triggered by broader IT production and use will be nurtured from:

i) Intermediate and Final Demand of Industry;
ii) Government Purchases;
iii) Private Household Demand;
iv) Infrastructure Investment.

a) Intermediate and Final Demand of Industry

With increased pressure for structural adjustment and changing demand patterns, investment in industrial activities may again become more attractive than purely financial transactions. Such investment over the next decade is likely to be concentrated on technologically advanced equipment, systems and services to increase productivity and flexibility so that changing economic circumstances and consumer demand can be better and more promptly met.

Alterations in the relative ability of firms to cope with information will lead to new competitive patterns, major redistribution of resources, and changes in management priorities.

Figure 3.   **SOME KEY EVENTS IN THE CONVERGENCE OF INFORMATION TECHNOLOGY**

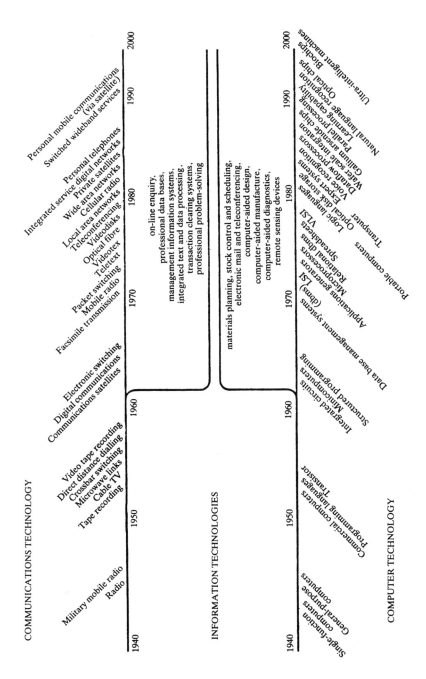

Source: Eric Arnold and Ken Guy *(op. cit.).*

Table 7. **Key applications of IT by economic sectors**

Agriculture, Forestry, Fisheries:

Remote sensing (to identify patterns in pest control, migration, and weather);
Farm management aids (including the use of artificial intelligence/expert systems for achieving optimum yields);
Communications systems for large farm operations/remote operations;
Advanced portable instrumentation (for moisture analysis, blood tests, etc);
Videotext and other databases (for access to market and other data);
Simple robotics and automatic/remote control systems (for operations such as tractor work, milking, poultry management, sheep shearing, picking and harvesting).

Primary Extractive Sector:

Remote sensing (for identification of likely deposits);
Expert systems (for prospecting and extraction management);
Advanced process monitoring and control;
IT-based management and distribution systems;
Integrated mining systems (combining extraction and finishing operations under hierarchical control);
Remote and automated extraction from hostile areas (deep sea robotics).

Construction:

Computer-aided design (architecture) and prefabrication;
IT-based management and distribution systems;
IT-enhanced power tools, surveying equipment;
Simple robotic construction machinery.

Manufacturing:

Computer-aided planning/scheduling/management;
Automated stockholding/warehousing;
Computer-aided design and draughting;
Automated handling and manipulation;
Automated manufacturing monitoring and control;
Automated testing and quality control;
Automated packaging and despatch;
Integrated, intersite communications (via local area networks and wide area networks).

Service Sectors:

Office automation technologies, combining processing (text, voice, image), storage/retrieval and communications in both integrated and stand-alone equipment (operating within local and wide area networks);
Automated operations in fields like banking via automated telling machinery (ATM) and in retailing via electronic point of sale equipment (EPOS);
Electronic funds transfer/point of sale linkages between banks and retailers;
Expert systems/artificial intelligence-based database search and retrieval systems, providing new forms of library-type services;
Electronic mail;
Videotex (including interactive systems);
Advanced telecommunications equipment (message forwarding, cellular radio type local/mobile communications, satellites);
Home computer-based service access (financial services, teleshopping, electronic mail/fax terminals).

Source: From Eric Arnold and Ken Guy (Background Paper).

Table 8. **IT applications by economic sector**[1]

System Type	|	Sector					
	1	2	3	4	5	6	7[2]
Integrated text & data processing	+	+	+	++	++	+++	+++
Transaction clearing	+	+	+	+	+++	+++	+
Online enquiry systems	+	+	+	++	+++	++	+++
Management information systems	+	+++	++	+++	+++	++	++
Professional problem solving	++	+++	++	++	+	++	+
Professional databases	+	++	++	++	+	+	++
Electronic mail & teleconferencing	+	++	+	++	++	++	++
Material planning stock control, scheduling systems	++	++	++	+++	+++	+	+
CAD and draughting	+	++	+++	+++	+	+	+
Computer-aided manufacturing		+	++	+++			
Computer-aided fault diagnostic systems	++	+++		+	+++	+ +	
Remote sensing devices	++	+++	+++	+	++ +		

1. + = Moderate signficance; ++ = High significance; +++ = Very high significance of IT equipment.
2. 1 = agriculture, etc; 2 = extractive; 3 = construction; 4 = manufacturing; 5 = goods services; 6 = information services; 7 = people services.
Source: Eric Arnold and Ken Guy (Background Paper)

These applications clearly show the engineering sector as the centre of microelectronics based innovations. It is largely by the use of these new products in other industries that IT induced change will proceed. In this sense the engineering industry – covering mechanical, electrical and electronic and instrument engineering, transport equipment and miscellaneous mechanical goods and precision instruments – will be a major recipient of compensation effects that arise in capital goods production as the new technology is used more extensively.

The other major activity to profit from increased IT diffusion seems to be office based services. The ITEP report suggests that this sector is likely to expand its share of employment especially given a high income demand elasticity for such activities.

b)   Government Purchases

A major IT user will be government, both as a leading edge customer and provider of services, and also through its responsibilities associated with defence. Again, massive use of advanced IT based equipment is spurred by expectations of IT gains from improved delivery of public services, including public administration itself. In times of severe budget constraints, increased social burdens and limited possibilities to raise tax revenues, the pressure to use IT to increase productivity and flexibility in such areas of government responsibility as education, health and environment protection is rising. IT growth may provide new room for manœuvre in government action, may encourage more citizen participation and may trigger multiplier effects up and downstream in the supplier industries.

c) Private Household Demand

Future IT applications in the home are of a peculiar economic importance both because of the sheer size of household expenditure in GNP and because IT is only now beginning to penetrate consumer markets. The large number of consumers for new potential IT goods and services promise attractive scale economies. Table 9, showing Objectives of the Fifth Generation Project launched in Japan, attempts to capture the rationale of this line of thinking.

Fifth generation computers are intended to use artificial intelligence techniques to permit effective interaction with people, and to facilitate reasoning about information.

Household demand for electronics will no longer be concentrated on entertainment goods and services, but is increasingly expanding in security, control and surveillance equipment to monitor, for example, energy consumption (see Figure 4). In addition, pronounced trends seem to be emerging towards "interactive and intelligent homes" incorporating such IT-based services as telework, teleshopping and banking. In the US in 1986 there were some 600 000 private subscriptions for on-line information services, and it is expected there will be 10 million in 1996. Spending on services is projected to increase from a 36 per cent share of private consumer expenditure in 1984 to around 50 per cent in 1995, largely concentrating on financial, legal and professional services. Health care and related services are estimated to become the fastest growing part of service consumption.

On the basis of current developments, domestic IT-based equipment over coming decades is likely to be increasingly:

- *Remote controlled* (e.g. infrared switches), leading to *multicontrol remote* (multiple devices operated by the same controller), and *distance or telecontrol* (e.g. controllable by telephoned instructions, as are telephone answering machines now, in a fairly primitive way);
- *"User-friendly"* (voice control; menu-type displays for control; more informative output displays, voice synthesised messages);
- *Programmable* (offering increased options to fit current user requirements, and automatic control which takes into account, for example, energy tariffs);
- *"Informed"* (memory to recall previous programming and data inputs – e.g. weight of dieter on successive days – and ability to interface with other devices to optimise performance, and with external information sources to achieve desired outcomes);
- *Portable* (smaller, more personal, devices; devices permitting greater mobility; devices for cooking, washing, etc., for single people and for fitting into small spaces, etc.; cordless devices for convenience of use);
- *Safety featured* (warning indicators, automatic fail-safe controls);
- *Breakdown featured* (diagnostics and easy repair);
- *Power conserving* (more energy-efficient devices, ability to take account of environmental temperatures and energy tariffs);
- *Integrating* different items of equipment around common monitoring and control systems (moving toward information handling services (IHS) for the home).

The attached Tables 10 to 12 amply illustrate applications which lend themselves to future growth areas in households ultimately operating in networking functions as Figure 4 suggests. In general, there is a trend towards making machines more ueful by making them smarter and more accessible to a wide range of people.

Table 9. **FIFTH GENERATION OBJECTIVES**

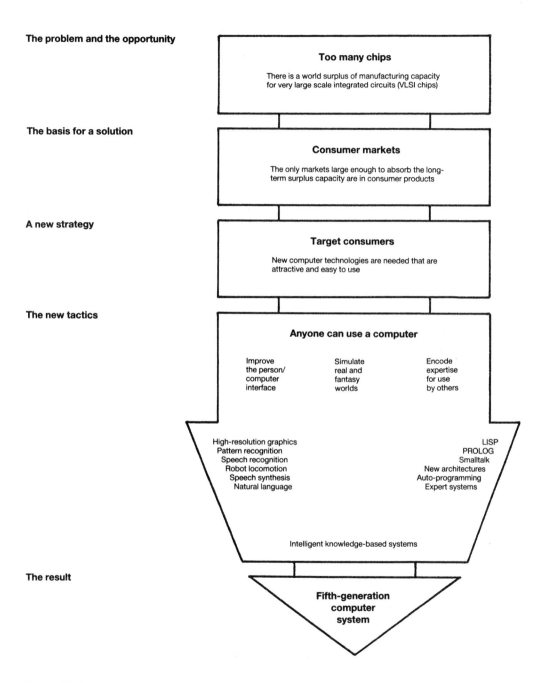

The problem and the opportunity

Too many chips

There is a world surplus of manufacturing capacity for very large scale integrated circuits (VLSI chips)

The basis for a solution

Consumer markets

The only markets large enough to absorb the long-term surplus capacity are in consumer products

A new strategy

Target consumers

New computer technologies are needed that are attractive and easy to use

The new tactics

Anyone can use a computer

Improve the person/computer interface

Simulate real and fantasy worlds

Encode expertise for use by others

High-resolution graphics
Pattern recognition
Speech recognition
Robot locomotion
Speech synthesis
Natural language

LISP
PROLOG
Smalltalk
New architectures
Auto-programming
Expert systems

Intelligent knowledge-based systems

The result

Fifth-generation computer system

Source: Eric Arnold and Ken Guy *(op. cit.).*

Figure 4. **THE NETWORKING OF HOUSEHOLD FUNCTIONS**

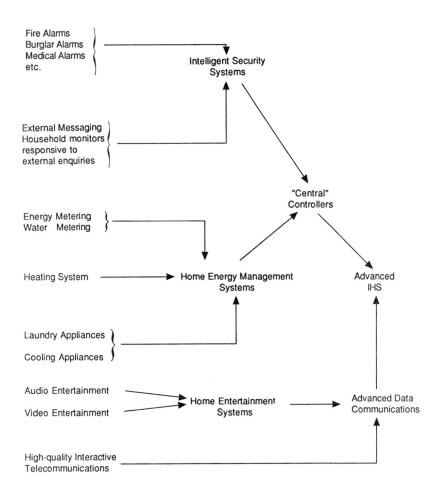

Source: Eric Arnold and Ken Guy *(op. cit.).*

d) *Infrastructure Investment*

The way that technologies for the factory, office and home develop is much dependent on appropriate communications infrastructure. All major telecommunications authorities are committed to digitalisation. With this comes the possibility of using computers to manage information flows in the telecommunications network, and the prospect of a wide range of new services being carried quickly and efficiently – be the data involved voice, image or text. Figure 5 illustrates the range of telecommunications services that is appearing. The integration of IT can be used to bring together all these divergent applications.

Table 10. Developments in "white goods"[1]

	Kitchen and household goods	Personal care and leisure goods
C. 1980		Baby alarms
	Timers on ovens, washing machines	Dolls and toys with voice and other sound synthesis
	Integrated washer/dryers	Electronic board games
		Video-games
	Specialised ovens	
	Frostfree freezers	Cordless baby alarms
	Cordless irons, cleaners	Digital thermometers, sphygamometers
	Self-setting microwaves Multi-power cleaners	Voice- and digital-output weighing with machines, memory
	Programmable tea and coffee makers	
C. 1990	Advanced knitting and sewing machines	
	Mains control of washers	Exercise machines with displays, memory,
	Multi-function fridges	programmed tests, etc.
	Mains control of cookers	Robotic toys
	Infra-red taps	
	Remote monitoring of details of operating	Electronic masseur
	status of major white goods	Biofeedback devices
C. 2000	Remote (e.g. telephone control of detailed operations of white goods)	IT incorporated in chairs, beds, baths, etc.

1. The chart above indicates the approximate period at which these items of consumer electronics are likely to be widely retailed and in use, not the date of invention: indeed most of them have already been developed at least as experimental models.
Source: From Eric Arnold and Ken Guy (Background Paper).

Table 11. Developments in "brown goods"

	Radio/Audio	TV/Video
C. 1980	Personal stereos	Teletext, Videotext Portable colour TV
	CD players	Videocamera, Videorecorder
	Digital Cassette Players	Personal TV ("Watchman") Camcorders
	Digital Cassette Recorders	Split-screen TV
C. 1990	Radio Data Broadcasts	"Stored TV"
	Narrowband Traffic Services	Stereo sound TV Peritelevision
	Digital Radio	Electronic still cameras
	Radiotext	Flat TV Widescreen/Videoprojectors
C. 2000	Advanced Digital Radio	Digital VTR High Definition TV Fully Digital TV TV Printers

Source: Adapted from Eric Arnold and Ken Guy (Background Paper).

Table 12. **Household services**

	Telephony	Computer/ Communications	Computers
C. 1980	Answering machines	Videotext	Home computers
	Memory phones	Multi-standard modems	Floppy discs Dot-matrix printers
	Remote-access answering machines	Bulletin Boards	
			Early teleshopping, telebanking
	Cordless phones	MIDI interface to synthesisers	
	Multi-line households		
	Telephone alarms	Computer hobbyist networking	Video digitisers Laser printers
C. 1990	Home cellular phones	Home Videotext systems	Laser cards
			Laser disc storage
	Electronic mail		Special-purpose domestic robotics
	Telephone interrogation of domestic equipment	Teleworking	Portable terminals with large capacity
		Sophisticated teleshopping	Computer control of equipment
	Electronic messaging systems	Networking	
C. 2000		Sophisticated teleservices	
		General purpose portable computer-communicator	

Source: Adapted from Eric Arnold and Ken Guy (Background Paper).

The prospect of continued digitalisation of telecommunications and the support this may give to convergence have promoted the idea of the Integrated Services Digital Network (ISDN) as the appropriate goal for the medium term in telecommunications infrastructure. The timescale for ISDN deployment is relatively lengthy – twenty years or more before full implementation in many countries. There are, however, competing concepts, such as the Japanese Wideband Integrated Network System (INS). The choice of ISDN builds in a bandwidth bottleneck, impeding the use of the network for broadband services. In its current configuration it does not allow experiment with emerging new services, though broader transmission bandwidth and higher transmission speeds eventually may be required.

32

Figure 5. **THE EVOLUTION OF DIVERSE TELECOMMUNICATIONS SERVICES**

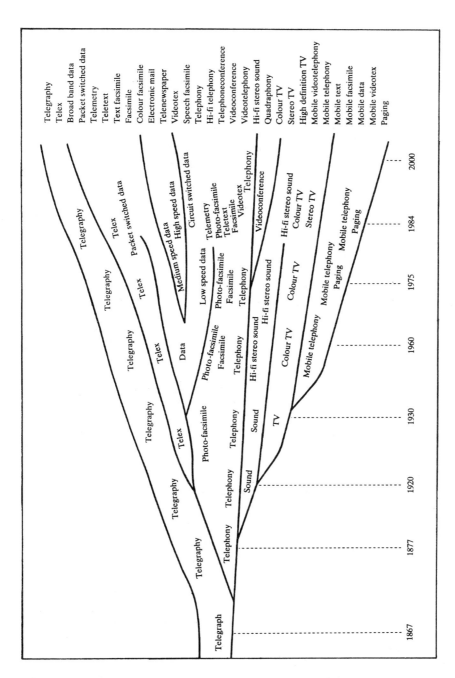

Source: Eric Arnold and Ken Guy *(op. cit.).*

33

Chapter IV

INFORMATION TECHNOLOGY:
THE HIGH-TECHNOLOGY SECTOR MYTH
AND THE CHANGING ROLE OF MANUFACTURING
AND SERVICES

It has been argued in the previous chapters that information technology and information as a resource will increasingly upstage land, labour and capital as the most important input into modern productive systems.

This has encouraged the development of a number of IT determined "futures" and various interpretations have emerged to describe likely IT-induced changes. The more developed concepts dominating the current policy debate consider IT as the core of a high technology sector and engine of future growth in its own right, or argue that modern economies are increasingly becoming service economies.

These concepts are based on dangerous simplifications and might rather obscure than reveal emerging trends. In order to avoid many of the current misinterpretations, it may be appropriate at this stage to consider this type of discussion. It is often argued that the new IT-based "sunrise" industries will increasingly eclipse the older "sunset" (smokestack) industries. This is not convincing. The fact is that high technology industries, however defined, produce a small fraction of total output only; on its own, IT will have only a limited impact on overall performance and standards of living. IT induced growth mainly depends on the capacity to deploy IT capabilities across a broad range of economic activities. The "cars-to-computers" policy approach therefore is both incomplete and misleading. This perspective obscures the fact that inefficient production processes and arrangements are the strategic parameters of economies and therefore the ultimate targets of change. Eradication of whole industries is neither necessary nor desirable.

The vision that modern economies are becoming service economies is another dangerous simplification. Whilst there is real growth in services, a great deal of service growth reflects a reclassification from "manufacturing" to services undertaken by specialists in new service-industry firms instead of being done within the manufacturing firms themselves. The boundaries between manufacturing and services are shifting, but the two remain interdependent. There is no contradiction with the statistically significant observation that goods-producing industries are expected to further decline as an important employment source. These observations must be considered in the context of changes in output and its composition. The relative decline in job creation in manufacturing is not a sign of de-industrialisation. Manufacturing matters and remains a major source of value added in GNP. As customised production gains momentum, the relative cost share of material processing per unit of output will decline, whereas the need for and cost of information for R&D, design, marketing, packaging, transport and delivery of goods and services will continue to grow. As the need for information and data increases information and knowledge-related services and occupations will expand.

Seeing the future industrial structure in OECD countries as a choice between manufacture and services is therefore misguided. Manufacturing and services are complementary and IT has a vital role in both, as well as in their increased integration. In many areas of personal consumption, goods are substituted for services (TVs for theatre, dishwashing machines for servants) alongside the trend towards contracting out services (financial, legal, marketing) as an alternative to performing these functions within the existing organisation.

Many of the reports on microelectronics and IT-based machinery (NC machine tools, microprocessor controlled robots) generated during the 70s correlated the spread of these new production technologies and related goods and services with increased unemployment. These reports often fell victim to the difficulties associated with the generalisation of case study observations at the company level. Though these investigations confirmed the large quantitative and qualitative productivity gains possible from the use of IT-based systems they failed to embrace these impacts in a macro-economic setting. More recent ICCP investigations have overcome this weakness and conclude:

i) There is no evidence that IT-based change has significantly contributed to the current high levels of unemployment;

ii) The various macro-economic feedbacks through cost/price changes and the relevant multiplier effects have often more than compensated for job displacements of direct productivity increases.

Low levels of investment in productive activities – as opposed to financial transactions – accommodated too little technical progress (not too much, as was often argued in the employment-technology debate) characteristic of the 70s and early 80s. IT may, therefore, have been the victim rather than the cause of poor economic performance in many OECD countries.

There is a further lesson to be learnt from the responsiveness of economies to the opportunities offered by developments in IT and its use during the recent past. In the United States, existing factor prices (or their expected developments) were such as to favour the exploitation of the new product and service potential of IT. The lead the United States still holds in space and defence related IT seems to have facilitated such development. Relatively low labour costs and high interest rates have encouraged US firms to hire additional labour in the face of expected output growth rather than to invest in expensive (and often risky) electronics based machinery. IT-product and service innovation was more dominant than IT-based process (rationalisation) innovation. This may, in part, explain why the US investment and productivity growth have been the lowest of all OECD countries in the period concerned.

In Europe and Japan, where real wage costs have risen dramatically over the last ten years, industry has tended to exploit the rationalisation potential of IT systems and services, often imported from the United States.

As a consequence, the US information industry has grown rapidly in terms of output and employment over the last 15 years and became a major provider of new goods and services, but not of IT to be incorporated in production processes. The relatively low number of industrial robots, programmable industrial machinery and the decline of the machine tool industry in the United States, compared with Sweden, Japan and Germany, also support this hypothesis.

The changes in trade flows and the emergence of trade surpluses and deficits between the main regions of the OECD which followed the different IT-diffusion pattern may, however, be reversed. New comparative advantages may rise as US industry redirects its focus and emphasis.

This is not to say that the mythical quality of high technology in general and of IT in particular has now been dispelled. That will not happen as long as high technology is regarded as an automatic and instant panacea for all manner of economic ills. The essence of a myth is that it can have value in the absence of analytical assessment, and high technology has had great value as political myth. As long as IT remains immune from critical assessment, one relies on good fortune alone for the benefits it brings. That situation is not acceptable, as Arnold and Guy are keen to stress. The cataclysm of mass unemployment forecast to result from the widespread adoption of technological change may not have come about, but it was not avoided through deliberate action based on deep understanding of the situation. The prospect of Freeman's jobless growth, whereby production and productivity may now be increased without concomitant increases in employment, still looms large.

Chapter V

CONSTRAINTS, BOTTLENECKS AND POLICY IMPLICATIONS

The trends presented here suggest that IT offers enormous opportunities for OECD economies and standards of living of its citizens. The changes likely to be induced or permitted by IT, as it comes to be more broadly used in homes, offices and factories, will involve adjustments. In addition, it must be kept in mind that there is nothing automatic or inevitable about the response of the market to the signals of emerging technological trends and opportunities, and there is no linear relationship between IT invention and broad commercial applications. The factors to be considered for capitalising on this potential to the fullest extent include technology and firm specific factors and external pressures as well as barriers. They determine whether the economy will respond at all and whether responses to the IT opportunities will be effective.

In the absence of appropriate IT policy, there is a danger that the adoption of IT products will be supplier-driven and piecemeal, with little integration of IT into the broader social and economic framework. The constant debate over compatibility of standards indicates that even the integration of IT equipment itself has not been achieved. Making IT compatible with the massive diversity of a whole economy will be much more difficult and will require government intervention if there are not to be considerable economic losses in both opportunity and welfare.

The report by Arnold and Guy involves several instances of barriers to this necessary integration.

Obstacles to broader IT production and use include:

-   Learning processes involved in developing and taking up the new technology, its know-how and associated services;
-   Social and cultural barriers (resistance to technological change);
-   Institutional and market rigidities (regulatory environment);
-   Supply and demand side factors (outdated industry structures and information deficiencies about IT-opportunities);
-   Trade barriers;
-   Inadequate legal (copyright, privacy) and technical infrastructures including telecommunications networks with bandwidth and standard limitations.

Other obstacles are emerging as IT advances. These include new threats to privacy and increasing opportunities for counterfeiting and forgery, with their serious implications for social stability.

Furthermore, the changing product nature of IT-based innovations creates new diffusion problems. As computer and communication technologies converge, they lose their commodity character and turn into infrastructures. This transition from commodity to systems hardly allows a piecemeal market introduction. Systems and networks in the home, office and factory

37

require from the beginning huge investment, the benefits of which are difficult to appropriate (externalities). Risks and uncertainty also make broad application, unaided, extremely difficult.

The paper by Arnold and Guy gives a good example of how there is no linear relationship between production of equipment and adoption in the economy in that independently-purchased pieces of equipment must be integrated before they can bestow much benefit. The argument can be taken further: not only must they work in conjunction with other IT equipment in the home and in other homes, but also with equipment and with systems of using information much further afield. In the same way, as Solomon points out in his paper, having the tools available for electronic publishing and a demand for the activity are not sufficient when there are obstacles to the integration of this innovation within a wider economic framework. The existing structure of the publishing industry, with its multitude of disparate functions, is a barrier to the adoption of electronic publishing, but more fundamental obstacles are posed by institutional systems which recognise the legality and authenticity of information only when it is contained on paper. With some of these difficulties the market will, though perhaps only eventually, be able to cope: with others there will be need for deliberate intervention to aid integration with broad social, cultural and economic systems. Obviously, the more association there is between not just IT systems and users, but also between IT suppliers and the real world, the more likely it is that equipment will be produced that is not just user friendly, but friendly in social, cultural and economic terms as well.

Chapter VI

POLICY CONSIDERATIONS

Clearly, IT already affects society and the economy in a variety of ways, and quite profoundly. Government policies, even though they may not be specific IT policies, affect the development and use of IT in a multitude of ways. Arnold and Guy in their paper make an attempt to list IT policy options classifying them in three categories: supply-side; demand-side; and bridging policies with the last aiming at coupling the other two. This is illustrated in Figure 6.

It needs to be emphasized that what is labelled demand side policy covers a vast territory as IT may be usefully applied in basically all sectors of the economy. Actions aiming at developing the use of IT in a particular context will furthermore require attention to a number of aspects other than the technology itself. This makes the whole concept of demand-side IT-policies intrinsically complex.

Arnold and Guy's list of policy options is complementary to the Background Report for the CSTP Ministerial Level Meeting in November 1987 on the contribution of science and technology to economic growth and social development. However, two additional policy areas may usefully be added to the list. One concerns the institutional environment and includes the legal and regulatory environment of innovation. The other concerns the need for appropriate data and tools for economic analysis on the level of the individual organisation as well as that of the national economy.

Most, if not all, countries have some explicit or implicit policies in the areas mentioned above. The nature of these policies and their mix will, however, vary between countries and will also change over time in each country.

Much of the attention of government IT-policy has been directed towards strengthening the domestic electronics industry. There has, however, been a clear shift in the ways in which governments have tried to support their electronics industries, moving from an emphasis on subsidies to individual companies towards a preference for providing incentives for collaboration between firms and between firms and research institutions including national laboratories. Among the EEC countries such co-operation has also been stimulated across national borders.

Governments' involvement in promoting the use of IT has, in comparison, been less visible partly because this involvement is more dispersed and therefore less obvious, and probably also because questions of IT utilisation have so far been given less priority than development of basic IT technology and IT industries. Nevertheless, it is possible to point to examples of government policy playing an important role in promoting the use of IT. Use of electronics and software in defence systems is the most striking example. Air traffic control systems and systems for weather monitoring and prediction are other examples where IT is today an absolutely crucial element. In many other sectors where local or national

Figure 6. **IT POLICY OPTIONS**

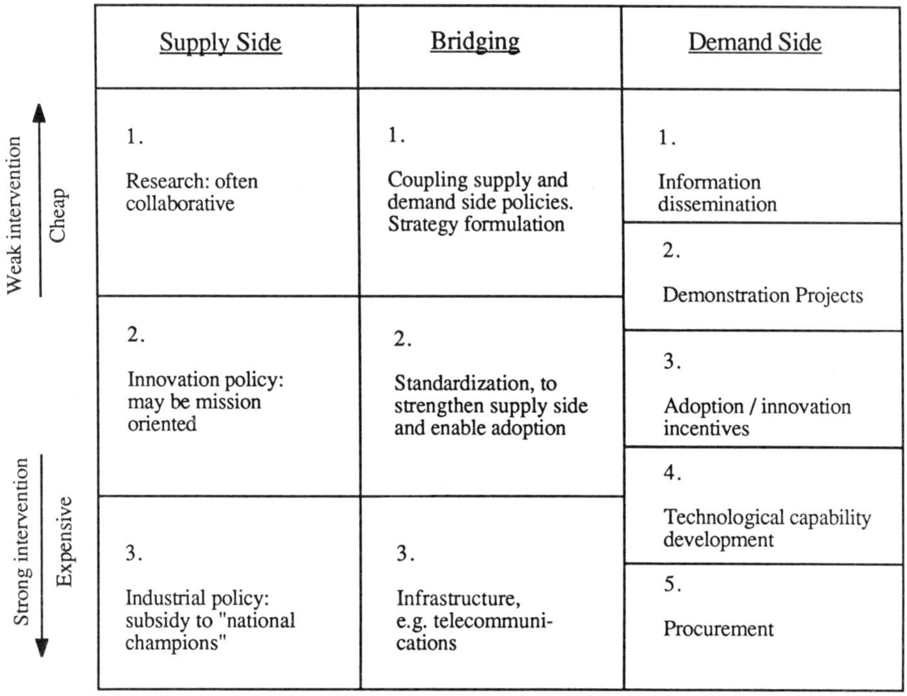

	Supply Side	Bridging	Demand Side
Weak intervention / Cheap	1. Research: often collaborative	1. Coupling supply and demand side policies. Strategy formulation	1. Information dissemination
			2. Demonstration Projects
	2. Innovation policy: may be mission oriented	2. Standardization, to strengthen supply side and enable adoption	3. Adoption / innovation incentives
Strong intervention / Expensive			4. Technological capability development
	3. Industrial policy: subsidy to "national champions"	3. Infrastructure, e.g. telecommuni-cations	5. Procurement

Source: Eric Arnold and Ken Guy *(op. cit.)*.

governments are providing services (health care, education, public administration, monitoring of environmental quality, etc.) the potential of IT has yet to be exploited on a systematic basis, although this does not mean that nothing has been done in these areas.

Governments have also engaged in supporting the diffusion of IT in the private sector by providing economic incentives, various kinds of technical and advisory services and training programmes. In this context, special attention has been given in technology based programmes to the diffusion of advanced IT-based manufacturing technologies such as flexible manufacturing systems (FMS) and computer-aided design and manufacturing (CAD/CAM), and to the use of electronic components in engineering products.

In some countries there have also been programmes to support the development of application software for particular functions.

There is, however, a growing recognition that exploitation of the real long term potential benefits of IT will require more attention to the "systemic" or "network" aspects of IT usage both within and across organisations than has so far been the case. As a consequence, interface problems of different kinds will predominate, a development which is discussed at length in the papers by Imai and Solomon.

The need for interconnectability of electronics and software systems is already widely recognised as indicated by the growing awareness of the need for standardization. Equally important, but less recognised are interfaces between the electronic systems and the "analog world" that they are designed to serve. Imai emphasizes the need for policies to encourage the creation of more "user friendly" interfaces, whether at the hardware or software level, between people and machines. In addition, there must be interfaces between electronic systems and other types of physical systems in the form of sensors, actuators, etc. In many cases these turn out to be critical elements for the utilisation of IT and require special efforts for their development.

The establishment of efficient networks usually requires more than well developed interfaces. The organisations or physical processes which become parts of such networks often will need to change in the way they function internally as well as externally in order for them to operate fruitfully in the network context.

Although no systematic evaluation of government policies towards IT-use has been undertaken here, it seems fair to say that governments have yet to explore the full significance of the emergence of an "information network economy" and to devise appropriate policies to further its development.

User involvement in the development of IT applications can be more or less intensive, spanning e.g.:

- Evaluation of products and systems offered on the market;
- Modification and adjustment of marketed products and systems to specific conditions in the user organisation;
- Development of user specifications which influence suppliers' development of products and systems;
- Active involvement in the conception, development and practical testing of new systems concepts or components thereof.

Many factors influence the need for, and capacity of, user organisations to participate intensively in the development of new IT applications.

Successful adoption of IT for particular applications will in many cases require a considerable amount of innovation in the users' own technology as well as their organisation. It can therefore be misleading to conceptualise the increasing use of IT as a process of diffusion of a fixed IT technology in a fixed economy. One could, in fact, argue that diffusion and innovation will occur simultaneously and will interact.

Development of appropriate IT applications requires a balanced combination of competence and development efforts from suppliers, users, research organisations, regulatory authorities, etc. As examples of factors that may hinder adequate inputs from users in the development of IT applications could be mentioned:

- The resources of individual user organisations may be insufficient for the R&D tasks at hand (application of IT in a special area may require significant advances in terms of basic knowledge or technology that go beyond the capabilities of individual organisations);
- User organisations may have insufficient IT-competence and meet with difficulties in recruiting the necessary IT-specialists in competition with electronics and software firms;
- The high costs and risks for a user to pioneer a new application that will ultimately be exploited also by other users may discourage users from ambitious development efforts;
- It may be difficult to attract the attention of IT firms to specialised application needs;

- In the case of systemic innovations requiring parallel development efforts by several different types of organisations, adequate mechanisms for co-ordination may be absent.

Co-operation between users that would be desirable from a systems point of view may not materialise. In part this may be because the exploitation of IT is seen as a strategic competition factor by users in a particular branch of the economy. This could hinder co-operation between users in the development of basic IT application knowledge and technology and lead to more fragmented and therefore subcritical development efforts. Competence and technology will differ among organisations. Some will see themselves as likely to give more than they receive and therefore be reluctant to enter into co-operation. To reduce such differences and resistance, government incentives for co-operation are often necessary. Joint efforts will have the effect of raising knowledge and technology to a level from which individual firms can develop their unique capabilities in relation to competitors.

Governments can help the development of applications through:

- Support of collaborative research that involves integration of IT and application of specific knowledge and technology;
- Supporting R&D efforts of innovative early users on the condition that the results of these efforts are made available to other users;
- Providing incentives to, and helping to organise joint programmes among users, with possible additional involvement of research institutions and suppliers, to develop systemic IT-applications.

In all these cases government support could be devised so as to be "competition-neutral", i.e. results of R&D undertaken should not be appropriated by a single organisation, but should be made generally available. The actual work may be performed either in some independent organisation (university, research institute) or by individual user organisations; in the latter case, general availability of results may be more difficult to achieve and special arrangements may have to be made. This fact is particularly relevant in the case of semi-conductors which represent the cornerstone of information technologies. In a recent investigation on innovations in the United States, von Hippel found that semi-conductor based product breakthroughs have been developed by users and later adopted by manufacturers.

Innovation in the IT-industry clearly stimulates diffusion by improving the performance to price ratios of electronic products and software. Such innovation will certainly continue to be useful and even necessary in order to make some envisioned applications economically feasible. As suggested above, this will however not be sufficient if IT is to play a critical role in revitalising the economy and contributing to social development. Special efforts must be made to develop IT-applications, and only part of these efforts will be technological in nature.

Bridging policies, in the terminology of Arnold and Guy, include standardization and infrastructure. Although their importance is widely acknowledged, they still offer difficult questions for policy. Both Imai and Solomon point to the danger that premature or too narrowly conceived standardization may stifle innovation. In terms of telecommunications infrastructure, there appears to be differing views on the desirability of early and demand-inducing investment in broadband networks as opposed to more conservative, gradual and demand-induced expansion of broadband communication capabilities.

As far as institutional aspects of IT are concerned, Solomon presents examples from the electronic publishing field which strongly suggest that technology in this area has developed far beyond what the existing legal framework can handle.

Examples of how government-industry joint application research could be organised are numerous. In the context of future IT standards, which often decide the shaping of commercial markets and technology, the US National Bureau of Standards (NBS) is testing – together with General Motors – an architecture for automated manufacturing systems as part of the programme to develop the Manufacturing Automation Protocol (MAP). With the co-operation of other firms, the NBS is also working on computerised manufacturing and design standards, such as the Integrated Graphics Exchange Standard (IGES) and the Data Definition Interchange (PDDI) both of strategic importance for the electronic printing and desk top publishing described in Solomon's paper.

Chapter VII

CHANGES IN POLICY FOCUS AND FUTURE WORK

It is widely accepted that the major economic benefit of IT will come from its use throughout the economy rather than through the growth of the IT industry itself. No matter how impressive the absolute growth of the global IT industry may be, it is dwarfed by the potential benefits to be gained from the use of its products.

To narrow the gap between the potential and actual benefits of IT, it is not sufficient to focus on the increase of the supply of IT and related services. To have a computer does not guarantee productivity enhancement.

To enhance productivity, user requirements and circumstances must be incorporated in IT and this is difficult for the IT industry to do by itself. It requires the active participation of users.

The market fails to establish the sort of information network incorporating users and suppliers that is so important for the rapid pace of innovation in the IT supply sector.

Government IT policies have traditionally focussed on IT hardware (catch-up objectives) and have failed to address what is a specific information market failure. In the same vein is Imai's thesis that the character of the new industrial society is one of constant innovation by linkages across rather than within the borders of specific industries. Indeed, such a characterisation seems to fit the electronics and software and "knowledge" firms – firms that have developed in other sectors.

The intense networking that is characteristic of the IT industry throughout the world seems to be essential to its dynamism and is facilitated by the products of the IT industry.

Rather than a single monolithic network, the IT industry networks are many, irregular and overlapping and some include a few innovative users. The mass of users, however, is virtually isolated from the IT industry's networks, and do their business along traditional, primitive communication channels to suppliers and customers of traditional material goods.

Not only are the linkages often poor between the two "worlds", but communications among the many users in the economy may also be poor. The proliferation of such linkages cannot be provided with government policy focussing on IT hardware, nor will the market provide them unaided. To advance the process, IT application-oriented policies may be more appropriate to help build networks and reap the qualitative IT-potential described above. Obvious areas for governmental involvement are information intensive societal functions such as education, research, health care, public administrative and social services, including environmental monitoring. Figure 7 attempts to illustrate this proposed change in policy focus.

44

Figure 7. **CHANGE IN POLICY FOCUS**

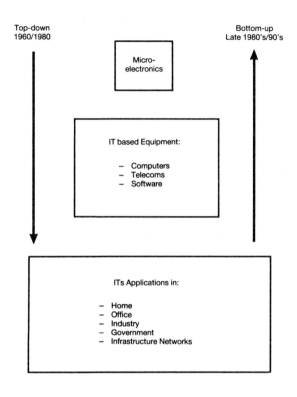

Top-down
1960/1980

Bottom-up
Late 1980's/90's

Micro-
electronics

IT based Equipment:

   – Computers
   – Telecoms
   – Software

ITs Applications in:

   – Home
   – Office
   – Industry
   – Government
   – Infrastructure Networks

Source: Dieter Kimbel, "IT-Diffusion, Changing Industrial Structures and Policy Implications", KAIST, Seoul, 1987.

BIBLIOGRAPHY

Information Technology and Economic Prospects, ICCP Report No. 12, OECD, Paris, 1987.

IT-Futures... It can work, Long-term Perspectives Group, National Economic Development Office, London, April 1987.

Kimbel, D. "Information Technology: Today and Tomorrow" in *Telecommunications Journal*, Butterworth & Co. Ltd., London, December 1987.

Flamm, K., *Targetting the Computer*, The Brookings Institution, Washington, DC, 1987.

Specialised Information Programme of the Federal Republic of Germany for Specialised Information 1985-1988, The Federal Minister for Research and Technology, Bonn, 1985.

Stoneman, P., *The Economic Analyses of Technology Policy*, Clarendon Press, Oxford, 1987.

Kimbel, D., "IT an Engine to Growth?" *OECD Observer No. 147*, August/September 1987.

CSTP Ministerial Meeting Background Report, "The Contribution of Science and Technology to Economic Growth and Social Development", Meeting of the Committee for Scientific and Technological Policy at Ministerial Level, SPT/MIN(87)2.

Freeman, C., "The Challenge of New Technologies" in *Interdependence and Co-operation in Tomorrow's World*, OECD, Paris, 1987.

Englander, S. and Mittelstadt, A., "Total Factor Productivity, Macro and Structural Aspects of the Slowdown", *OECD Economic Studies No. 10*, Spring 1988.

Ergas, H., "Does Technology Policy Matter?", in *Technology and Global Industry. Companies and Nations in the World Economy*, National Academy of Engineering, Bruce R. Guile and Harvey Brooks (eds.), National Academy Press, Washington, DC, 1987.

Kimbel, D., *IT Diffusion, Changing Industrial Structures and Policy Implications*, Korean Advanced Institute for Science and Technology (KAIST), Seoul, 1987.

von Hippel, E., *The Sources of Innovation*, Oxford University Press, New York, 1988.

Part II

RESEARCH PAPERS

POTENTIAL OF INFORMATION TECHNOLOGY AND ECONOMIC GROWTH IN JAPAN AND ASSOCIATE POLICY PROBLEMS

by

Ken-ichi Imai
Professor of Economics and Management Science
Institute of Business Research
Hitotsubashi University
Tokyo, Japan

TABLE OF CONTENTS

INTRODUCTION 50

I. A QUANTITATIVE ANALYSIS OF JAPAN'S INFORMATION INDUSTRY UP
   TO THE YEAR 2000 50
   1. The Changing Industrial Structure 50
   2. Predictions at the Semi-Macrolevel 52
   3. Supplementary Data on the Microlevel 55
   4. Implications for Investment, Employment and Trade 61

II. IMPLICATIONS FOR DIVISION OF LABOUR AND WORK ORGANISATION   65
   1. Transition to a New Industrial Society 65
   2. The Emerging Network Industrial Organisation 66
   3. Characteristics of the Network Industrial Organisation 67
   4. Examples of the Network Industrial Organisation 68
   5. Innovations in the Distribution System 70
   6. Reshuffling of Organisational Boundaries 71
   7. Implications for the Future 71

III. SCENARIOS FOR GOVERNMENTAL POLICIES 74
   1. The Technology Driven Scenario 74
   2. The Market Driven Scenario 75
   3. The Policy Driven Scenario 76

NOTES AND REFERENCES 79

INTRODUCTION

This paper presents a quantitative and qualitative overview of the growth potential of information technology(IT) and related industries and discusses the government policies required to realise such potential. In section one, I present a quantitative prediction for Japan's information industries until the year 2000 at the macro, semi-macro, and microlevel and estimate their impact on long-term employment, investment, and trade structures. In section two, I provide a qualitative discussion of the implications of IT for the division of labour and organisation of work in Japan. My primary focus in this section is upon the evolutionary development in Japan's industrial structure toward a network system, the changing pattern of the division of labour in industry and recent innovations in the distribution system. Finally, in section three, I introduce several government policies, including a new version of Schumpeterian policy, designed to encourage the growth and standardization of an information network.

I. A QUANTITATIVE ANALYSIS
OF JAPAN'S INFORMATION INDUSTRY
UP TO THE YEAR 2000

1. The Changing Industrial Structure

Technological innovation and its induced structural change within industry are the major driving forces behind progress in industrial society. Figure 1 statistically confirms the remarkable structural changes that have occurred in the labour composition of both American and Japanese societies and notes the growth of the information sector, which has now become the leading sector, surpassing all other sectors of the economy. Figure 1 divides the economy into four sectors – agriculture, manufacturing, information and the service industries – in terms of employment using statistical estimates provided for the United States by Mark Porat and for Japan by the Research Institute of Telecommunications and Economics. The three turning points for changes in industrial structure are depicted by A_1, A_2 and A_3 in the case of the United States and J_1, J_2 and (J_3) in the case of Japan. A_1 and J_1 indicate the year that the manufacturing sector surpassed the agricultural sector, A_2 and J_2 the year that the information sector overcame the manufacturing sector, and A_3 and (J_3) the year when the service sector eclipsed the manufacturing sector. In the United States the information sector began to absorb the largest share of labour in approximately 1960; in Japan the same phenomena occurred around 1980. Although Japan's structural changes follow the American pattern, they have taken place in a much shorter time span.

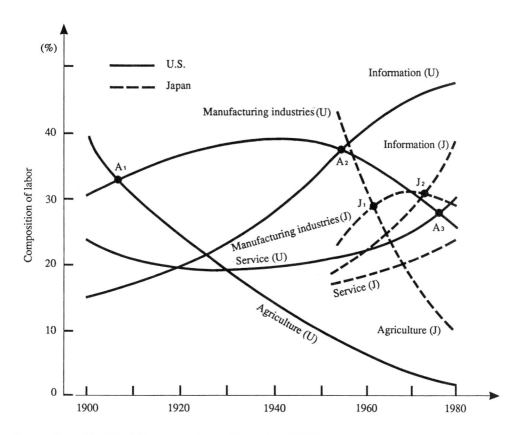

Figure 1. **CHANGING INDUSTRIAL STRUCTURE IN JAPAN AND UNITED STATES**

Source: Research Institute of Telecommunications and Economics (RITE), Tokyo.

A major concern is whether the curve for employment in the information sector will continue to rise well into the future or will flatten out in the near term. Charles Jonscher at MIT has predicted, on the basis of a comprehensive econometric study of the United States' information industry, that the share of employment in that industry will peak during the 1980s and thereafter decline until it reaches an equilibrium approximately in the year 2000. Jean Voge, using a statistical study comparing value added per capita between the real goods manufacturing industry and the information industry in the United States for the period 1900-1980, noted that value added per capita in the real goods manufacturing sector will reach a maximum value when the ratio of information industry's value added per capita to that of the economy as a whole becomes 50 per cent[1].

These opinions suggest that even though output or the added value of the information sector will increase in the future, there is a limit to the share of the information sector in the economy as a whole. The emerging information society and its economy will thus be based on the diffusion of IT into other sectors of the economy rather than on the growth of an independent information industry. In other words, IT will be used to revitalise agriculture and manufacturing, and the service sector will grow as a result of the utilisation of IT and through joint ventures with firms in the information industry.

I believe the above holds true not only in the United States, but also in the case of the Japanese information industry. It can be seen from Figure 1 that the Japanese information industry has in the past expanded its share of employment at exponential growth rates, but I do not expect that trend to continue[2]. Therefore, the focus of this investigation will be on the manner in which IT will diffuse throughout all sectors of the economy and the extent to which this diffusion will contribute to the future growth of the Japanese economy.

2. Predictions at the Semi-Macrolevel

I first wish to present a quantitative assessment of the Japanese information industry to the year 2 000 based on a report by MITI's Special Committee of the Industrial Structure Council, which I belong to as an academic member. The predictions that follow were produced utilising an input-output table, dividing the economy into four sectors. These four sectors include electronics, telecommunications and information as well as another classified as "other". The four sector input-output table for 1984 was used as a base year table and this table was integrated with a basic table consisting of 406 x 541 sectors. Predictions were then made for the years 1990, 1995, and 2000.

Predictions were arrived at in the following way:

  i)   An assessment was first made of final demand based on the assumptions made in the macro framework predictions mentioned below;
  ii) Output (domestic production) was then estimated for the three information industries by integrating forecasts provided by related industrial associations and research institutes;
  ii) An input-output coefficient which satisfies both final demand and output levels was then established; and
  iv) Final adjustments were made so as to provide a consistent input-output table by considering such factors as plausibility of changes in input-output coefficients.

The result of these predictions is shown in Table 1. The upper figure indicates actual values for 1984 and the lower figure indicates predictions for the year 2000, while the figures in parenthesis show percentage changes from the base year.

These predictions are based on an assumed growth rate for the Japanese economy of 5 per cent per annum until the year 2000. These predictions constitute a potential growth path for the Japanese economy given a stable environment. The estimates by sector should thus be considered within the larger framework of constituting economic policy designed to realise the targeted 5 per cent annual growth rate. Note that these predictions are not, however, merely a linear projection of current patterns of growth. Required structural changes are assumed. In the case of final demand the ratio of Japanese exports is assumed to decrease, while in the case of technological coefficients (input coefficients) the use of electronics is assumed to increase substantially in all sectors. This prediction thus illustrates the type of industrial structure which will be realised when Japanese economic growth relies mainly on domestic demand and the diffusion of innovations utilising electronic technology[3].

Table 1 shows that while sectors other than the information industry are expected to expand at relatively moderate rates of 1.84 times (2 000/1984), the expansion rates for each

Figure 2. **INFORMATION WORKFORCE AS A PROPORTION OF TOTAL NON-AGRICULTURAL WORKFORCE (C. Jonscher)**

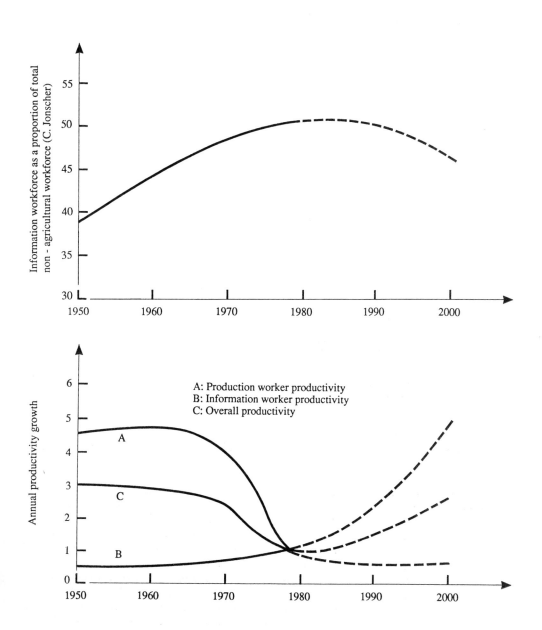

Source: Charles Jonscher (MIT) "Information Resources and Economic Productivity", in *Information Economics and Policy,* 1983, pp. 13-15.

53

Table 1. **Semi-macro prediction of Japan's information industry,
4 Sectors input-output table of 1984 and 2000[1]**

To	Firm Electronics	Telecommu- nications	Information Service	Other Industries	Sub Total	Final Demand	Domestic Production
Electronics[2]	8.0	0.6	0.3	1.5	10.5	17.2	27.7
	40.7	3.6	8.5	27.4	80.2	148.7	228.9
	(5.1)	(6.0)	(28.3)	(18.3)	(7.6)	(8.6)	(8.3)
Telecommu- nications[3]	0.2	0.07	0.04	3.1	3.4	1.5	5.0
	1.7	0.4	0.8	4.8	7.6	10.9	18.5
	(8.5)	(5.7)	(20.0)	(1.5)	(2.2)	(7.3)	(3.7)
Information Services[4]	0.2	0.02	0.1	2.7	3.0	0.02	3.0
	3.6	0.2	3.0	11.0	17.7	20.9	38.6
	(18.0)	(10.0)	(30.0)	(4.1)	(5.9)	(1 045.0)	(12.9)
Other Industries	10.6	0.4	0.7	30.7	31.8	288.1	606.5
	132.3	0.7	4.9	461.0	598.8	516.9	1 115.8
	(12.5)	(1.8)	(7.0)	(15.0)	(18.8)	(1.8)	(1.8)
Sub Total	19.0	1.1	1.2	314.0	335.3	306.9	642.2
	178.4	4.8	17.1	504.1	704.4	697.4	1 401.8
	(9.4)	(4.4)	(14.3)	(1.6)	(2.1)	(2.3)	(2.2)
Value Added	8.7	3.8	1.8	292.5	306.9		
	50.5	13.7	21.5	611.7	697.4		
	(5.8)	(3.6)	(11.9)	(2.1)	(2.3)		
Domestic Production	27.7	5.0	3.0	606.5	642.2		
	228.9	18.5	38.6	1 115.8	1 401.8		
	(8.3)	(3.7)	(12.9)	(1.8)	(2.2)		

1. Upper figures: 1984; lower figures: 2000; figures into brackets: 2000/1984.
2. Computer and its ancillary apparatus, other associated electronic equipment, electron tubes, semiconductor devices/IC, communication and related equipment, measuring instruments, radio and television receivers, acoustics.
3. Telecommunications industries of the first kind like NTT and KDD. Services by the second kind are included in Information Service.
4. Information processing, software and information supply service.
Source: The Report of MITI's Special Committee of the Industrial Structure Council, 1987/6.

of the sectors in the information industry are quite substantial; in Electronics the expansion rate will be 8.3 times, in Telecommunications it will be 3.7 and the Information Services will achieve 12.9.

Predictions for the intermittent years prior to 2000, as outlined in Table 2, suggest several important points for policy discussion. First of all, it is obvious that the electronics industry will be the force propelling the Japanese economy forward in terms of both supply and demand. On the supply side, as seen in the changing pattern of input coefficients (see Table 3) technologies will be used extensively within the "Information Service" and "Other" industries, providing the basis for incremental innovation and increased efficiency within these two sectors. On the demand side, as is seen from the remarkable expansion of domestic production and the increase in purchases from the "Other" industries (the input coefficient increases from 0.38 in 1984 to 0.58 in the year 2000), the "Electronics" industry will contribute to an increase in final demand and stimulate domestic demand in all other sectors.

Secondly, in the "Telecommunications" industry the ratio of final demand to total domestic demand will remain in the range of 30 to 40 per cent until 1990, but after 1996 it

Table 2. **Predicted main indicators for the information industry**

	Share of value added to gross output in %			Ratio of final demand to total demand in %		
	Electronics	Telecommu-nications	Information service	Electronics	Telecommu-nications	Information service
1984	31.3	77.4	60.8	62.0	31.1	0.7
1990	28.6	76.2	58.5	57.5	38.7	16.5
1995	25.4	75.1	57.2	60.6	52.2	36.4
2000	22.1	73.8	55.6	64.9	58.8	54.1

Source: See table 1.

Table 3. **Comparison of input-output coefficients: 1984/2000[1]**

	Electronics	Telecommunications	Information service	Other Industries
Electronics	0.290	0.128	0.112	0.003
	0.188	0.196	0.220	0.025
Telecommunications	0.008	0.015	0.013	0.005
	0.007	0.021	0.021	0.004
Information service	0.006	0.004	0.034	0.004
	0.016	0.009	0.077	0.010
Other industries	0.384	0.079	0.232	0.506
	0.578	0.035	0.126	0.413

1. Upper figures: 1984; lower figures: 2000.

will exceed 50 per cent. This implies that in the near term telecommunications technologies will be used chiefly to increase efficiency in the intermediary products sectors, including transportation and distribution, but in the latter part of the period under study the demand for telecommunications services will increase due to the stimulas provided by the spread of new media to the household sector.

Thirdly, the ratio of final demand to total demand in the "Information services" industry jumps suddenly from 0.7 per cent in 1984 to 36.4 per cent in 1995 and again to 54.1 per cent in the year 2000. Such rapid growth reflects the expectations of many experts in this industry and a policy stance of MITI that a growing number of information services, such as the software which interfaces man and machine or services which make machines and telecommunications networks "user friendly", will be required for the household market, and the quality of these services should be promoted so as to realise a balanced development of the information society in terms of both efficiency and human convenience.

I will discuss policy issues related to these points in the third section of this paper. I would at this stage, however, like to present in more detail the statistical forecasts that are underlying the semi-macro predictions presented in this section.

3. Supplementary Data on the Microlevel

First, I would like to present a statistical overview of Japanese high tech investments (see Table 4) in order to illustrate the importance of investments in microelectronics as a share of

Table 4. **Japan's high tech investments in selected industries, 1984**

Billion yen and percentage

	High tech related investment					Ratio of microelectronics related investment to total fixed	
	Total fixed investment	Micro electronics-related	Bio-related	New material related	Others	Investment 1984	Contribution to increase of investment
All industries	15 094	3 096				20.5%	51.8%
Material related industry	2 563	205	10	141	75	8.0	30.8
Processing and assembly industry	3 897	1 527	10	2	14	39.2	66.6
Energy industry	4 231						
Service industry (including construction & utilities)	4 404	1 366	7	1	0	31.0	45.7

Source: Japan Development Bank.

industrial investments in all sectors of the economy. From Table 4 we find that microelectronics-related investments account for 20.5 per cent of total investment and contribute to 51.8 per cent of all increases in total fixed investments. I envisage that this pattern will continue for some time into the future.

Tables 5 and 6 provide more detailed forecast figures for the various sectors within the "Telecommunications" and "Information service" industries. From Table 5 we are able to confirm the previous assertion that demand for new media services in the household sector will increase substantially in the future; the production of data transmission and cellular telephones for automobiles is expected to increase 100 times. Table 6 indicates that within the "Information service" industry, software production and information services such as databank services, will expand dramatically during the next fifteen years. Moreover, Japanese imports of information services will increase substantially in response to an assumed bottleneck in the domestic production of software. The above facts suggest that, within the Japanese information industry, growth in hardware and software will proceed roughly in tandem, and interaction between the two will be necessary for the growth of the industry as a whole.

Microelectronics contributes not only to an increase in the efficiency of the manufacturing sectors, but also to non-manufacturing, and particularly service sectors. Telecommunications enable new linkages between the manufacturing and service sectors, and between the household and service sectors. All of these activities increase the demand for software, and the production of software in turn creates additional demand for microelectronics and telecommunications which meet the expanding needs of the software itself. The reciprocal and interdependent relationships between the above three sectors represent an important element in my projections for future growth. A comparison of the inverse matrix of input-output coefficients in Table 7 illustrates how these interactions will evolve in the next fifteen years. I would like to discuss these interactions from the perspective of data which was produced by a research committee formed by the Ministry of Finance for the investigation of "Softnomics".

Table 5.   **Prediction of telecommunications domestic output by subsectors**

Unit: Billion yen

Subsectors	1985 (A)	2000 (B)	(B)/(A)
Telephone	4 234	11 002	2.6
Exclusive use	251	1 025	4.1
Data Communications	153	958	6.3
Data Transmission	10	1 188	118.8
Wireless Call	70	507	7.2
Cellular Telephones for Automobiles	15	1 582	105.5
Total of Domestic Telecommunications	5 091	17 142	3.4
International Telecommunications	216	1 397	6.5
Total	5 307	18 539	3.5

Source: See table 1.

Table 6.   **Prediction of information service demands by subsectors**

Unit: Billion yen

	1984 (A)	2000 (B)	(B)/(A)
Information Processing	631	4 570	7.2
Software	512	7 867	15.4
Information Supply Services	97	3 386	34.9
Export	5	1 761	352.2
Import	23	3 024	131.5

Source: See table 1.

Table 7.   **Comparison of inverse matrix coefficients, 1984/2000[1]**

	Electronics	Telecommunications	Information Service	Other Industries	Total
Electronics	1.42	0.19	0.17	0.01	1.79
	1.27	0.26	0.32	0.06	1.91
Telecommunications	0.02	1.02	0.02	0.01	1.07
	0.02	1.02	0.03	0.01	1.08
Information Service	0.01	0.01	1.04	0.01	1.07
	0.04	0.02	1.10	0.02	1.18
Other Industries	1.11	0.31	0.62	2.04	4.08
	1.26	0.32	0.55	1.77	3.90
Total	2.56	1.53	1.85	2.07	8.01
	2.59	1.62	2.00	1.86	8.07

1.   Upper figures: 1984; lower figures: 2000.

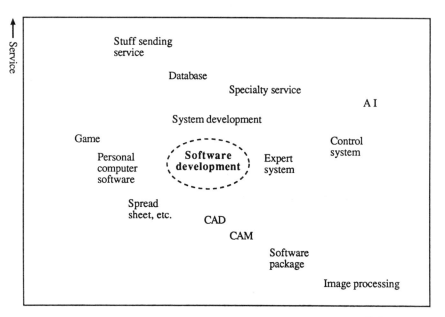

Figure 3. **BUSINESS OPPORTUNITIES OF THE SOFTWARE SERVICE INDUSTRY**

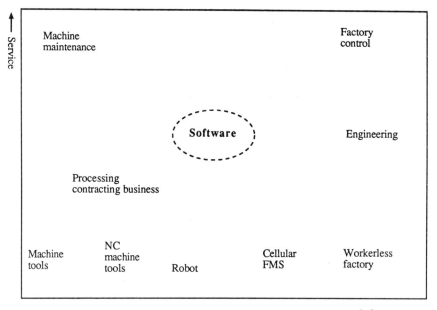

Figure 4. **BUSINESS OPPORTUNITIES OF THE FA INDUSTRY**

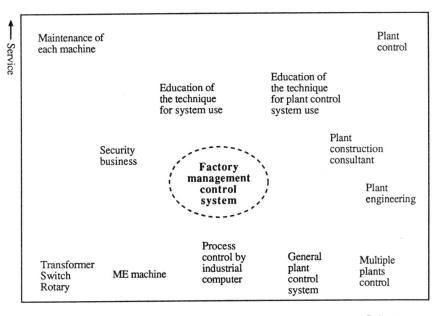

Figure 5. **BUSINESS OPPORTUNITIES OF THE HEAVY ELECTRIC INDUSTRY**

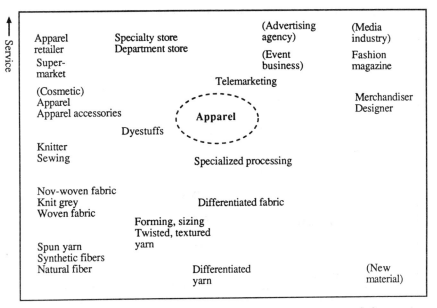

Figure 6. **BUSINESS OPPORTUNITIES OF THE FASHION INDUSTRY**

59

Figure 7. **BUSINESS OPPORTUNITIES OF THE HOUSING AND URBAN INDUSTRY**

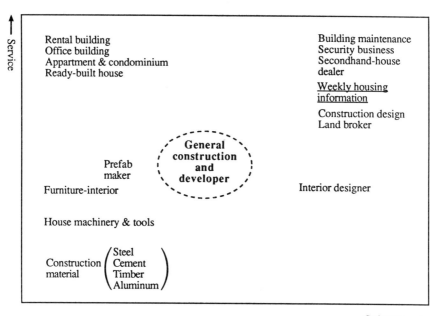

Figure 8. **BUSINESS OPPORTUNITIES OF THE RETAILERS**

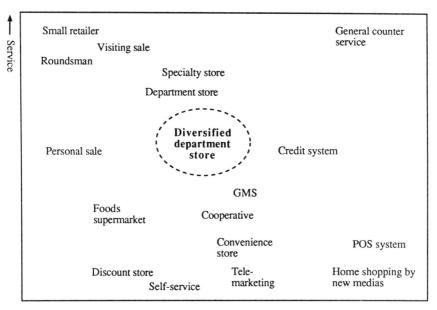

Figure 9.   **BUSINESS OPPORTUNITIES OF THE LEISURE INDUSTRY**

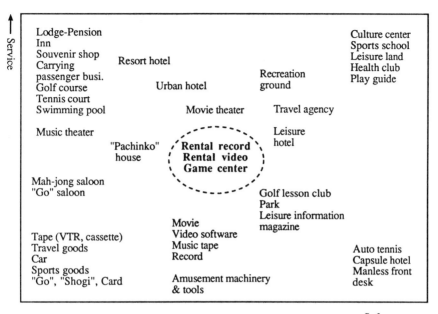

Figures 3-9 illustrate some of the new business opportunities now emerging in Japan. The basic idea of this chart is that goods and services are supplied as a combination of real goods, software, and human services. The pattern by which the three are combined is depicted in the chart in which the horizontal axis represents the degree to which software is utilised; the vertical axis indicates the degree to which human services are utilised: the origin represents real goods. For example, because a computer requires roughly equal inputs of both software and services, the computer business is drawn in the centre of the chart, at the intersection of the appropriate values from the x and y axes.

In these seven figures a variety of industries are provided as examples. In all of these cases, however, the most promising business opportunity is situated in the centre of each chart. This means that an appropriate combination of real goods, software and human services is required to meet the needs of the future. The so-called information society cannot be based solely on information; it also requires real goods and services. The projections for Japan's information industry have been made from such a perspective.

4.   Implications for Investment, Employment and Trade

Substantial investments are required to create and interface an efficient information system with a complex hardware-software network. Investment in information systems comprised 11.1 per cent of all capital investment in Japan in 1984 and by the year 2000,

61

Figure 10. **DEVELOPMENT OF THE INFORMATION INDUSTRY**

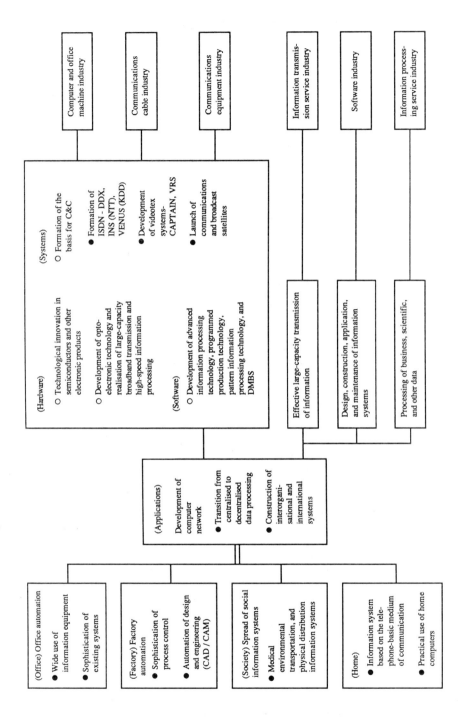

Source: *Japan's High Technology Industries*, The Industrial Research Division, The Long-Term Credit Bank of Japan, May 1983.

62

68 trillion yen will be required for such investment. As total capital investment is expected to approach 206 trillion yen, approximately one-third of all investment will be devoted to information systems. It is important to note that this investment creates a virtuous cycle in the sense that the new investment in information systems necessitates further fixed investment, while such capital investments in turn create new demands on the information industry. Figure 10 shows how investment creates a diversity of information systems in the Japanese economy and how these information systems are then linked to the development of specific information industries.

The impact of these developments on employment is shown in Table 8. The "Electronics" and "Information Service" industries create substantial new employment opportunities: 1.45 million positions in the "Electronics" industry and 0.9 million positions in the "Information Service" industry. The information industry as a whole is expected to add

Figure 11. **CHANGING PATTERN OF EMPLOYMENT STRUCTURE (BY EPA)**[1]

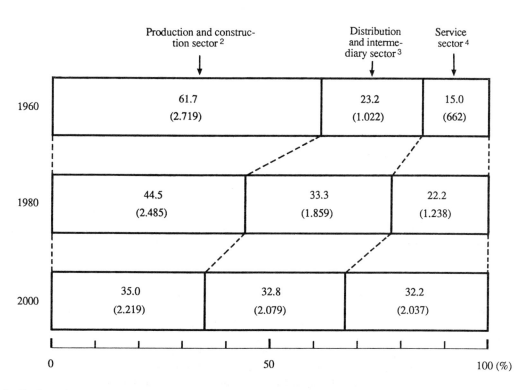

1. The figures in parentheses indicate the number of people employed (unit: ten thousand persons).
2. Production and construction sector: Agriculture and fisheries, mining, manufacturing and construction.
3. Distribution and intermediary sector: Commerce, transportation, telecommunications, banking, insurance, real estate, electricity, gas and water supply.
4. Service Sector: Service, public sector, education, medical care, etc. (includes non-classifiable).
Source: *Technological Innovation and Employment,* Economic Planning Agency, 1986.

Table 8. **Prediction of employment growth in Japan**[1]

Industry	1984 (A)	2000 (B)	Increase (B)-(A)
Electronics	0.91	2.36	1.45
Telecommunications	0.32	0.47	0.15
Information Services	0.37	1.27	0.90
Sub Total	1.60	4.10	2.50
All Industries	57.66	63.35	5.69

1. Unit: million person.
Source: See table 1.

Table 9. **Employment structure of the year 2000**[1]

	1980 (A)	2000 (B)	(B)-(A)
The Primary Industry	5.8	3.1	−2.7
The Secondary Industry	24.7	24.5	−0.2
Chemicals	1.8	1.2	−0.6
Primary Metals	0.7	0.4	−0.3
Machinery	5.4	5.3	−0.1
General ma.	2.4	1.8	−0.6
Electric ma.	1.6	2.3	0.7
Transportation ma.	1.0	0.8	−0.2
Precision ma.	0.3	0.4	0.1
Others	6.0	4.5	−1.5
Construction	5.5	7.8	2.3
The Tertiary Industry	30.2	41.3	11.1
Electricity, Gas and Water Supply	0.3	0.3	0
Finance, Insurance and Real Estate	1.9	3.0	1.1
Transportation and Communication	3.5	4.6	1.1
Wholesale and Retail Trade	12.5	13.0	0.5
Service	12.0	20.4	8.4
Total	60.7	68.9	8.2

1. Unit: million Number of Employment.
Source: Economic Planning Agency, *Technological Innovation and Employment*, 1986.

2.5 million new jobs, which will constitute nearly 50 per cent of Japan's total employment growth (5.69 million jobs by the year 2000).

These employment projections provided by MITI do not allow us to produce a more detailed and comprehensive picture of Japanese employment because they use sectoral forecasts developed by the Economic Planning Agency (EPA) only as a framework. I have provided figures from the EPA's report on Technological Innovation and Employment (1986) in Table 9 and Figure 11 for reference. Figure 11 shows that even though employment will decrease in the manufacturing and construction sectors due to changes brought about by the microelectronics revolution, employment in the service sector will more than compensate for the losses, while the distribution and intermediary sectors will maintain their approximate present share in the total employment picture.

The structural changes so far described will have a favourable impact on the structure of Japanese trade from the standpoint of reducing international trade conflicts. There will be a decline in the ratio of exports to GNP in nominal terms from 16.4 per cent to 11.5 per cent by the year 2000, and an increase in the import of information services can be expected due to the need to break the bottleneck imposed by a shortage of qualified personnel in the Japanese software industry. Japanese foreign direct investment will proceed to the greatest possible extent, but it is probable that Japanese firms will encounter some difficulties in establishing truly successful manufacturing facilities in foreign countries. Table 10 provides a forecast for foreign direct investment as envisioned by JERC, the research centre of the *Nihon keizai shinbun* (Japan's foremost economic newspaper). It is possible that these projections may be somewhat conservative.

Table 10.   **Forecast of Japanese foreign direct investment by JERC**[1]

	1985	2000	Average growth rate	Composition in 2000
North America	5 495	63 000	17.7	42.0
Europe	1 930	27 000	19.2	18.0
Asia	1 435	30 000	22.5	20.0
Middle and Near East	45	3 000	32.3	2.0
Middle and South America	2 616	22 500	14.4	15.0
Africa	172	1 500	15.5	1.0
Oceania	525	3 000	12.3	2.0
Total	12 218	150 000	18.2	100.0

1.   Unit: Million dollars.
Source: JERC (Japan Economic Research Centre).

II.   IMPLICATIONS FOR DIVISION OF LABOUR AND WORK ORGANISATION

1.   Transition to a New Industrial Society

The production and distribution system of the economy is built upon an infrastructure which includes roads, harbours, transportation systems, telecommunications systems, various stocks of information, etc. The quality and functioning of such an infrastructure exerts a great influence on the types of divisions of labour and work organisations within a society.

In America for example it can be said that large scale production and mass marketing emerged almost immediately after the completion of the transportation and telecommunications infrastructure in the 1880s. According to Professor Alfred Chandler, the establishment of this infrastructure transformed the "invisible hand" of the previously dominant market economy into the "visible hands" of the large corporation.

Japan also exerted great efforts to build an infrastructure of roads, harbours, and railway transportation during the initial years of the Meiji period (1868-1912), and this infrastructure

65

was largely responsible for creating the market mechanisms of prewar Japan. Japan has now undertaken the construction of an infrastructure designed to carry it into the twenty-first century, based on microelectronics, telecommunications, and information services. A quantitative prediction concerning that emerging infrastructure was made in the previous section of this paper and I would now like to present a qualitative discussion of the coming information society and the infrastructure on which it will be built.

I would like to define the newly emerging society as an "Information Network Society". An information network society is a society formed on the principle of organisation through networking, whose advancement is motivated by the creation and propagation of information. The Japanese society is inexorably moving toward the creation of such an information network society, driven by innovations in information and telecommunications technology and by the changing relationships between organisations and people, as will be later explained.

2. The Emerging Network Industrial Organisation

Japan's industrial organisation has evolved from *zaibatsu* to "business groups" to, most recently, "network industrial organisations". The worldwide industrial reorganisation which followed the recession of the 1930s contributed to the formation of Japan's financial cliques, or *zaibatsu*. The dissolution of the *zaibatsu* following the war produced another perceived crisis which was resolved by the competitive postwar Japanese industrial reorganisation. More recently, the oil shocks of the 1970s brought about yet another fundamental industrial reorganisation.

The oil crisis made it imperative for Japanese business enterprises to utilise all available technologies, and specifically the microelectronics technology, in order to conserve energy resources. As a result, the specialisation and division of labour associated with technological improvements advanced at an accelerated pace. Each company, including small sized companies, undertook lengthy studies of a variety of rationalisation techniques designed to achieve the highest degree of specialisation possible. Big business implemented these new techniques and systemetized them. The resulting acceleration in specialisation and division of labour was not a new phenomenon, but the way in which these developments were adopted in firms and industrial groups, and were accompanied by the transfer of technology, exhibited a special character which may be referred to as the formation of networks.

The formation of networks, however, left an important and special characteristic of the Japanese company intact. This characteristic was the tendency to create linkages within the specialised work force. Thus, while the business groups have been rearranged in response to the requirements of the market and were moving toward looser linkages, they maintained the organisational and market linkages which were to become the basis for the formation of networks. The specialisation of the work force which had been advanced by the most recent industrial reorganisation was different from both the isolated specialisation of labour in the market economy and the planned specialisation seen in large corporations. This type of specialisation of the work force, in which each unit retains autonomy and yet remains in close interdependence, is a phenomena which may be termed "network specialisation of the work force[4]". This type of specialisation, unlike the static division of labour which Adam Smith described using the example of the manufacturing of pins, is characterised by self-organisation. As a consequence, newly-developed technology is able to find its own niche and create its own demand or market.

This type of specialisation of the work force has been noted by M.J. Piore and C.F. Sabel[5], who refer to it as "flexible specialisation". They go as far as to say that this development has created a second divide in the industrialisation process, entirely different from the conventional mass production system. The network specialisation of the work force gives rise to both the specialisation of technologies and the simultaneous creation of their markets, advanced by the tendency for self-organisation.

At the same time, in a world of highly interdependent and interpenetrating technologies and markets, a more specialised work force necessarily creates solidarity among the firms engaged in related production. This is because individual enterprises that perform highly specialised tasks cannot reach their full potential by merely interacting in the market. They need to work and progress as a network. Hence, network activity, or activity conducted with consideration for one's "position" in the network and "distance" from other firms in that network, becomes the mode for action.

The specialisation and advancement of technology thus resulted from an ever higher specialisation of the work force. New technologies then become linked across the boundaries of firms and form a grid, utilising the sophisticated market functions created by recent developments in information technologies, allowing those firms to function in a loosely integrated "network industrial organisation". The network industrial organisation can, therefore, now be defined as an interorganisational configuration of a variety of independent firms having mutual ties with each other through a network within an industrial system.

3. Characteristics of the Network Industrial Organisation

In order to further clarify the characteristics of the network industrial organisation as described above, and to provide a comparison with *zaibatsu* and business groups, I have defined the features of each type of organisation in Table 11. Some basic differences between the various types of organisations can be noted from this table. First of all, it becomes evident that the relationships between companies have changed from such formal systems as mutual stockholding or the exchange of directors between companies, to informal relationships in which the exchange of information is of primary importance. Secondly, the handling of information has undergone a drastic change. In the case of the *zaibatsu,* the organisation functioned to collect information on the affairs of the outside world; in the jargon of the economist, the information can be said to have been exogenous. In the case of business groups, however, it is endogenous in nature in that the internal transmission and processing of information, while important, has been of less importance than the arbitrating activities based on that information. This type of information utilisation is common to the trading company, which has not itself engaged in a high degree of information creation.

In network industrial organisations, information is created through interaction, and the creation of information itself becomes the driving force of business activity. The term "creation of information" may sound like the activity of geniuses; that is, the creation of something from nothing. However, that is not the sense in which the term is used here. Information creation can be said to be merely the means of creating a new context in the process of normal decision making. The information that is initially produced is not, however, linked to economic decisions. Only after it is further distilled and its meaning progressively defined does it become information with significance for decision making and action. During the course of this distillation the information undergoes a variety of selection and screening processes, which may result in the discovery of unexpected connections. It is thus the network which creates this stock of information and reveals the relationships of various aspects of that information. The market fails in such activities. The network industrial organisation has thus created a mechanism to obtain positive externalities, in contrast to the *zaibatsu* and business

67

Table 11.   Evolution of business networks in Japanese industry

	Zaibatsu	Business Group	Network Industrial Organisation
Nature of Technology	• Import of inventions, patents	• Large capacity, mass production technologies	• Small scale, small-batch engineering
Nature of Information	• Exogenous • Special route	• Endogenous • Hierarchical • Arbitrage-related	• Creation • Interaction
Inter-business	• Control by stock holding, assignment of directors (strong ties)	• Mutual stock holding, presidents' clubs, assignment of directors (strong and loose ties)	• Affiliation, co-operation (loose ties)
Management	• Control	• Authority	• Leadership and rules
Advantages	• Concentration of decision making	• Rapid growth	• Dispersed decision-making • Creativity
Disadvantages	• Financial control, suppression of entrepreneurial freedom	• Groupism, cartels, excessive competition	• Instability

groups which were forced to cope with the lack of mature markets or the possibility of market failure associated with uncertainty.

Innovation, as Schumpeter has said, is to carry out something new. To advance this concept further one might say that innovation is nothing other than the creation of new information. Network industrial organisations may therefore be considered to be organisations which continually execute incremental innovation based on information analysed at its source.

This constant incremental innovation produces the fundamental advantage of the network industrial organisation. In the case of the former *zaibatsu*, only innovations which occurred on the order of once every hundred years, such as a great discovery or its patenting, were imported and implemented. In the case of the business group, the nurturing of the major technical innovations, which had accumulated over a very short time span due to the great advancement in science and technology in the 1930s, was of major importance. Network industrial organisations, however, link large and small scale improvements and innovations and attempt to carry out a constant flow of innovation. The character of the new industrial society is one of constant innovation by linkages across, rather than within, the borders of specific industries. Japanese industries and business enterprises, by carefully integrating internal and external business networks, have steadily advanced innovation across the spectrum of industry and thereby formed such network industrial organisations.

4.   Examples of the Network Industrial Organisation

Network-type organisations are ubiquitous in the modern Japanese industrial scene. Examples include:

   i)   The "Toyota Group" or "Honda Group";

ii) Heterogeneous R&D networks formed by a variety of competing companies and government agencies (such as the VLSI research and that for the fifth-generation computers); and

iii) The multifaceted network among manufacturers, wholesalers and retailers in the household goods industry.

Examples of *i)* and *ii)* may be better known, so I have provided a sketch of *iii)* in Figure 12. Eight household goods manufacturers including Lion, Unicharm, and Shiseido are joined by Intec, an enhanced telecommunications service supplier, to form a communications network consortium known as Planet. Planet provides a linkage among a variety of actors involved in production and distribution. It also includes hundreds of independent wholesalers who conduct business transactions through the network. It also functions as a code centre; computer software is being developed through joint efforts at Planet. The Planet network is thus essentially a synergy-creating enterprise.

An important aspect of the Planet network is that Planet itself acts as an information infrastructure so that its members are able to organise various kinds of subnetworks by their own initiative without worrying about basic communication facilities and services. Such subnetworks include Coronet, Act, Gruppe, and Soryu Forum, as is shown in Figure 12. Soryu Forum, for example, is a voluntary study group consisting of Unicharm and several wholesalers which discusses methods for optimal collaboration between wholesalers and manufacturers and joint retail support. New members are constantly being added to this subnetwork. A multifaceted complex of this type symbolises the configuration common to the

Figure 12. **MULTIFACETED NETWORK IN THE HOUSEHOLD GOODS INDUSTRY**

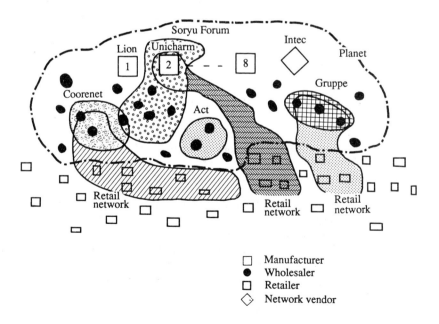

network industrial organisation. It is worth noting that an important characteristic of this type of organisation is the coexistence of competition and co-operation as a result of the co-ownership of the physical communications network.

5. Innovations in the Distribution System

Innovation within the distribution system has recently brought changes that are just now beginning to be felt in markets throughout the world. The foundation for such innovation is the application of information and telecommunications technologies which have led to the creation of POS (point of sale) and VAN (value added network) systems. These systems, when combined with an enhanced telecommunications network, are destined to fundamentally change the structure of wholesale and retail business.

These systems will, first of all, give distributors instant access to combined data as to where, when, and to whom any particular good was sold. This appears to be an exceedingly modest innovation at first glance, but by having access to such cumulative data on the microlevel, it is possible to construct a relationship between micro and macro behaviour. If, for example, a product sells particularly well in a certain region, an investigation into the reasons can be quickly made. Through such comparative investigations more complete marketing information will be gained. Marketing departments will gain new insights about optimum marketing strategies if they are able to confirm the threshold level of sales of a particular good beyond which consumers make purchases in response to the good's popularity and status as the most recent fashion or fad.

A second point to be noted is that instantaneous statistical comparisons make it possible for marketing personnel to discern those particlar areas where important qualitative information can be gathered. Recently, in Japan, marketing methods have begun to change from statistical methods which utilise large data samples to new methods which place emphasis on qualitative information gained through extensive interviews with consumers. This new method places a premium on "on-the-spot" information. The problem with this method, however, is that there are an innumerable number of possible "spots" from which information can be gained. Continuous, instantaneous statistical summations of micro data provide important clues concerning the most productive "spots" for seeking new data. When this is achieved, there will be significant advances in the integration of qualitative and quantitative information.

A third, and perhaps most important, point is that these technological and marketing innovations will change the competitive nature of relationships between firms. While detailed sales data has formerly been a closely guarded secret, recently certain firms have begun to publish such data in order to make analysis of aggregate data possible so as to be able to more clearly establish the position of one's own products in the market. This represents a monumental change from a competitive strategy based on protection of one's own turf through information blocking.

These innovations clearly represent the trend for future developments in the distribution system. Of course, comparison of micro and macro data has been undertaken for decades and is not in itself a new development. However, previous methods did not allow instantaneous comparison, and normally entailed considerable time lags. There is a fundamental difference between the sequential analysis of the past and the instantaneous feedback possible using recent developments in information technologies. The latter type creates a so-called "holonic" loop between sellers and consumers.

6. Reshuffling of Organisational Boundaries

The previously mentioned network division of labour, or flexible specialisation, and the new developments in the distribution system are easily and effectively linked. In fact, these new marketing methods are much more easily adapted to flexible specialisation than they are to fixed divisions of labour.

Under the fixed division of labour regime, a manufacturing process is hierarchically divided into detailed subprocesses involving parts manufacturing, and further subdivisions generate a more complex hierarchical relationship. Production planning, however, is based on sales targets for finished products. If those sales targets are not fulfilled, substantial misallocation of resources will occur at all levels of the hierarchy. Consequently, sales promotion activities rely extensively on mass media advertising to achieve sales targets. However, under this system the linkage between consumers and producers is indirect and remote, and it is only natural that the producers will attempt to assert control over this relationship through sales promotions. The relationship between distributors and producers thus becomes a power game.

In contrast to this situation, producers operating under a flexible division of labour market their products according to the principle of "producing the necessary volume just in time", and are careful to note to whom their product has been sold. The linkage between producers and customers is thereby more direct and there is a strong incentive for both producers and distributors to supply goods which more closely fit the consumer's true needs. Such a system also provides producers and distributors with information about consumer demands that have not yet been met and thus contributes to increased consumption and demand. A virtuous cycle is thus created in which flexible specialisation adapts to and profits from the new marketing system and the marketing system itself contributes to the efficiency of the flexible specialisation system.

The difference between the fixed and flexible divisions of labour seems subtle at first glance. However, because the pattern for the division of labour is the fundamental integrating mechanism for a society, a change from one system to the other will necessarily have important repercussions on the economic and social organisation of society. Those changes are even now beginning to affect the structure of Japanese society and the Japanese industrial system. The movement to a flexible division of labour is creating a basic restructuring of intra- and interorganisational relationships as well as reshuffling the organisational boundaries of firms. The previously mentioned innovations in the distribution system are also beginning to create new vertical linkages between producers, distributors and consumers. These changes represent nothing less, in my opinion, than a redefinition of society and the establishment of the "Information Network Society".

7. Implications for the Future

How will Japan's corporate network evolve from now on? This paper may not provide the appropriate forum for conjecture; however, for the purpose of clarifying the implications of the preceding analysis, I would like to suggest some tentative conclusions. The special characteristics of the Japanese industrial system, which has evolved in the above-mentioned manner, may become clearer if they are contrasted with those which have been created in the United States during the course of its industrialisation.

The American industrial system was predicated on a typical pattern of capitalistic production, with the special conditions for economic development based on the virgin lands of America. With an abundance of land and resources, steady economic growth proceeded in tandem with the expansion of the railways and eventually produced the conditions facilitating the creation of the American mass production and mass marketing systems. Starting with the skillful mastery of British scientific technology, traditional craftsmanship and technical refinements were eventually discarded in favour of standardization and functionalisation. The American manufacturing system became the model for production throughout the world and techniques other than those employed in America were rapidly discarded.

The creation of this model of industrial production also set the direction for the functioning of the market. A business environment, based on contracts was created by standardization; not only financing, but also the labour force became "quantifiable". The development of the stock market, in which the many conflicting evaluations of investors were numerically combined, produced an environment in which enterprises could also be easily bought and sold.

The American industrial system, thus formed, was a natural development given the factors reflecting the availability of resources and the conditions of the labour market. However, the development of the American production system, based on the standardization of parts and fixed specialisations, eventually reached its limits. The mass production, mass marketing and financial systems combined to produce the prototype of the capitalistic production and financial system as the world entered the information network age. Although at one time this system was considered as having attained the highest measure of rationality and efficiency, it became apparent that the supply of manpower exceeded the demand. The industrial system had reached a crossroad in its development. On the other hand, the Japanese industrial system, which developed after the American one, created a structure based on the axis of human networks. To put this in extremely oversimplified terms, whereas the American industrial system operates on a network of finance, that of Japan operates on a network of people. Japan's industrial system has so far succeeded as a flexible human network. However, as the world enters a new stage of development, the disadvantages of this system will also begin to become apparent.

In the Japanese network organisation, the exchange of information involves intense interaction among network members. Consequently, a large amount of resources is needed merely to maintain such human networks, which form the basis for information gathering. However, in most cases a price is not paid for each individual transaction. Information exchange, whether involving technology transfer or consulting services, has traditionally been a long-term bilateral exchange in kind (information), rather than an economic transaction with monetary compensation. Some types of information, such as computer software, have, of course, recently become commodity goods transacted in the market. However, even in such cases the prices paid for such software are lower in Japan than in the United States as a result of the Japanese tradition of not paying, monetarily, for information exchange. This tradition in part explains the slow development of the Japanese software industry, which even now remains in an infant stage.

This type of information exchange devoid of direct payment has in the past provided a hidden source of Japanese competitiveness in manufacturing. If the tradition continues, however, Japanese industries will be unable to create much added value in the coming age of the advanced information society. This is a point of some concern and represents the Achilles' heel of the Japanese corporate network.

Japan's prospects in the area of venture businesses, run by a new type of entrepreneur destined to play a major role in the development of the future industrial society, also differ from those in America and Europe. Venture businesses in these countries are either organisations which bring into the market the technology which they themselves develop or that find and fill a need in the market place. If these businesses are successful they reap tremendous capital rewards when they bring their stock public. These businesses are created by entrepreneurs who utilise the market system to the fullest extent, even if that means selling their own company. Japan, on the other hand, maintains strict standards for the issuance of stocks and investors are generally reluctant to commit their capital to ventures promising high returns at the cost of high risk. Entrepreneurs also are reluctant to sell their own company or acquire other companies through the stock market.

Even Japan will slowly adapt to the new entrepreneurial environment. If the evolutionary process of industrial organisation is influenced by socio-historical factors, however, the same will also be true of the path taken in the development of venture businesses. I have previously defined the fundamental characteristic of the japanese industrial organisation as "the interpenetration of the market and organisation[6]". This means that in a favourable situation the advantages of both market and organisation are utilised, whereas in an unfavourable instance of interpenetration the advantages of both the market and the organisation are lost and the venture fails.

Japanese venture businesses now function under these constraints. Successful ventures in Japan do not receive compensation from large capital gains alone, but in a broader sense they are compensated with moderate profits, the formation of good interorganisational and personal relationships and a favourable exchange of human resources, etc. There are many instances, however, in which the venture failed due to the failure to fully utilise both the market and organisations. Under these circumstances, the disadvantage of interpenetration appeared. Japanese venture business can thus be said to lack the genuine spirit of venture. A point of issue in Japanese corporate behaviour has been, as is often pointed out, its inclination to move in lockstep. I expect venture businesses to begin to break this mold, but there are reasons for scepticism on this point.

I would like to once again call attention to the fact that the characteristics of the Japanese network industrial organisation were inherited from behavioural traits formulated during a period of rapid economic growth. The long-term competitive behaviour in intra and interfirm activites was conditioned by expectations for the future growth of the firm. The behaviour typified by the tendency to seek cost reductions became dominant only after the oil crisis and was a product of the expectations by workers that their company would once again achieve high rates of growth if severe reductions in cost could merely be implemented. The result of this type of behaviour has been a rush to the export market.

Movement into the export market has now also been halted due to recent trade friction. It is clear that Japanese firms and industries have to find a new way of doing business, to increase domestic demand by creating a new context for the industrial society. To that end each firm has had to restructure its managerial resources and technological base. However, as I have previously mentioned, Japanese companies are not able to accomplish that restructuring through the more efficient and quick means of merger or acquisition. Nor can venture businesses be expected at this stage to provide the initiative for such restructuring. The Japanese position in the software industry, which will be a key industry in the future information society, also remains weak and one therefore cannot expect rapid relief from this sector. Although the positive attributes of the network industrial organisation still remain[7], the necessary restructuring will move slowly and yield few immediate results. There are therefore serious obstacles to quickly implementing the structural adjustments that are pressed for by the outside world. It will be the task of the Japanese industrial network to deal with this dilemma in a positive and resourceful manner.

III. SCENARIOS FOR GOVERNMENTAL POLICIES

The policy direction of the Japanese government is now clear, though perhaps still expressed in rather abstract terms. Recently, the *Maekawa Report,* which was presented by Prime Minister Nakasone in Washington on 13th April, 1987, offered seven national goals:

  i)   Increasing domestic demand;
 ii)   Transforming the industrial structure;
iii)   Further improving foreign access to Japanese markets and promoting imports of manufactured products;
 iv)   Fully co-operating to international efforts to stabilise exchange rates and further liberalise and internationalise Japan's financial markets;
  v)   Promoting international co-operation and making contributions to the world economy that are commensurate with Japan's new international economic position;
 vi)   Changing Japan's fiscal and monetary policies; and
vii)   Following up on the proposals contained in the report.

These goals are clearly desirable in principle, but crucial problems remain with regard to their implementation. There has been heated debate in Japan as to whether predictions about the transformation of the industrial structure, along the lines described above, towards the creation of a more balanced structure emphasizing increased domestic demand, are realistic or "painting an imaginary world". My own stance on this point is that if policy goals are desirable we should try to create the long-term policy framework to achieve such goals. More concretely, as it has become evident that a new context for the Japanese industrial structure is being created, policy should be designed to promote the realisation of these structural changes and efforts should be made to increase domestic demand. The essence of this new context, as mentioned in previous sections of this paper, is a transition from a fixed division of labour to a flexible one through the use of microelectronics technologies and innovation in the distribution sector through the use of expanding telecommunications networks. It should be a national goal, I believe, to combine these two by providing policy support for information networking. Such an approach to national policy could be termed Schumpeterian in the sense that it accentuates technological innovation, rather than short-term Keynesian expansion or monetarist factors which are devoid of any structural element.

In discussing policy objectives that focus on IT and information networks it is possible to imagine three future scenarios. The first scenario is the "Technology Driven Scenario", which seeks to realise all feasible technological possibilities in both the information and telecommunications systems. NTT's Information Network System (INS) is an example of this scenario. The second scenario is the "Market Driven Scenario", which emphasizes competition in the market and the transformation of Japan's information network on the basis of factors of supply and demand. Finally, the third scenario is the "Policy Driven Scenario", which attempts to correct the defects of the above two scenarios and seeks evolutionary development in accord with basic policy objectives.

1. The Technology Driven Scenario

In this scenario immense investments of capital are made in such areas as "intelligent cities" and telecommunications infrastructures such as Integrated Services Digital Networks (ISDN) in order to realise the greatest possible number of technological advances. The main feature of this scenario, from the perspective of information networks, is the emphasis placed upon the technological standardization of the telecommunications system and related subsystems and the desire for the highest quality equipment. Such standardization creates the advantage of economies of scale on the supply side, which frees a greater portion of funds for R&D work in such capital intensive areas as satellite communications.

Major companies play a key role in the achievement of this scenario. Japanese industry is at present compelled to restructure intra-firm and inter-firm networks in order to deal with technological innovations in distribution and finance. This restructuring will not only reshape the fundamental structure of manufacutirng and marketing systmes within each industry, it will also provide the opportunity to reshape the basic telecommunications system. Large firms will certainly be among the actors who decide the shape that the information and telecommunications systems will assume in the future. Thereafter, those companies not directly concerned with the issue of telecommunications, will have no choice but to accept the innovations offered by the system as a whole.

NTT, along with certain VAN and CATV firms, will assume a central role in this new telecommunications network. Business firms will position themselves at points around the centre and implement telecommunications strategies designed to promote systematization and technological standardization. Although it is likely that one dominant telecommunications standard will eventually emerge, the degree of competition that this system allows will be determined by whether that standard is developed by a single dominant firm or an alliance of two or three large firms. If the accepted standard is the product of two or three allied companies, the established prices for telecommunications services will be either monopolistic, if the firms act in collusion, or will approach a competitive market price, if the firms actively compete with each other for market share. If one company alone determines the standard, the price for telecommunications services will be a monopolistic price, subject only to pressure from smaller firms offering competitive services on the periphery of the system.

The intrinsic problem of this scenario is that there is little incentive to cut costs. Without such an incentive, there is little reason to believe that the prices charged for telecommunications and information services will be held to their minimum. Certainly, the potential for competition within the system exists to at least a certain extent, as does the possibility that costs for services might fall due to technological innovation. However, in the event that the dominant firm or group of firms functions as a public utility able to recover any and all capital costs, there may be a tendency to seek excessively high quality and promote excessive investment. This point will become clearer when we look at price incentives in the following section.

2. The Market Driven Scenario

This scenario assigns the role of promoting the development of information networks to the market. In this scenario, the telecommunications industry would be deregulated to the greatest possible extent. Entrepreneurs would assume the function of identifying and meeting the various demands created by the market. Under these circumstances, of course, it is highly probable that there will be at least some duplication of services and excess capacity. However, through competition and the process of market selection, Japan's information network would develop in an evolutionary manner.

In this scenario, when the demand for a new media exceeds a certain threshold level due to precedent-setting price cuts by a pioneering entrepreneur, a period of intense competition and rapid advancement in technology is sure to follow. During this stage a general restructuring will occur within the industry forcing certain players to leave the field while enhancing the competitve advantage of others. However, after this restructuring has been completed, the intensity of competition will abate and the pace of technological innovation will slow down. This will be due in part to the tendency for disorder created by a lack of leadership by dominant firms, but the lower rate of investment in the R&D necessary to provide the vitality for future development will also be a factor.

The technological focus of this scenario is upon market-oriented developments. Technological development is particularly important to properly interface the consumer with the telecommunications system. This can be achieved only by technological excellence in combination with consumer education through marketing, as is true of any effort to create consumer demand for new products and services. Management must remain responsive to the needs of the market and be alert for chances to stimulate demand through such techniques as precedent-setting price cuts or the combination and repackaging of diverse services.

The creation of the initial demand for new media, such as CATV, which is aimed at households is difficult if the initial investment (subscription fee) and monthly fees are too high, even if the product attracts the user's attention. The introduction of new goods and/or services requires that demand be expanded through low costs in the initial stage of production so that a threshold level of demand may be achieved. This often requires that the entrepreneurs have access to a source of surplus funds so that the low prices for the product or service may initially be subsidized by the company. Today in Japan, however, there is widespread debate about the feasibility of creating an economically viable CATV network so the risk is perceived as being too great even for companies with deep pockets. It is therefore necessary to approach the project of building a CATV network with a certain amount of caution, constructing the network step by step and utilising the present infrastructure to the greatest extent possible. This entails expanding the cable network from its presently small base, which was created either by government policy designed to provide television reception to those areas which were unable to receive broadcasts by conventional means or by companies attempting to create a simple two-way interactive system. Due to the fact that the expanded system would attempt to tap market demand on a variety of levels it will be necessary for the CATV industry to accommodate a diverse number of small and medium sized enterprises. Thus, although NTT will remain the dominant actor in this market driven scenario, CATV and VAN firms will also play an increasingly important role within the telecommunications and information system.

As can be seen from the above discussion, this scenario assumes that vigorous competition will occur within the marketplace. This competition increases in intensity with the entrance of small-scale entrepreneurs or renewed activity on the part of existing firms. This suggests that the level of competition in the information services industry is also taken into consideration. The problems faced by this scenario due to such excessive competition include the high failure rate of companies, the possibility that any telecommunications standard will fail to emerge, the certainty that there will be no predetermined, overall direction for the development of the industry, and the lack of incentives for future-oriented large-scale R&D.

3. The Policy Driven Scenario

This scenario may overcome the disadvantages of the previously discussed scenarios by proposing a plan which will allow the coexistence of the technology driven and market driven scenarios. It should be said, first of all, that this proposal envisions not one but a number of goals to be achieved in tandem, with quasi-public and private systems in competition and co-operation in the areas of basic telecommunications, value added communications, and software. Due to the fact that the potential for the creation of immense social problems exists with the implementation of any one particular system, the type of problems being dependent upon the particular system being constructed, it would be too dangerous to focus on only one system or move in only one direction. Therefore, a policy which encourages development along a number of tracks, an essentially pluralistic approach, must be followed. In this way, the tendency for high cost exhibited by the technology driven approach and the disorder inherent in the market driven scenario may be controlled.

In more concrete terms, I propose that:

i) A weak federation of private networks be formed as a counterbalance to the NTT affiliated system. As I have indicated in my discussion of the market driven scenario, it is likely that a diverse number of VAN and CATV networks will eventually emerge. There is, of course, some question as to the future of CATV in Japan, but on the whole it appears that the possibility exists for the development of a system consisting of a number of partial networks with varying degrees of technological quality and size. A federation of such partial systems would find it difficult to compete with the basic communications services offered by NTT and on its own would not constitute one of the development tracks described. However, an integrated network could be constructed if some quasi-public company, such as a large electric power company, would assume leadership of the federation. Local governments might also provide support for building such a network of smaller companies;

ii) NTT would be responsible for the information and telecommunications system as a whole. It should take a leading role in promoting easy access and interfacing with the system and allow free linkage with other partial systems. If necessary it should also be prepared to provide linkages between CATV systems. Should NTT take advantage of its superior position to exclude private VAN systems, its right to function as a monopoly would be revoked in accordance with antitrust laws. The amount of power to be held by the privately-held VAN systems is still a question for consideration. If, however, it can be assumed that institutional restrictions on entry into the network can be completely removed and any secret attempts on the part of NTT to exclude private activities can be controlled, then the VAN system should develop to its fullest potential and incorporate a wide variety of actors, including foreign firms;

iii) The co-existence of small-scale, club-like or regionally-based networks with large-scale, nationwide networks should be encouraged, either through policies such as "Technopolis", which encourage the diffusion of technology throughout the country. The large-scale, nationwide networks would be quasi-public networks similar to utilities companies and would handle travel reservations, banking and credit card transactions, medical information, etc. As these types of networks will be able to utilise economies of scale, it is anticipated that they will develop as a natural consequence of the desire by large corporations to enhance profits. The small-scale, club-like networks are also likely to become widespread as a result of market demands. The regionally-based networks will, however, probably require special nurturing through favourable government policy in order to succeed. It is quite clear that CATV will develop largely as a response to regional needs. It is difficult to perceive the benefits, however, of a regional CATV centred on pornographic entertainment, and steps must be taken to forestall such tendencies. The ability of entertainment to foster the spread of CATV networks cannot, of course, be negated, and strong restrictions on content by the government would only serve to dampen developmental energies. Therefore, policies should be geared merely toward encouraging certain types of regional entertainment and programming, such as broadcasts of children's track and field events, PTA meetings, city council meetings and shopping information. These regional networks also provide an excellent forum for news concerning volunteer activities, and the dissemination of such information is also to be encouraged. Once again, it should be emphasized that the government should engage in efforts to promote certain types of programming rather than discourage or ban competing programs, and in this way foster the growth of these regional networks as well as providing direction for regional economic policies;

iv) In recognition of the fact that certain types of information serve the public good, policies should be formulated with the goal of creating such services as public databases offering access to diverse types of information at a low cost. As Japan is notably behind in the formulation of policies in this area there is a strong need to promote such policies on both the national and regional level. Through such a measure the government should upgrade the quality of software supply by the Japanese software industry which is still in an infant stage owing to the reasons mentioned in the above section. The creation of such an information infrastructure might even result in the development of a new media, distinct from the existing mass communications media, utilising the infrastructure created by the policies outlined here;

v) In terms of information network policy, I strongly urge the adoption of the liberalisation policy advocated by MITI, which would guarantee "freedom of entry", "freedom of activity", and "freedom of use". In order to assure that these freedoms will in fact be guaranteed, however, it is necessary to devise concrete plans to provide flexible linkages between networks. Such plans would thereby guarantee what has been called the "interoperability" of information networks. If standardization is pushed too strongly it could stifle the creative energies of individual firms, resulting in a loss of vitality for the system as a whole. Standardization should thereby be pursued in the spirit of creating guidelines, not ironclad rules which attempt to anticipate future developments but establish only the minimum requirements for assuring that the various systems will be able to link up through the information and telecommunications network. Even if NTT takes a leading role in formulating standards, it is necessary to allow other enterprises, including other information and telecommunications manufacturers, sufficient opportunities to express their desires and opinions. Designing a standard which ensures "interoperability" but does not limit options for the future should therefore be a primary concern of information network policy makers;

vi) The creation of demand in the household sector for information and telecommunications services is of crucial importance in this policy driven scenario. It is clear from the semi-macro predictions of Section 2 of this paper, that the prospects for the development of the Japanese information industry will in large part depend upon the degree of demand from the household sector. All planning and policies must take this into consideration.

In regard to technology, policies should promote the spread of information technologies to the household sector by encouraging the creation of more "user friendly" interfaces between people and machines, whether at the hardware or software level. A large percentage of public R&D resources should be used for this purpose, rather than expending these resources for the advancement of basic technology *per se,* as advocated by the technology driven scenario. Meanwhile, in the area of marketing, policies should be formulated which provide government support for such semi-public markets as medical care, education, and public information services, rather than merely relying upon the efforts of private companies to achieve market penetration in these areas.

Finally, I believe that the "Technopolis" plan of MITI should be promoted as a policy for the diffusion of technology, and the "Teletopia" plan of the MPT and the "New Media Community" plan of MITI should also be developed so as to provide important information infrastructures and software for the household sector. The urgent task for Japanese policy makers is to devise a means for co-ordinating and combining such diversified efforts and directing their synergy into actions to increase domestic demand.

NOTES AND REFERENCES

1. We found the following relationship: $V_{inf} = 0.0315V^2$.
   Here, V_{inf} refers to value added per capita in the information industry and V refers to that of the economy as a whole. If we designate V_{phy} as value added per capita in the real goods manufacturing industry, we obtain:

   $$V_{phy} = V - V_{inf} = V - 0.0315V^2 \text{ when } V_{inf}/V = 0.5.$$

   See Voge, J., "The Political Economy of Complexity – From the Information Economy to the Complexity Economy", *Information Economics and Policy*, 1983.

2. My point here is not to predict that the share of the information sector will peak soon, rather, to indicate that a simple extrapolation is not appropriate.

3. In the *ad hoc* expert meeting a question was raised as to whether this prediction is a target or not. The prediction is not a target in a usual sense, rather it should be considered as a quantitative framework for policy discussions.

4. For more details refer to: Imai, K., Nonaka, I. and Takouchi, M., "Managing the New Product Development Process: How Japanese Companies Learn and Unlearn", in K.B. Clark, R. Hayes, and C. Lorenz (eds.), *The Uneasy Alliance – Managing the Productivity-Technology Dilemma*, Harvard Business School Press, 1985.

5. Piore, M.J. and Sabel, C.F., *The Second Industrial Divide – Possibilities for Prosperity*, Basic Books, 1984.

6. See Imai, K. and Itami, H., "Interpenetration of Organisation and Market – Japan's Firm and Market in Comparison with the US", *International Journal of Industrial Organisation*, 1984.

7. See Imai, K., "Japan's Industrial Policy for High Technology Industry", in H. Patrick (ed.), *Japan's High Technology Industries*, University of Washington Press, 1986.

NEW INFORMATION TECHNOLOGY
AND INDUSTRIAL ORGANISATION*
EXPERIENCES AND TRENDS IN ITALY

by

Cristiano Antonelli
Politecnico di Milano
Milano, Italy

TABLE OF CONTENTS

I. INTRODUCTION 82

II. THE INDUSTRIAL ORGANISATION APPROACH 82

III. THE DIFFUSION OF NEW INFORMATION TECHNOLOGY IN THE ITALIAN ECONOMY 85

IV. THE EFFECTS OF NEW INFORMATION TECHNOLOGY 86
   1. Information Technology and the Production of Goods and Services 87
     a) Procurement 88
     b) Manufacturing 88
     c) Marketing 89
   2. Information Technology and the Governance of Transactions 90
     a) The Governance Transactions within the Firm 90
     b) The Governance of Transaction among Firms 91

V. CONCLUSIONS AND POLICY ISSUES 93

NOTES AND REFERENCES 97

BIBLIOGRAPHY 98

---

* Mr. Dieter Kimbel at the OECD and Mr. Roger Noll at Stanford University have been very helpful in commenting upon and suggesting improvements to earlier drafts of this manuscript. Any remaining errors are entirely of my own making.

I. INTRODUCTION

New Information Technology can be defined as a set of latent technological and organisational innovations characterised by more communication intensive techniques of production and co-ordination of transactions[1].

By changing the costs and conditions of retrieval, processing, evaluation and storage of information necessary to co-ordinate separate activities such as plants and production units, New Information Technology has important effects on the organisation of firms[2].

By changing the cost and condition of use of information necessary within the production process to co-ordinate different machines, New Information Technology has also important effects on the structure and scope of production units[3].

For these reasons the economic analysis of the impact of New Information Technology on firms and industries requires a specific framework. New Information Technology is in fact a major technological innovation, with major organisational and production implications.

With reference to the organisational aspects, New Information Technology can be described as a radical innovation in the use of information in the management of firms. New Information Technology therefore has important effects on the strategy and structure of firms and industries by changing the information environment and the relations between markets and organisations.

With reference to the production features, New Information Technology can be described as a radical innovation in the use of information within the entire production process. As a consequence, New Information Technology has important effects on the size of plants and productive units by changing the minimum efficient size of production.

To assess the complex and subtle chain of organisational and productive changes induced by the introduction of New Information Technology, the industrial organisation approach as developed in industrial economics and transaction cost economics seems best suited[4].

II. THE INDUSTRIAL ORGANISATION APPROACH

In *Limits of Organisation,* Arrow has emphasised the strategic role of information for the optimal outcome of economic activity in a market system. The possibility of using the price system to allocate, co-ordinate and monitor the economic activity under optimal conditions, is determined by the access of economic agents to information. Arrow has also shown that uncertainty can only be internalised in a competitive equilibrium system when all individuals have access to the same information under the same conditions. The price system fails when these conditions are not fulfilled and access to information is imperfect among the economic agents. Transactions have a cost as such and because markets are imperfect[5].

When the administrative integration of information exchange reduces these costs, organisations take the place of markets. Markets and "Hierarchies" of firms can be considered as alternative modes of co-ordination, allocation and monitoring of production inputs.

According to the industrial organisation approach, all economic activity is organised either within or outside the firm depending on the relative weight of hierarchical (co-ordination) and market (transactions) costs. Co-ordination costs have always been considered a major factor in limiting the size of firms. As Simon (1982) argues, they counterbalance production costs and limit the growth of the firms even in the presence of technical economies of scale[6].

The size of a firm and its strategy are determined when the costs of internal co-ordination of economic activities, the costs of production and the costs of purchasing the production factors on the market are jointly taken into account. The size of firms depends not only on technical economies of scale but also on organisational forces as uncertainty and information deficiencies play a strategic role[7].

The strategy of firms, their size and their internal organisation, are the result of a balance between co-ordination and transaction costs. Firms expand until the marginal costs per unit of input allocated, co-ordinated and monitored internally, equal its marginal revenue, and the cost of the same product bought on the market[8].

Firm structures and strategies depend upon the information environment and its changes. All innovation regarding the management of information is expected to modify in depth transaction and co-ordination costs and consequently the conduct of firms and industrial structures.

More generally it can be stated that within the industrial organisation approach, production costs and transaction costs are regarded as the two determinants of industrial structures.

Production costs shape the minimum efficient size of production activities.

Transaction costs shape the minimum efficient size of firms.

More specifically, production costs depend upon the corresponding production functions or production technologies, i.e. the sets of productive techniques available, and their characteristics, namely indivisibilities and consequently economies of scale. It can therefore be argued that production technologies determine the minimum efficient size of production activities.

An industrial structure with no transaction costs would be characterised by firms which are never larger than the minimum efficient size of production units. No discrepancy would exist between the level of technical concentration and the level of economic concentration. Economies of scale shape the size of firms and, for given levels of demand, the structure of the sector. Firms would have no interest to run productive plants larger than the efficient size and the industrial structure, i.e. the distribution of typical firm sizes in a particular industrial sector would be governed by the ratio between minimum efficient size plant and demand.

In the real world, however, firms are usually larger than the optimal sized plants; economic concentration is often much larger than technically justified.

According to the traditional industrial economics approach, the discrepancy between the theoretically efficient size of plants and the real size of firms is the result of monopolistic conduct[9]. In this economics tradition, the boundaries of firms are in fact regarded as rigidly determined by the features of available production technologies[10]; the concept of the firm and the concept of the production function coincide.

The growing industrial organisation literature proposes that the concept of the firm as a production function must be integrated with the concept of the firm as a governance function[11]. Transaction costs and the features of the governance function, i.e. the set of organisational techniques available to govern transactions within the firm, determine the minimum efficient size of firms, i.e. the number and size of production activities co-ordinated within the same firm.

The industrial organisation approach considers the firm also as the outcome of the specific features of the governance function. As production functions shape the efficient size of production activities to minimise production costs, governance functions shape the efficient size of firms, i.e. the efficient number and collection of technical activities, at minimised transaction costs. As the efficient size of plants is determined by economies of scale, the efficient size of firms when larger than minimum efficient size of plants is determined by economies of scope, i.e. the reduction in total transaction costs, both internal and external, for the appropriate collection of technical activities.

The firm internalises the transactions between technically separable production activities when the "use cost" of markets is larger than the "use cost" of the managerial hierarchy.

The level of transaction costs, or use costs of exchanging goods among technical units (plants) depends upon the characteristics of the production process. The more idiosyncratic and specific the assets, the higher the rate of market failure, i.e. the lower the efficiency of prices as appropriate signals to convey information about the production costs of goods.

More generally, transaction costs can thus be defined as the opportunity costs of any localised inefficiency in prices to deliver correct signals. Transaction costs are thus the costs of acquiring relevant information not provided by prices.

Use costs of managerial hierarchies depend upon the organisational technology used within the firm to internally co-ordinate the transaction between different efficient technical units. Co-ordination costs consist of the cost of managing the internal flow of information relevant for each productive unit. Co-ordination costs also include the cost of acquiring information on the performance of the communication activities. Co-ordination costs limit the efficient size of firms with respect to both technical economies of scale and economies of scope. Fast rising marginal co-ordination costs cause the failure of firms. In this situation, markets become an alternative to minimise transaction costs.

The size of firms beyond the minimum efficient size of each plant depends upon features of the governance function, i.e. the relative cost of market transactions with respect to co-ordination costs.

An industrial structure with high levels of transaction costs, low levels of co-ordination costs and small size of efficient plants would be characterised by a large number of average sized firms. In such a case, the size of firms would be in fact much more the result of the features of the governance function than that of the production function.

In conclusion, within an industrial organisation framework, the firm can be considered a substitute for arm's length arrangements (trade) when market failures make transactions more expensive and less reliable than internal co-ordination.

Firms are the result of decisions to internalise productive, financial and technological factors or commercial opportunities, when these opportunities are not perfectly exploitable through market transactions. Any internalisation decision made by the firm is also the result of a specific advantage (i.e. higher factor productivity) which the firm possesses in terms of technology, managerial organisation or market control of which it cannot make perfect use of through the market transaction of goods. In the face of market imperfections, the firm accepts extra costs in order to take full advantage of its higher productivity. The costs involved are partly those of co-ordinating geographically dispersed operations and heterogeneous products.

The internalisation decision therefore involves a comparison between a number of factors: the price of goods on the market and the real cost of the production process; the cost of acquiring the information necessary to combine these in an internalised productive process; the cost of communication of relevant information within the managerial structure.

Within industrial structures the number of firms in a market and their size, the relationship between the size of production activities and the size of firms, i.e. the ratio of technical concentration, are governed ceteris paribus by demand, by the joint effect of the production function, transaction costs, and governance functions.

This analysis supports the conclusion that industrial structures are governed by the joint evolution of two broad categories of costs: production and transaction costs.

III. THE DIFFUSION OF NEW INFORMATION TECHNOLOGY IN THE ITALIAN ECONOMY

A variety of indicators suggest that New Information Technologies spread very fast in the Italian economy[12].

The Italian industrial structure is characterised by specific and localised pattern of adoption and incremental change. New Information Technologies are favouring the introduction of a wave of organisational changes both within and between firms.

The Italian economy falls into the category of late industrialised countries[13], i.e. countries whose industrialisation process took off late in the nineteenth century. It has long been characterised by a number of specific features, namely, low factor productivity, strong relevance of traditional sectors, the polarisation of firms around two types: a small number of "modern" firms with high total factor productivity, high wages and advanced managerial structures. These firms have command over skilled input factors. They operate at the forefront of technological advance. There is, however, a large number of "traditional" firms with low total factor productivity, operating at backward technological and managerial levels. These traditional firms survive in making use of the low wage workforce and by avoiding fiscal burdens.

This industrial and economic dualism is the result of an historic process of leapfrogging. Italy started its industrialisation process when other countries were already established on international oligopolistic markets and well ahead in the Schumpeterian competition based on innovation and technological advance. Italy, thus, given the low levels of accumulated tangible and intangible assets, specialised its economy in low capital intensive activities with low levels of output per worker. Over time, however, a few firms were able to take advantage of new technological trajectories in reducing the innovation lag and the productivity gap with the early industrialised countries. The process of reshaping the factors of comparative advantage and accumulating scarce intangible assets, however, is costly, risky and long-term thus reducing the number of firms able to modernise. Until recently the Italian industrial structure seemed to be characterised by two categories of firms; one able to compete on international markets with techniques and production functions similar to those of early industrialised countries; the other group, in order to compete internationally, applying a different set of techniques, i.e. making use of less tangible and intangible assets and employing low-skilled labour.

This dualism also characterised the factor markets. As a consequence, the Italian labour market used to be strongly segmented, with a large share of low paid and poorly skilled manpower and a small fraction of trained workers.

Major changes in the seventies challenged this traditional structure. The spread of higher salaries from the tiny modern sector to the large traditional one has been very rapid in the 1970s as a result of strong innovation patterns, sharp reduction of unemployment rates, high levels of unionisation and the very active behaviour of unions. This pressure diminished as the economic basis of the traditional sector of the industrial structure has squeezed the price-cost margins, pushed firms towards more productive uses of labour, and applied more innovative strategies.

The changes in the international division of labour caused by the entry of new competitors, the growing differentiation of demand and customisation in traditional markets such as textiles, apparel and footwear have also favoured this development.

In the 1970s and 1980s, the Italian industrial structure has been shaken by the strong increases in prices of oil and other primary factor inputs, by the changing character of the internal labour market, and by the entry of new competitors in international markets. These changes affected the market position of Italian firms and generated falling rates of profitability.

Firms adopted the New Information Technology as a tool to cope with the growing economic problems: Information Technology was perceived as a major opportunity to modernise an obsolete industrial organisation and to introduce in the fabric of traditional activities major technological and organisational innovations[14].

New Information Technology was introduced to rejuvenate traditional "low-tech" manufacturing activities such as textile, apparel, footwear, and obsolete tertiary sectors such as small shop retailing. This has increased total factor productivity without dramatic disruption. The Italian evidence seems to suggest that the New Information Technology can help to blend traditional industrial structures based on small firms with trends towards customer sophistication and market segmentation both in consumer and capital goods.

IV. THE EFFECTS OF NEW INFORMATION TECHNOLOGY

The features of the Italian industrial organisation have been described as comprising strong industrial dualism with a small number of big, modern firms and a large number of small, traditional firms; these, and the existence of a major economic crisis have, to a large extent, propelled the diffusion of the new technology.

The diffusion of New Information Technology in the Italian industry has in fact favoured the appearance of a new institution: the network firm.

The network firm is first of all the result of the introduction of new communication intensive techniques by large modern firms in the governance of "vertical" transactions with smaller subcontractors and retailers.

Network firms also tend to cluster around communication channels introduced to manage "horizontal" transactions among firms of the same industry to achieve a better division of labour.

The emergence of such a network firm also seems to be the result of the differentiated effect of New Information Technology on the production process as distinct from the transaction governance process.

A clear separation of the analysis of the effects of New Information Technology on the production of goods and services as distinct from the analysis of the effects on governance functions seems to be a preliminary condition to understand the overall economic effect of New Information Technology on industrial structures. Only in a second step will it be possible to consider the global effect resulting from the joint evaluation of the production and the organisation effects of New Information Technology in terms of efficient size of firms, performance and new industrial structures.

Such a two-step methodology, consistent with an industrial organisation approach, seems necessary to organise the large body of conflicting empirical evidence about the effects of New Information Technology on the Italian industrial structure.

In order to analyse the organisational changes which parallel the adoption of new information technologies, we now turn to consider the evidence provided by a number of case studies. An indepth case study approach, to reach the microanalytical (functional) level *within* the firms considered, has been applied to better focus the contingent and specific features of the process of change within the organisational structure of those firms adopting New Information Technologies. More specifically, it can be argued that such a process of change by trial and error is part of the dynamic interaction of technological and organisational changes (learning by doing and learning by using) which characterise the diffusion and incremental improvement of major innovations.

The empirical evidence gathered to date suggests in fact, that the effects of New Information Technology on production functions tends to be basically centrifugal, reducing the role of technical economies of scale by lowering the minimum efficient size of production units. Its effects on governance functions appear to be rather centripetal, increasing the weight of economies of scope and the average size of governance structures. From this point of view, it seems confirmed that the overall result of such a conflicting mix of centrifugal and centripetal forces generated by the introduction of New Information Technology is a growing trend towards the appearance of a new institution: the *network firm,* characterised by the large size of its governance structure and small size of separate production functions and technical units managed by means of hierarchical co-ordination and quasi-integration[15].

1. Information Technology and the Production of Goods and Services

To assess the distinctive effects of the New Information Technology on each component of the "collection of activities that are performed to design, produce, market, deliver and support (its) products[16]" by each firm, a step by step approach seems appropriate.

The growing quantity of information made available by the New Information Technology is pushing towards radical changes in the design and management of the production activities within the firm.

The sharp decline in the relative cost of information is in fact generating a wave of induced innovations in manufacturing, marketing, procurement and finance. Because of major changes in the terms of trade between information costs and other input costs and a consequent increase in the opportunity cost of information, the production process of goods and services is being dramatically redesigned towards new techniques which are both more communication-intensive and more productive[17].

To highlight these changes a number of Italian case studies will briefly be reviewed to show the effects of New Information Technology in such activities which are sensitive to information technology such as procurement, manufacturing and marketing.

a) Procurement

The increased quantity and quality of information made available by the introduction of new communication intensive techniques within the procurement function has strong effects in terms of reductions in site-specificity of suppliers with increased access to multisourcing and global scanning, and reductions in the time specificity of suppliers. This leads to a major reduction in the stock of inputs and important reductions in transaction costs per unit procured.

In the case of a leading garment firm, access to electronic information markets for standardized inputs, makes it possible to evaluate much more easily a broader range of potential suppliers including those located abroad.

In the same case, on-line contacts between suppliers and a third party specialised in quality control make it possible to:

- i) Reduce litigation on quality standards;
- ii) Share the costs of quality controls performed jointly only once by a third party instead of twice by supplier and customer; and
- iii) Reduce the time-specificity of procurement functions introducing just-in-time techniques and thus reducing the stock of inputs[18].

A large amount of empirical evidence suggests that both the average costs and the minimum efficient size of procurement services shrank consistently after the introduction of new communication intensive techniques including data bank services, on-line connections with third parties, and internal capacity to elaborate, retrieve and store larger quantities of information made possible in a medium sized computer.

It seems apparent today that small procurement units, much smaller than before the introduction of information technology, can provide efficient services.

The overall effects of such new communication techniques on procurement can be summarised as leading to:

- Reduction of stock of inputs;
- Reduction of paper work;
- Reduction of litigation;
- Reduction of prices;
- Better quality control.

b) Manufacturing

The introduction of new communication intensive techniques in manufacturing has strong effects in terms of reduction of the minimum efficient size of production runs with a consequent reduction in the physical and site specificity of fixed capital assets. In a large mechanical firm the creation of a telecommunication network between headquarters, R & D labs and remote plants to establish on-line communication between Computer Assisted Design units and Computer Assisted Manufacturing centres made it possible to:

- Distribute, to a large number of plants and manufacturing centres, basic designs and engineering information with enhanced levels of technical economies of scope, i.e. fungibility of designs, components and parts;
- Increase the number of products that can be manufactured by the same machining centre thus reducing the effects on optimum size of plants of product specific scale economies and more generally the multiplant economies stemming from the specialisation of plants in specific segments of production[19];

- Tighten the interaction between after-sale assistance quality control, manufacturing and R&D with a major increase in quality standards, the rate of incremental product and process innovation, and the appropriation of learning effects;
- Customise the efficient production of specialised goods;
- Reduce the minimum efficient size of manufacturing centres because of higher interchangeability of each specialised asset.

It seems that the introduction of new communication intensive techniques in manufacturing in northern Italy has led to a reduction of the traditional gap between rigid mass production with large economies of scale and flexible craft production characterised by small sized production units. In the textile and garment industries, for example, a large number of medium sized manufacturing units are able to manufacture a wide range of differentiated products with production costs much closer to former large plants specialised in rigid mass production than to those of small craft shops, by means of CAD-CAM and CAL (Computer Assisted Learning) techniques[20].

In addition, the introduction of more communication intensive techniques has led to a reduction in the size of manufacturing (and R&D laboratories) centres and more cost effective communications among manufacturing units (and R&D laboratories). This has had important effects on the location of specialised production units and has minimised transportation costs[21].

c) *Marketing*

The introduction of more communication intensive techniques has also had major effects on the commercial strategies of the firm including:
- Enhanced product and market differentiation with widespread adoption of niche strategy and price discrimination;
- Global scope of operation;
- Increased product customisation;
- Increased after-sale assistance for durable goods;
- Reduction of time specificity relevant to physically perishable goods (food) and fashion products;
- Reduction of invoicing lags.

The effects of the adoption of a computerised infrastructure system for distribution has been especially evident in a large Italian group active in the food and beverage markets. In this firm, production costs accounted for only 60 per cent of total costs, while distribution and advertising accounted for up to 35 per cent. The structure of production within the company was such that stocks of intermediate products and final goods were very important. Consequently, the amount of working capital needed was extremely important, which led to heavy financial costs. The customer base is extremely wide and diverse, ranging from large customers such as catering companies, chain-stores and hotels to small shopkeepers with very specialised and limited requirements. Consequently, selling conditions are extremely diverse, and distribution, terms of payments and delivery times vary greatly. The adoption of a computerised distribution system made it possible to reduce stocks by 31 per cent and to increase the flexibility of production lines to the changing requirements of final demand, to introduce a custom-based distribution system specialised for different market niches. This dramatically reduced the need for working capital.

The overall effects on performance have resulted in:
- Higher quality standards as perceived by customers;

- Reduction in delivery lags, invoice lags, reduction of float and reduction of stock of final goods with decreasing working capital;
- Higher sustainable prices.

2. Information Technology and the Governance of Transactions

The introduction of information technology-based management information systems has major effects both on internal co-ordination costs, i.e. the costs of governance of transactions within the firm, and on the costs of governance of quasi-integration, i.e. the governance of long term transactions among independent firms.

a) The Governance Transactions within the Firm

Co-ordination costs may be broadly defined as those costs accruing from the continuous control of the production process and related activities.

Co-ordination costs have threshold effects on the capacity of managers to monitor ongoing operations, review and control financial performances, take corrective action and finally to undertake strategic planning for the future development of the firm.

The rapidly rising slope of average co-ordination costs is a traditional factor limiting the efficient size of firms[22].

The use of new Management Information Systems (MIS) *reduces co-ordination costs* as a result of the broadening of control. This, in turn, causes the progressive inefficiency of hierarchical structures because of the limited capacity of central managers to keep the disparate evolution of various firm activities under control.

Management Information Systems which enable information to be retrieved, processed and stored at a much lower cost particularly affect the co-ordination costs of all those processes that require real-time monitoring and feed-back. In this way, Management Information Systems completely change the conception of processes, fostering the introduction of automatic techniques. This type of transformation is already visible in some specific managerial tasks: the organisation and management of production; the design of logistic plans; the reorganisation of productive cycles among factories and firms; the management of finance, that is, all fields in which a real-time control allows a further degree of automation. The introduction of new Management Information Systems in a large retailing chain has made it possible to:

- Eliminate the tremendous amount of paper work which is now part of everyday business activity;
- Better plan careers and personnel skills;
- Optimise internal financial situations by minimising working capital;
- Optimise internal infrastructures of supplies, storage and distribution;
- Avoid shirking of duties and hence to reduce monitoring costs;
- Increase the number and specialisation of organisational units in the company.

In a few large Italian firms the introduction of New Information Technology seems to support a trend towards the creation of matrix organisational structures with regionally dispersed, specialised production units. This, in return, requires more centralised control activities. Strategic decision making becomes more and more centralised, while the implementation of global strategies in each market is decentralised to specialised functional units.

With the adoption of New Information Technology, firms are more and more characterised by a network of commercial affiliates, which sell worldwide the products manufactured by a few, highly efficient and specialised small monoproduct factories, supported through IT by global product divisions and central service centres including finance, procurement, advertising, R&D, electronic data processing (EDP) and transport facilities.

The use of New Information Technologies seems to be paving the way to a trend towards functional specialisation in manufacturing and marketing within the firm. Each unit is becoming more and more similar to a quasi co-ordinated firm which internalises a limited amount of resources without the constraint of a fully integrated structure.

Strategic management and monitoring of the performances of the global manufacturing divisions, the commercial units and the other specialised functional units, is provided at the corporate level by central staff, responsible for the overall planning, strategic decision making and the electronic network.

Relations among the network of quasi-functional (or co-ordinated) firms and the corporate staff seem to be characterised more and more by new forms of "quasi co-ordination" based on shadow prices.

By means of electronic accountancy and on-line reporting each quasi co-ordinated firm is free to trade its products within internal markets at shadow prices, bidding with the others to obtain new investments or placing surplus resources into new investment projects.

The corporate management acts as a controller and auctioneer favouring the allocation of all available resources (financial, productive, commercial and technological) to meet strategic goals.

The larger the corporate network of quasi co-ordinated firms, the larger the chance of having a sustainable mix of fast growing and profitable business units able to generate a continuing flow of financial resources available for new undertakings.

It seems clear that the downward shift of average co-ordination costs induced by the adoption of new communication intensive organisational techniques has major effects on the efficient size of the governance activities, i.e. the minimum efficient size of firms, by delaying the maximum efficient size, thus allowing larger firms to operate efficiently[23].

b) The Governance of Transaction among Firms

Most importantly, computer networks make it possible to elaborate new forms of "electronic quasi-integration", i.e. long term contractual agreements among independent firms based on a shared computer communication infrastructure.

Electronic quasi-integration is based on long term contracts among firms which decide to share hardware and software standards with major constraints on the freedom to change all of the informatic infrastructure without previous agreement of all the parties. The cost of "exit" and switching from one network to another depends on the variety of standards and their differentiation; the costs of "exit" are estimated to be in the order of 100 per cent of the informatic infrastructure investment. These costs are a major barrier for smaller parties, but a source of contractual power for a larger party. This asymmetry in "exit" costs is of major advantage for larger firms.

An array of new forms of electronic quasi integration among independent firms has emerged with the introduction of computer networks, including:

- Electronic franchising and electronic retailing;
- Electronic subcontracting;
- Electronic joint-ventures in research and design.

These forms of electronic quasi integration seem characterised by important economies of scale with the asymmetry in exit costs, and even more importantly, with network externalities[24]: the larger the network, the lower the operating costs, and the larger per unit revenue. More specifically, we see that the larger the network, the larger the opportunities to appropriate the externalities generated by the circulation of information and the distribution of intangible assets.

Computer based distribution systems make new forms of retailing by means of "electronic franchising" possible. Shops owned by independent third parties can be linked electronically to the computerised distribution network with important implications in overall sales and reduction of fixed capital assets and direct personnel costs per unit of sale. By "electronic franchising", firms are able to increase their capacity of governance of distribution and marketing at decreasing rates of managerial co-ordination costs. The analysis of a leading apparel firm shows that electronic franchising makes it possible to better enforce franchising contracts, to keep sales and stocks of each commercial unit under control, and thus reduce the scope for opportunistic behaviour of contractors. Moreover, electronic franchising makes it possible to increase the appropriation capacity of network externalities: the larger the number of distribution points the higher the quality of information on market trends and the lower the unit cost of EDP resources committed to the distribution system.

The advantages for the firm adopting this electronic franchising concept are evident:

i) Almost no additional investment is required to build the distribution chain and no additional employment hiring to run the shops which are owned by independent entrepreneurs;

ii) Low levels of working capital both in terms of stocks of finished products and credits to the shopkeepers.

If the independent shops linked to a computer based distribution system keep their commercial name, experts speak of electronic retailing. Electronic retailing seems to open the way to a radical change in the traditional retailing system in Italy based on small independent shopkeepers. The growth of electronic retailing chains seems in fact able to increase the overall efficiency of the retailing sector without reducing the autonomy of each business. In a large commercial company for example, the management of the electronic retailing network provides each contractor with a variety of services such as procurement, delivery, intermediary stocks and in some cases accountancy. The results have been dramatic. Overhead costs have dropped by 25 per cent within three years in each sub-contractor unit and profit levels for the commercial company operating the electronic retailing network have increased comparatively.

In-house CAD-CAM systems linked to external computer-based machining centres open new forms of "electronic subcontracting". The production process of independent subcontractors is governed and instructed by CAD-CAM centres owned and managed by larger firms responsible for research and development, product design, input selection, quality control, incremental product and process innovation.

Electronic subcontracting also helps to better enforce subcontracting relations with sophisticated and innovative products characterised by high risk, opportunity costs of learning effects, and low appropriability of technological leadership. Experience in a large engineering firm shows that electronic subcontracting makes the governance of a large number of small efficient plants and manufacturing units at low marginal co-ordination costs possible. Major economic advantages of this system include:

– Important economies of scale in costs for R&D, EDP, design and engineering, input allocations;

- Reduction in fixed capital asset requirements per unit of sale;
- Reduction in direct employment per unit of sale;
- Better quality control of the production of subcontractors;
- Better enforcement of opportunistic behaviour of subcontractors responsible for the production of technology-intensive components or spare parts.

Computer links between data banks, central processing units of research and development laboratories and engineering service centres owned by independent firms help to create important forms of electronic joint-ventures in research and engineering design. These electronic joint-ventures are characterised by selectivity and specificity of co-operation. The case of a leading firm producing investment goods, for example, shows how such computer links provide a selective interface with specialised partners, both customers and competitors. This has improved the division of labour, specialisation, reduction of total costs and higher quality of results. In this case, it became clear that the larger the size of R & D laboratories, the larger the size of R & D projects which are either multidisciplinary or whose results are considered fungible for different firms and technologies, the larger the number of potential partners with whom to develop each section drawing on the specialised intangible resources and skills available to each partner[25].

V. CONCLUSIONS AND POLICY ISSUES

The cases analysed and the empirical evidence found, seem strong enough to provide some stylised facts and the drawing of some generalisable trends about the diffusion of Information Technology in the Italian manufacturing industry, and to assess some basic policy issues.

The diffusion and implementation of New Information Technology as a set of major latent innovations is generating a swarm of incremental changes both in the production and governance functions. The reduction in the relative cost of information processing induced the introduction of new production techniques which are more communication intensive and more productive. At the same time, the diffusion of New Information Technology has strong effects on the governance of transactions among production units within firms and on markets. To assess the impact of New Information Technology on industrial structures, a specific approach is necessary to encompass the twin and combined effects on production and governance functions.

The industrial organisation approach, a result of the merging of industrial economics and transaction cost economics, seems to fit the need of a joint evaluation of the effects of new technology on both the production functions, which express the relationship between inputs and products and the governance functions which express the relationship between production units and firms. The results of the analysis of the empirical evidence are summarised in Table 1.

The adoption of new communication intensive techniques induced by lower communication costs seems to have strong centrifugal effects lowering the minimum efficient size of production of goods and services, and reducing the threshold of efficient operations in many manufacturing and service industries.

New communication intensive techniques seem also to be characterised by higher levels of total factor productivity because of:

Table 1. **The effects of adoption of new communication intensive technology**

Production of Goods and Services	Governance of Transactions
– Increased access to multi-sourcing – Global scope of procurement – Reduction of stocks of input – Reduction of paper work – Better control of quality standards	– Use of specialised intermediary agencies to enforce quality controls – Reduction of litigation and other negotiating costs
– Reduction of minimum efficient size of production *lots* and production *units* – Foot-loose location of new plants – Valorisation of latent economies of scope among different product unit and business units – Enhanced customisation of small production – Increased advantage of specialised location – Increased flexibility of the production process – Reduction of stock of intermediate products	– Increased use of quasi-integration by means of electronic sub-contracting – On-line enforcement of quality control and opportunistic behaviour of subcontractors – Increased use of quasi-co-ordination by means of internal markets and shadow prices – Increased co-operation on specific projects with third parties both customers and competitors – Increased co-ordination between R&D, manufacturing and markets
– Niche strategy based on differentiation – Global scope of operation – Reduction in delivery lags – Reduction of stocks of final products – Reduction of working capital – Reduction of financial risks on customers – Reduction of invoicing lags	– Increased number of quasi independent business units – Increased interaction of top and middle management – Strengthening of the central superdivisional management – Electronic franchising – Increased interfunctional co-ordination – Creation of internal data banks with unified information on each customer (and supplier)

i) *Reductions in the amount of working capital* per unit of sale after reduction of the levels of stocks of finished products, intermediate and primary inputs and the order-invoice time lags;

ii) *Reductions in the "idleness" of physical assets* dedicated to rigid mass production after the introduction of flexible techniques widening the scope of efficient fungibility.

The introduction of New Information Technology in the governance function has induced the adoption of new communication intensive co-ordination techniques within firms. This has led to important reductions in average co-ordination costs and increased the maximum efficient size of the governance structure. Most important however, New Information Technology has induced new forms of "electronic quasi-integration" which seems to have strong centripetal effects largely based on the possibility of internalising important network externalities.

The result of such a competing mix of centrifugal and centripetal forces induced by the introduction of New Information Technology seems to be the development of new network organisation forms with specific strategic and structural features. Such strategic features of the network firm include:

– Selective vertical and lateral integration of production phases;
– Intensive domestic and international subcontracting;
– Strong use of "new forms" of investments such as joint ventures, management

94

contracts, production sharing, franchising where non-equity contracts are enforced by means of on-line communication;
– Footloose location of plants, laboratories and offices;
– Global scanning for sourcing;
– Customisation of large-scale production processes;
– Aggressive centralisation of specialised services, namely international finance, transportation, telecommunication, EDP.

Major structural features of the network firm seem to support the growing centralisation and internalisation of allocative functions (sourcing, finance, transportation, communication) and intangible asset intensive activities (research, development, advertising and strategic planning) and the quasi-integration of geographically dispersed manufacturing and marketing activities performed by small efficient units not necessarily (fully) owned[26] by the holding organisation.

The diffusion of Information Technology in the Italian economic system in the seventies and early eighties[27] has been favoured by a variety of factors:

   i) The economic problems of large firms caused by the increasing costs of labour, the obsolete managerial structure and the need to reshape the internal organisation;
   ii) The low levels of financial requirements and fixed capital investments necessary to adopt new communication intensive techniques;
   iii) The high level of compatibility with previous communication and information processing equipment;
   iv) The high levels of vertical integration and diversification of large Italian companies and financial groups and the opportunity for rationalisation of internal flows of intermediate products, services and financial resources permitted by new communication intensive techniques;
   v) The strategic role of marketing and distribution in fashion intensive activities and the opportunity offered by new communication intensive techniques to rejuvenate traditional industries such as textile, garment and furniture by reducing delivery lags and enhancing niche-strategies based on the aggressive quasi-customisation of large scale produced goods;
   vi) The high levels of inflation in Italy in the seventies and the opportunities offered by new communication intensive techniques to reduce the financial burden of the working capital of inventories of both finished products and intermediate inputs and the time lags of the order-invoice cycles;
   vii) The growing international competition and the increasing level of internationalisation of Italian firms to become multinational corporations to cope with worldwide differentiation of demand; the shortening of the product cycle of innovation in consumer goods and the opportunities offered by new communication intensive techniques to expand the scope of co-ordination of managerial structures beyond domestic markets.

Available data suggest that smaller firms, i.e. the bulk of the dualistic Italian industry, have major problems in imitating the sophisticated technological and organisational innovations applied by large firms because of an external environment which is not yet conducive to the diffusion of new information technologies. Major obstacles to the diffusion of New Information Technologies in and among small firms include:

   i) The lack of standards in software, hardware and communications. Interaction among independent parties is seriously limited by the variety of technical and organisational standards resulting in duplications of costs;

ii) The small size and the low levels of sophistication in the supply of information processing services due to the high levels of internalisation in the provision of updated services within large firms and financial groups;

iii) The lack of manpower specialised in managing New Information Technologies both on the technical and the organisational sides;

iv) The backwardness of the Italian telecommunication infrastructure still based at 90 per cent on electromechanical switching;

v) The institutional framework which guarantees the monopolistic supply of telecommunication services to SIP, the state-owned telecommunication company, under the control of PPTT.

Further developments in the diffusion of New Information Technologies in the Italian industrial structure therefore depend on the possibilities of smaller firms to adopt and use the new system. This, however requires major changes in the supply of telecommunication related skills and services.

At this stage, diffusion patterns are rather erratic; this is due to low technical sophistication of the services provided by the public network; high quality services within large Italian firms; rapid intra-firm but slow interfirm diffusion of IT-based services in the small and medium sized business and industry community. To improve this situation it seems important to rethink user-supplier links.

The findings of the case studies suggest that business users have a significant demand for privately owned telematic systems. Business users seem to first consider the advantages of supply-conditions of the new services currently available and compare them to the old non-telematics solutions to their problems. Only at a second stage do they compare prices and qualities of services with existing alternative telematics choices. Thus, the opportunity-cost level is more important than the absolute cost-level of the telematics business services. If there is only one telematics-choice available, demand would be rather unelastic to the price. As a result, in the take-off phase of new telematics services it is not the absolute lowest price which counts, but rather, the possibility of organising the new service around the need of users.

For this reason, when private telematics networks are available, business users do not compare the supply conditions of such private services and networks to the supply of the telematics services incorporated in an advanced, say ISDN, public network. They compare them to the conditions of the non-telematics solutions for their problem. Therefore, when private systems prove to be profitable, they are adopted sometimes despite their costs and performances because of the future opportunities provided by national networks.

Moreover, private telematics systems are even more advantageous as they provide more flexibility when questions of extending their capabilities are up for discussion. Any possible increase in the number of new potential points interconnected with the primary system can be obtained through expansions of the private system itself, but also through gateway interconnections with the public infrastructure. This enables further links with other points on the territory without any necessity for new investments in private telematics systems. This approach would assure that a decision to adopt a private system of telematics in the first phase will not prevent the users from exploiting the future technological opportunities offered by an advanced public network. Indeed, this could justify a decision of developing a private network as an immediate solution to meet pressing information processing and communications needs to improve the efficiency of transformation-transfer activities in the absence of appropriate public telematics services. Once public services become available, it will be cost-benefit analyses which decide over the most viable solution.

This discussion suggests that a continuum of alternative solutions exists, between public and private services (and networks) as well as different degrees of combination of the public infrastructure and private undertakings[28].

Recent trends of externalisation by diversification, and vertical disintegration of internal telematic service units from large firms can be considered a major step towards the creation of an advanced market supply of new services also available to small firms. In the last three years, a number of firms have proceeded in this direction: FIAT entered the market with INTESA a joint venture with IBM; Olivetti with SEVA, a joint venture with SEAT of the STET group; Montedison with TELEVAS, a joint venture with STET; ENI with ENIDATA; FINSIEL, a large state-owned company is increasingly offering its services on the market; Pirelli recently created a new company "Pirelli Informatica" externalising the existing internal information processing unit. Most of these firms have been created by large manufacturing firms in a process of diversification to exploit the expertise built up in the provision of internal services as well as to better utilise available internal excess capacities.

This suggests that major progress can be made with the help and factual assistance of public authorities to create an open market for telematic services. A means to achieve this goal is to provide standards that all potential partners in the market can use.

Diffusion policy tools such as fiscal incentives, dissemination of information etc., reductions of prices of hardware and software and training of skilled manpower can successfully be applied to help existing supply capacities to grow and the latent demand of potential users to enter the market[29].

NOTES AND REFERENCES

1. See Pool (1977).
2. See Antonelli (1981) and *ICCP Report No.12* (1987).
3. See Antonelli (1979).
4. See Williamson (1986).
5. See Arrow (1974).
6. See also Robinson (1931).
7. See Williamson (1975).
8. See Chandler (1982).
9. "Inasmuch as the natural boundaries of the firm are therein defined by technology, any effort by the firm to extend its reach by recourse to non standard contracting was presumed to have monopoly purpose and effect.", Williamson, O.E., (1985), page 26.
10. "Regarding the firm as a production function to which a profit maximisation objective has been assigned led to the aforementioned view of technological determinism. Transactions either belonged in firms or they belonged in markets. Any effort to tamper with this natural order was accordingly suspect.", Williamson, O.E., (1985), page 163.
11. "A common characteristic of the new line of research is that the concept of firm as a production function is supplanted (or augmented) by the concept of firm as governance structure.", Williamson, O.E., (1985), page 16.
12. The rate and the level of adoption of new information technology in Italy, as measured by the diffusion of modem seems very high by international standards and suggest that a long term learning process on their effects and opportunities has already taken place.
13. See Fua (1985).

14. The Italian position on international markets and the Italian dualistic industrial structure and labour market, shows that a special framework is necessary to understand the mix of factors determining the rate of adoption of new information technologies and generally the relationship between innovation and economic growth in the Italian case: the *"failure inducement" model*. See Antonelli (1988).

15. See Antonelli (1988).

16. Porter, M.E., (1985), page 36.

17. The change in the slope of relative price consequent to the reduction of communication costs induces more communication intensive techniques and an overall increase of productivity.

18. See Antonelli (1988).

19. For the distinction between plant specific scale economies and product specific scale economies see Scherer *et al.* (1975).

20. See Antonelli (1988).

21. Communications make it possible to reduce the constraints of location, when it is *tied* to that of other industries or *linked* to that of other industries.

22. See Robinson (1931).

23. The adoption of Management Information Systems induces a downward shift of average co-ordination costs which in turn, for given costs of use of the markets, pushes the maximum efficient size to the right.

24. See Wilson (1975).

25. This case suggests that because of network externalities the larger the research project, the lower the costs of the network infrastructure, the higher the opportunity to build upon specific skill of partners and to appropriate the advantage of the innovative output.

26. These emerging trends in the Italian industrial organisation seems to follow similar trends found in the Japanese industry by Imai-Itami (1984), Aoki (1984) and more specifically Yokokura (1986).

27. See Antonelli (1988).

28. See Williamson (1985).

29. See Stoneman (1987) for an outstanding analysis of technology policy and diffusion policy instruments.

BIBLIOGRAPHY

Antonelli, C., "Innovation as Factor Shaping Industrial Structures", *Social Science Information*, 18, 1979, pp. 877-894.

Antonelli, C., "Transborder Data Flows and International Business. A Pilot Study", *DSTI/ICCP/81.16*, OECD, Paris, 1981.

Antonelli, C., "Multinational Firms International Trade and International Telecommunications", *Information Economics and Policy 2*, 1984, pp. 333-343.

Antonelli, C., "The Diffusion of an Organisational Innovation. International Data Telecommunications and Multinational Industrial Firms", *International Journal of Industrial Organisation*, 3, 1985, pp. 109-118.

Antonelli, C., "The International Diffusion of New Information Technologies", *Research Policy 15*, 1986, pp. 139-147.

Antonelli, C. (ed.), *New Information Technology and Industrial Change: The Italian Evidence*, Kluwer Academic, Dordrecht, 1988.

Aoki, M., "Innovative Adaptation through the quasi-tree Structure: An Emerging Aspect of Japanese Entrepreneurship", *Zeitschrift für National ökonomia Suppl. 4*, 1984, pp. 177-198.

Arrow, K.J., *The Limits of Organisation*, W.W. Norton & Co., New York, 1974.

Benjamin, R.I. *et al.*, *Effects of Information Technology and Market Structure and Corporate Strategies*, MIT Centre for Information Systems Research, Working Paper 137, 1986.

Chandler, A.D., *Evolution of the Large Industrial Corporation: an Evaluation of the Transaction Cost Approach*, Harvard Business School, (Mimeo), Boston, 1982.

Ciborra, C., "Markets Burocracies and Groups in the Information Society", *Information Economics and Policy 1*, 1983, pp. 145-160.

Dioguardi, G., *L'impresa nell'era del computer*, Edizioni del Sole-24 Ore, Milano, 1986.

Ergas, H., "Corporate Strategies in Transition", in A. Jacquemin (ed.), *European Industry: Public Policy and Corporate Strategy*, Clarendon Press, Oxford, 1984.

Florence, P.S., *The Logic of British and American Industries*, Routledge and Kegan, London, 1953.

Fua, G., "Les voies diverses du développement en Europe", *Annales, Economie Societiés, Civilisation*, 3/1985.

Goddard J. and Pye, R., "Telecommunications and Office Location", *Regional Studies 11*, 1977, pp. 19-30.

Hirschman, A.O., *Exit Voice and Loyalty*, Harvard University Press, Cambridge, 1970.

Imai, K. and Itami, H., "Interpenetration of Organisation and Market. Japan's Firm and Market in Comparison with the US", *International Journal of Industrial Organisation*, 2, 1984, pp. 285-310.

Jonscher, C., "Information Resources and Economic Productivity", *Information Economics and Policy 1*, 1983, pp. 13-35.

Pool I. (de Solla) (ed.), *The Social Impact of Telephone*, MIT Press, Cambridge, 1977.

Porter, M.E., *Competitive Advantage*, The Free Press, New York, 1985.

Robinson, E.A.G., *The Structure of Competitive Industry*, Nisbet & Co., London, 1931.

Scherer, F.M. *et al.*, *The Economics of Multiplant Operation: an International Comparisons Study*, Harvard University Press, Cambridge, 1975.

Simon, H.A., *Models of Bounded Rationality*, MIT Press, Cambridge, Mass., 1982.

Stoneman, P., *The Economic Analysis of Technology Policy*, Clarendon Press, Oxford, 1987.

Williamson, O.E., *Markets and Hierarchies: Analysis and Anti-trust Implications*, The Free Press, New York, 1975.

Williamson, O.E., *The Economic Institutions and Capitalism*, The Free Press, New York, 1985.

Williamson, O.E., "Vertical Integration and Related Variations on a Transaction - Cost Economics Theme", in J.E. Stiglitz and G.F. Mathewson (eds.), *New Developments in the Analysis of Market Structure*, MIT Press, Cambridge, 1986.

Wilson, R., "Informational Economies of Scale", *Bell Journal of Economics*, Spring 1975, pp. 184-195.

Yokokura, T., *Emerging Corporate Information Network: An Overview of Regulatory and Industrial Policy in Japan*, Center for Information Policy Research, Program on Information Resource Policy, Harvard University, October 1986.

ELECTRONIC AND COMPUTER-AIDED PUBLISHING: OPPORTUNITIES AND CONSTRAINTS

by

Richard Jay Solomon,
Research Program on Communications Policy and
The Media Laboratory, Massachusetts Institute of Technology,
Cambridge, Mass. 02139, United States

TABLE OF CONTENTS

I. INTRODUCTION AND SUMMARY 103
   1. Forecasting: Positive and Negative Feedback Modelling 103
   2. Technology 105

II. SCENARIOS 105

III. PARADIGM SHIFTS IN PRINTING 106

IV. INTEGRATION OF PRINTING AND PUBLISHING 109

V. ELECTRONIC PUBLISHING TECHNOLOGIES 110
   1. The Computer 110
   2. Page Makeup 111
   3. Recursive Graphic Building Blocks 111
   4. Memory and Processing 112
   5. Telecommunications 112

VI. OPPORTUNITIES 114
   1. Complementary Substitution 114
   2. New Publishing Activities 115
   3. Transfer of Information 115

VII. PROBLEMS 117
   1. Standards 117
   2. Broadband ISDN 118
   3. Trade Issues 119
   4. Intellectual Property 119
      a) Copying 122
      b) Piracy and Counterfeiting 123

VIII. THE COMPLEXITY OF CIGA – A REVIEW AND EXAMPLE 125

  IX. THE PLANNING PROCESS 126

   X. CONCLUSIONS 129

GLOSSARY 130

NOTES AND REFERENCES 130

I. INTRODUCTION AND SUMMARY

Emerging computer and telecommunications technologies are likely to change the nature of today's printing, distribution, graphics, photographic, writing, and allied industries by the end of this decade. This will create new opportunities for information accessibility and industrial growth in the generic publishing area. By definition, publishing in the electronic era will encompass all forms of textual and graphics distribution including full-motion video.

In this diffusion process these technologies will create a number of problems, for example:

   i)   Intellectual property;
   ii) Telecommunication standards and interconnection;
   iii) Industrial re-structure, labour mobility; and,
   iv) Protection against fraudulent documentation.

Information can now be produced, stored, retrieved, and transmitted in ways that bring out anomalies in the old methods and which create and amplify connections which were impossible before. Mechanisms which access numerous online data sources involving multiple jurisdictions, and which use Artificial Intelligence (AI) techniques to automatically combine, re-write, and modify this input in order to re-distribute the information ("publish") electronically also do not fit well with conventional views of copyright. These issues are discussed in more detail below.

1. Forecasting: Positive and Negative Feedback Modelling

The new publishing technologies – based on digital computers, and their extension, digital telecommunications networks – are recursive: i.e. they feed upon themselves, with one changing the other in ways that are extremely difficult to predict. Therefore, the potential of new publishing industries cannot be examined as simple, linear extrapolations of print technology as we know it.

In general, erroneous forecasting models come in two varieties: failures of assessment, and failures of imagination[1]. Failures of assessment occur when one looks backwards and attempts to make simple linear extrapolations. Not only is this error based on insufficient history or misleading cases, but more important is the false belief that such processes are, indeed, linear. Complex series of non-linear equations are unsolvable; more important, feedback from externalities generated by the innovative process may "seed" a random event with totally unpredictable consequences somewhere down the road – now understood as the "chaos" factor[2].

Failures of imagination are more complex. Here relevant facts are known, but process innovation is ignored. Such "forecasting" lacks the ability to look forward. To avoid such pitfalls one has to consider feedback in its positive and negative forms[3].

An example of a positive feedback model in electronic printing is desktop publishing: inexpensive laser printing technology has launched a whole new set of publications within a short period of time. This was an easy, short-term projection once the initial set of conditions were understood. Though a complex forecast, it was linear, solvable, intuitively correct, and not very interesting. The positive feedback component of the model was that easy-to-use software and machines could eliminate many of the former critical skills necessary to produce camera-ready, slick-looking typeset pages. (This did not take much insight, as we describe below.) As desktop devices proliferate (more software, more computers, more laser printers, and more people familiar with the process), positive feedback continually adds further input to the process, so that desktop publishing grows linearly, and predictably.

In some processes positive feedback may be part of its internalized algorithm permitting its stabilization (a thermostat). In other processes, feedback has no such built-in stabilizing factor so unpredictable events occur (the discovery of electromagnetic waves and the application of vacuum tubes leading to the growth of entirely unexpected industries such as television broadcasting).

Like any fundamental technological process, electronic publishing technologies do not contain discernable stabilization components. Moreover, since the definition encompasses wider and wider ranges of information dissemination, positive feedback (more and better software, equipment, and skilled individuals) will surely cause this new industry to grow in ways we cannot easily imagine with information based solely on the initial set of conditions.

The other form of feedback is called "negative," though both terms have neutral value connotations. While positive feedback uses current information to control or influence processes, negative feedback uses information which correctly predicts the future. For example, most automobile steering systems merely respond to the driver's control and to immediate information from the suspension system; under rapidly changing conditions this may lead to catastrophic instabilities. But more advanced steering systems predict road conditions (based on various movements of the car) using negative feedback to prevent over- and understeering and to stabilize the ride – a particularly valuable technique on slippery roads.

Though subtle, negative feedback could be usefully employed in modelling and to prevent processes from reaching undesirable states, but only if process innovation is fully understood. That means that details count.

For example, functionality is not an additive process. Often when you change just one key element, you can change the process – an underpinning of chaos theory. Assessing the past in order to understand what the future may bring requires an uncanny ability to understand which technologies are key, and how today's technology expands – feeds back – to fit tomorrow's applications.

Feedback – positive or negative – plays an important role in determining government policies. For electronic publishing there are two pitfalls. One is correctly quantifying the problem as it relates to employment and industrial output, and another are attempts to control "copying" under the novel regime of computers and electronics. These are discussed in this paper, along with the basic characteristics of electronic, computer-aided publishing. Beyond that, it is quite impossible to predict specifics of how the systems may evolve, and therefore where feedback may take place in the policy process. Why this is so is also an important consideration; the final section of the paper is devoted to a discussion of the planning problem for electronic publishing in the light of chaos and feedback theory.

2. Technology

The basic technological factors of electronic publishing include:

i) Office automation software and associated hardware (specialized electronic printing processors) can now emulate, with relative ease, virtually any graphic and textual mode created by the conventional printing process;

ii) Computer-based tools permit visual creations impossible in using manual methods, and access to information in ways radically different from that found in conventional print media. Interactive retrieval can be used to customize print output, typography, and graphics, with quality equal to or exceeding that common today. Display substitutes for print may go even further – animated graphics, mixed video/textual media, etc. None of this is beyond the current state of the art;

iii) For the first time since the invention of the stored-programme computer, digital telecommunications is advancing in power and cost-effectiveness faster than that of equivalent computer technology. These switched, broad- or wideband technologies are essential for advanced electronic publishing applications;

iv) Advances in semiconductor and optoelectronic technology have made powerful processors relatively low-cost commodity items, creating larger market opportunities for electronic publishing products.

II. SCENARIOS

Electronic publishing is at a similar embryonic point as office automation was about 15 years ago. The new tools are sufficiently different from the past, so that basic skills and organisational structures for electronically-aided publishing are unlikely to resemble current models.

Analogies are misleading. The new computer-aided publishing media are not just faster and more flexible printing presses, distributed instead of centralized. Computer-integrated graphics is not just an automated drafting table, which allows the untalented to become artists. Word processors are not just better typewriters with added features correcting spelling and grammar, and offering telecommunications. And electronic mail is not just a faster Telex. Once one part of a system is changed, change becomes endemic.

Distributed printing and remote access to text means printing on demand, when it is needed, combined with material from diverse sources, and abstracted or expanded as necessary. Computerized graphics means unique displays of data in different forms (again combined from different sources), customized for the user, enhanced dimensionally, temporally, with color, or even with animation. Word processing, coupled with distributed printing or electronic mail, page makeup and graphics software is a publishing medium, with profound implications for policy makers; even though this can serve as functional substitutes for print and telegraphy, electronic publishing follows few of the rules of print which today offer a modicum of protection for intellectual creations or against fraud.

Another example: Text takes up far less physical space on digital storage media. It is far cheaper for an author even today to mail a 3½ inch mini-floppy, which may hold 200 pages of text (formatted for typesetting), than to mail the equivalent amount of paper. Books then may be printed on-demand in libraries or book "stores," or anywhere remote from the place of storage, permitting drastic reduction of inventory and distribution costs. The future impact on both transport and paper industries is unknown. Display may take place on a color laser printer, a terminal, or in some hybrid system. Such data can be readily encrypted, or disguised, so that information flow could not be readily censored.

All of these examples are already being offered in some form as products, inexpensive, and with hundreds of thousands or millions of users. Computer-aided publishing can go much further, reach more economic sectors, and blur lines of demarcation that could never be touched by print. For instance off-the-shelf, personal computer software is being used for spreadsheets programmed to automatically capture data via telecommunications lines from different databanks. The spreadsheets then plot graphs customized for (or by) the user. These graphs are then pre-linked to page creation software so that illustrations automatically change when data changes. The pages are then printed on laser printers with a minimum of human intervention. For narrowly-targeted audiences, the laser output is normally less expensive than other forms of printing, and the quality often higher than offset. But the laser printers can be half a world away linked by highspeed modems and the public switched telephone network; the latest twist is to send this presentation-quality graphics directly from the microcomputer to any standard high-resolution facsimile printer in the world, again without human intervention.

These examples contain the kernel of the new publishing environment, using equipment readily available to anyone, and costing less than $10 000 (in U.S. computer discount houses), including good-quality laser printers. It does not take any leap of imagination to see how the scale can be increased to serve larger readerships, nor how positive feedback is rapidly expanding the scope of information dissemination *via* these tools.

III. PARADIGM SHIFTS IN PRINTING

Computer technologies have already had such a significant influence on publishing and graphics that future historians will see what is occurring as a "paradigm shift" – a new model of how things work[4]. Such changes appear to occur at regular generational intervals, perhaps for reasons that only chaos theory may yet explain. While the details are unpredictable, the broad changes seem to fit a long-cycle pattern of some 50-60 years.

A number of key industries have changed in the past this way, and most revealing, they tend to change together. That is because fundamental infrastructure is used in common. Steel, railroads, and automobiles are one example of such dynamic, yet coupled change in the early 20th century. Telegraphs, telephones and radio underwent fundamental alterations in concert around World War I for similar reasons. Today a new model is evolving for information industries, of which electronic publishing is more infrastructure than result.

This new model will likely be exploited by new entrepreneurs – an example of negative feedback at work. And while it is probable that these new information and publishing tools will promote economic growth, such growth may be in sectors quite different from the traditional printing and publishing industries which it emulates. To wit:

   i) The new tools for the production and dissemination of visual information require new and different skills, and different organisational behavior. The computer is a versatile device permitting the crossing of older divisions of labour (and capital), particularly when networked. Use of computers immediately requires treatment of all information, and tools which use this information, in terms of a logical database. Accepting the concepts of networked information as a universal database (which is not the same as access to online databases) will be the first paradigm shift;

ii) Robotics in the publishing, graphic arts, and printing industries is subtle. The machines may superficially resemble typewriters, cameras, and rotary presses, but the robots are embedded in software and have become an invisible part of the infrastructure! In fact, now the software code is the machine! And the software, like in all digital computers, is recursive – it may modify itself and become a new machine, a form of machine learning;

iii) Labor and capital inputs for the new publishing technologies may shift from specialized, labour-intensive, concentrated, highly-capitalized loci to low-capital investment, distributed hardware, using generalized skill inputs, and distinguished by electronic distribution (see Table 1). To speak of more or of less skill may be irrelevant, since when dealing with networked, computer database technologies the gestalt of electronic publishing and production is radically different;

Table 1.   **Shifts in factors of publishing**

From print and paper:
Highly specialized labour (press operators, typists, typographers, artists, writers)
Low interskill mobility
Centralized presses
Visible media for storage and retrieval
Physical transport for distribution

To electronics:
Highly articulate labour skilled in a wide variety of modes
High interskill mobility, adaptable
Distributed printing on-demand
Electronic distribution and display
Computer storage and retrieval, with intersecting databases

iv) Semi-conductor and photonic devices have become functional substitutes for paper-based storage and information transport. Information (text, graphics, and numbers) stored as a database on programmable digital machines, makes retrieval and manipulation far more flexible than just emulating file cabinets, shelves, and bound volumes. Information may be stored in numerical form (all binary), but these numbers can represent anything a human can hear, see, feel, touch, or even smell. Reproduction accuracy of graphics and sound often surpasses the original because of digital enhancement. Text formats and fonts are not restricted to the original input, but can be altered at will, or by design.
Most important, information can point to and "call" other information, independent of its ultimate form of output. Machines can, and do, this without human intervention or even instruction, and machines can communicate and modify data among themselves. As more and more information and concomitant storage media are added to the worldwide telecommunications networks, the universe of

information which interacts will get sufficiently complex so that the originators of information lose the ability to track use of this information. Once data is let loose to the network, the originator has little, if any, control over its destiny – the principal copyright dilemma with electronics. Print and presses, on the other hand, offered some modicum of control;

v) Whether paper can be completely replaced, or may have a new role in the future, cannot yet be determined. Predictions of whether paper consumption will rise or fall will be difficult during the transition towards electronic publishing. There seems to be concern that pulp and paper markets may become destabilized by the impact of electronic publishing.

The new graphics software makes it reasonable to emulate any paper output from a press, including typesetting, color, and grey-scale resolution. Since information need no longer be stored in paper formats, nor be created in hard copy until it is needed to be read, total demand for paper over time will not be dependent on the growth of information, per se. Where (and if) paper is still superior to other displays, or may be needed as an interface between incompatible information processing systems, paper may be produced on demand. Where paper is used to overcome system incompatibility, standards can make a big difference;

vi) Electronic displays can do things for human information transfer that paper cannot do. There is some indication that paper use per person drops dramatically once confidence in the reliability of electronic systems is reached. The probability of a transition to all-electronic publishing depends on further understanding of how the human brain processes information, and particularly how eye/brain, visual/skeletal, and other sensory interactions work. Display of information for human interaction and human absorption goes beyond just developing high-resolution, multi-color, flicker-free display hardware. The utility of paper for human information transfer depends on complex visual and skeletal motor processes which have not yet been clearly modeled by researchers. However, recent advances in this field of knowledge, which incorporates physiology, neurology, and psychophysics, are quite promising in pointing towards new optoelectronics mechanisms which may completely replace paper;

vii) The most dynamic area for electronic publishing is the oft- predicted merger of computer/communications and publishing. This has finally begun to surface in selected, but fast-growing niches. These may offer a working vision of the future. "Desktop publishing" is the catch-all phrase for this merger, using state-of-the-art, low-cost but powerful software, high-resolution printers, and most recently, combined word- processing/graphics/facsimile telecommunicating devices;

viii) The most startling advances may be in the graphics part of electronic publishing. We shall give this new industry the name "Computer-Integrated Graphic Arts" (CIGA), with strong parallels to the industrial design technologies in Computer-Integrated Manufacturing (CIM) and CAD/CAM. Desktop publishing is evolving as a marriage between CIGA technology, intelligent word processing, and advanced, highspeed, digital telecommunications. The downside is that CIGA technology creates opportunities for fraud and piracy.

IV. INTEGRATION OF PRINTING AND PUBLISHING

Computer-driven integration has had its major impetus from outside of the conventional publishing structure. As a result, certain key elements in the existing publishing chain are becoming redundant, while others may be enhanced. In general, print production is de-emphasized for publishing, while product creation and retrieval become more important. The author becomes the "publisher," while the role of editors and publishers either vanish, or merge into that of the carrier. This transition will take a long time before it is complete, but the trends in some areas are already clear.

Novels are being written that can be read online, as each section or chapter is complete. Technical papers are authored by several individuals, in diverse locations and then transmitted to interested readers (or stored for future access) – all without any paper copy, publisher, or, perhaps unfortunately, editor. Even for the conventional press, many of the steps in editing, type composing, page layout, and printing have been eliminated through the use of computers; entire books have been written and printed this way. Periodicals are being published without any paper except at the readers' computer terminal. And journalists typically file stories directly from word processors to wire services which are automatically accessed by other computers, using expert systems programmes to scan for content; these stories are then automatically assembled into personal "newspapers" for users, who often read the story (or story segment or abstract) directly from the screen. This is only one form that electronic publishing takes.

The elimination of the publisher's filtering/editing function is all too obvious in some of these endeavors, but no mechanism to replace this function has yet been developed. The closest thing we have is automatic spelling/grammar programmes, which is not the same thing.

Table 2 illustrates some of the conceptual shifts which the future electronic environment may bring to publishing.

Table 2. **Shifts in emphasis for the publishing chain**

From:		*To:*	
	Centralized publishing		Self-publishing
	Printing, Binding, Warehousing		Indexing, Online Data Storage, Database Pointers
	Multiple copies, few editions		One copy, many variations
	Verification of original via inspection		Encryption necessary for verification registration, publication
	Publication easily defined		Publication meaningless word
	Physical Distribution		Broadband Telecommunications Access to Databanks
	Editors, Publishers as Gatekeepers		Extensible Access (Hypertext) With AI Filters
	Editors, Peer Review		Little or No Review
	Fancy Printing		Computerized editing, Page makeup
	Charging by the print (easy)		Charging by access (difficult)
	Payment for publication (easy to enforce)		Payment by use or citation rights (difficult to enforce)
	Copy Rights		Usage Rights
	Author/Publisher Control of Distribution		Reader/User Control of Materials Uses

V. ELECTRONIC PUBLISHING TECHNOLOGIES

Several specific technologies have converged to make electronic publishing possible. These are:

  i) Powerful microprocessors working with 32-bit address space;
 ii) Rapid reduction in size and cost of megabit or larger random- access memories;
iii) Similar order-of-magnitude changes in storage media;
 iv) Imminent implementation of very highspeed switched telecommunications in the 1 to 10 megabit per second range;
  v) Near-term potential for even higher switched public telecommunications networks working in the 135 megabit per second to gigabit per second range;
 vi) Highspeed laser and other directed beam printers which equal or exceed the resolution of the conventional printing process;
vii) Low-cost scanning devices for the input of paper-based graphics or text;
viii) Low-cost optical character readers capable of recognizing multiple fonts and distinguishing between text and graphics; and
 ix) Software which ties all of the above hardware together.

It is difficult to isolate any of these items to determine which is primary and which secondary. In general, software is considered the key technology driving electronic publishing; but sophisticated applications could not have been built without very large memory space in which to run these applications. Similarly a way to print high-resolution typesetting and presentation-quality graphics is essential, and laser printers would not work without large memories and without their own microprocessor-based engines. So these technologies are all fundamentally synergistic.

We shall briefly describe some of these technologies in order to build a working definition of "electronic publishing" as a new medium.

1. The Computer[5]

The utilization of stored-programme machines for information retrieval, word process-ing, typesetting, and distribution cannot be compared to mere technological changes which amplify or improve existing products. Because of characteristics inherent in the way digital computers work – including communications, self-modification, and ability to emulate any machine process through programming – it is a unique process in the history of technology.

Through the application of Boolean arithmetic and microelectronics, the digital, stored-programme computer permits an ease of storage, retrieval, manipulation and transmission of information using techniques completely at odds with current notions based on the printing press. The cost of powerful machines based on 32-bit microprocessors, plus the cost of memory, has sufficiently dropped so that technologies which have had about two decades of development could finally be introduced for the mass market. These include page makeup software for bit-mapped typesetting and graphics, and laser printers to print these bit-mapped pages.

On the immediate horizon is the introduction of inexpensive, highspeed switched telecommunications based on a total computerization of the network: the Integrated Services Digital Network (ISDN), and Broadband ISDN. We will discuss the influence of the computer first.

2. Page Makeup

Text is stored and manipulated by computers by assigning numbers (binary numbers) to the alphabet, numerals, and a set of standard signs and symbols. It is a trivial task to translate them from one to another, and there are several ways to display this text on a screen or paper. In general teletext and videotext systems have failed to visually emulate print, and this may be one of the reasons teletext/videotext have yet to replace print in use, though basic alphanumeric information can be transmitted.

Telex, Teletex (highspeed telex), and conventional electronic mail terminals have even less of a visual impact than teletext/videotext. But because there are a substantial number of these devices in place, this rudimentary text method is heavily used for simple electronic publishing today.

3. Recursive Graphic Building Blocks

Using the trick of "escape" sequences, a virtually unlimited superset can be defined with special alphabets or characters on fairly conventional terminals. But there are other ways to present visual information on a computer which draw points and lines with the ability to be moved across a field ("translated"), rotated, enlarged or reduced ("scaled"), and displayed in part or whole ("windowed").

Any graphic can be defined in terms of its points, lines, and text parts ("strings") and stored as a database; in fact, with digital computers, this can be recursive, in that a smaller graphic can define a larger one, and can modify these definitions according to its programme. The graphic, for example, can combine a standard encoded character text string, with additional point and line information about serifs, character spacing, kerning and ligatures, and data about lines, gray scales, up to page layout and even information about paper size, color, and surface tooth.

The point and line information are stored in the database as vectors, data which tells the output device which direction a line is moving, how it is to be rotated and translated, whether it has a shadow, is screened (for fine dots, halftones, or gray scales), etc. Other data is stored for scaling, so the text, in the defined font, can be 8 points high on 9 point "leading," or 24 points high in boldface. All of the art and science of printing has been re-captured and defined in computer database terms this way. The result is not just a database which defines the page completely and perfectly, but a database which can be further manipulated for different effects, tailored, perhaps, to user needs. Most interestingly, this database technique of defining, storing, and perfectly replicating a page uses less computer space than facsimile, and displays a better image, either on paper or a screen. Such a database can be readily converted to facsimile, or to other formats, including a return to plain encoded text.

Today software for page manipulation is quite sophisticated and makes use of page description languages – true high-level computer languages, with conditional branching, and recursion, and with commands optimized for graphics, typesetting and page description. A page written in PDL format can be telecommunicated to any other machine which uses that PDL for a perfect reproduction. Several universal standards have been adopted in practice, though not yet officially by international standards organisations.

This is strikingly different from Telex, Teletex and videotext/teletext systems, and especially different from facsimile or video-based systems, which store and transmit images by scanning them and reproducing an analog of the scan. However fine the resolution of these systems, their storage requirements, bandwidth, and lack of extensibility make them far inferior to digital computer graphics for electronic publishing. Furthermore, PDLs and other database techniques for retrieval and presentation-quality display fit in well with the future microcomputer-based distributed processing and broadband ISDN environment.

4. Memory and Processing

Graphics and database software have enormous appetites for memory and processing power. While the new generation of inexpensive, commodity-issue, computer central processing units (CPUs) are more than adequate for most graphics and relational database applications, cost-effective memory hardware, like telecommunications, has lagged far behind CPU power.

The 32-bit microprocessors found on all high-end personal computers today can address 2 to 32nd power (4.2 billion) words of machine code, which would permit quite sophisticated electronic publishing applications including those using AI or expert systems techniques, such as hypertext or hypermedia, described below. Moreover, the concept of a universal receiver/terminal, based on microcomputer parameters, which can display text and video, is gaining currency because of the common cost savings using digital processors[6].

Memory is a critical technological constraint. To manipulate graphics, or generate fonts for typesetting, memory has to be used for temporary processing. For fast response with human interaction in page design, for example, it is preferable to have much of the work stored in main memory; sorting very large amounts of data, such as pointers to text or pictures in the form of a relational or hierarchical database, works faster if most of the database can be transferred to main memory.

But memory is still relatively expensive. And while cost of random-access memories are dropping rapidly, a more likely scenario would be for 32-bit (or larger) microprocessors to share application code and databases by addressing this space in a virtual mode. Current applications do this within an office environment on local-area networks (LAN). LANs are not yet fast enough to swap data in and out of processor memory to permit true virtual memory for microcomputers (the programmes work, but response time is unproductive for, say, artists trying to clean up an image). The concept of shared, complex graphics software, however, may work well over the new fibre-optic LANs, or via the equivalent, a broadband public network. The evolution of microcomputer shared-user and multiple job operating systems will have to follow that of highspeed telecommunications control software for these new networks to be useful in this regard.

5. Telecommunications

The main impetus to electronic or desktop publishing will not be from the fact that computers make page makeup easy, nor from the fact that computers permit easier manipulation of data and databases, but from the scale, speed, and power of computer network technology. The introduction of ISDN will begin this process.

ISDN, working at speeds of 64,000 to 160,000 bits per second (bps) will transfer 2 to 7 pages of raw text per second. "Made-up" pages, emulating typesetting and with perfect presentation graphics will take somewhat more time, but with PDL and compression techniques, not significantly more. Switching and connect time is to be no more than 2 seconds between any user terminal, and generally much lower. ISDN will be much more flexible than existing public switched networks, including such features as user-to-user signalling to help establish application protocols before connection, and point-to- multipoint transmissions. The first commercial, public ISDN networks are scheduled for 1988, and several private ISDN exchanges have already being implemented.

ISDN, however, is too slow, though this may seem an odd thing to state where most data users today struggle with 300 and 1200 bps modems. The ISDN rates are barely an order of magnitude change above this, and furthermore, are slower by a factor of 10 to 100 than the speeds used by desktop computers to transfer data between memory and their storage media. And connection times must be able to handle CPU-to-CPU interactions for direct memory access.

What is needed is a telecommunications network that works in the range of 10 to 100 megabits per second and is a "connectionless" system, with no chance of call blocking, and with switching based on statistical demand profiles. Such a system would be even faster than coaxial cable or copper pair LANs. Fibre optics happens to fit that need, and currently the telecommunications carriers are debating the option of skipping narrowband ISDN and moving directly to broadband ISDN (B-ISDN) via fibre, at least for service to the office, if not the home.

Fiber is being accelerated by favorable economics for intercity and intracity trunking, and for local distribution, in any case. The primary questions are whether fibre should be used in the last segment from the distribution nodes, and what physical methods should be used for broadband switching. There are many quite promising options for near-term implementation of this technology, which are beyond the scope of this paper.

B-ISDN systems[7] are scheduled for introduction by 1991-2 by some administrations, and installation of the distribution hardware has been underway for several years in several countries. It appears likely that B-ISDN via fibre will be the standard for all public telecommunications in developed regions by the early 21st Century, and this will have a major impact on publishing of any kind. With B-ISDN working at speeds that permits data transfers from main computer memory even faster than access to typical local disk drives, virtual memory via the network becomes feasible.

Proposed B-ISDN fibre standards use data frames structured as a "labelled matrix" (or relational database) for switching, customer, and network interfaces. Data manipulation along the fibre will become inherent for such a system. While B-ISDN frames are routed through the system in a manner having surface similarities to packets, B-ISDN operations and network architecture will be quite different from that of proposed narrowband ISDN, value-added networks (VANs), and existing packet-switched data carriers. Though B-ISDN operations and user applications will be difficult or impossible to separate, customers gain considerable control over the operations of the network, and without carriers losing access to critical operations, administration and management functions (OA&M).

Powerful expert systems can be implemented on B-ISDN, to search, massage, retrieve, and creatively display any data on connected machines, using the distributed processing power of network nodes coupled with customer terminal microcomputers. However, on B-ISDN, the database "memory space" needed for this software transcends all boundaries between "publisher" and "reader," between carrier and customer, and among sovereign nations. It will be necessary to find ways to account for use of this virtual space in order to do things like charge for use, and prevent piracy or counterfeiting of materials. This is similar to the problems found on timesharing machines, but on a global basis – no mean feat. Shared control raises some unusual regulatory questions, and also will be have profound implications for publishing, intellectual property and piracy (discussed below).

VI. OPPORTUNITIES

Hardly anyone anticipated the multi-billion dollar hardware and software industry that arose with the microcomputer less than a decade ago. This is a good example of the failure of imagination at work. While spreadsheets, word processing, computer graphics, page makeup, typesetting, and even games were all prototyped on mainframes as long ago as the 1950s, the concept that such applications could be performed on one's desk, and on tens of millions of desks, brought disbelief until microelectronics became cheap.

The forecasters, attempting conventional linear assessment in a non-linear world, could not envision the power, cleverness, and ease of use of the software that quickly evolved to take advantage of the electronics. As noted, we face a similar problem in trying to forecast the opportunities for electronic information transfer or publishing that the next generation of microcomputers and telecommunications will bring.

The intractability of prediction is due to chaos theory, which will be discussed in the final section. Three problems of assessing future developments are briefly outlined here:

  i)   Complementary substitution effects;
  ii) New and different publishing activities;
  iii) Increases in the transfer of information.

1. Complementary Substitution

The explosion of published materials – albeit not by today's publishers – is a form of complementary substitution. Predicting the success of desktop publishing (a positive form of feedback from the new technology) was a safe bet: Computer-integrated graphics is easy to use. There is no way to describe this in print. It is sufficient to set someone in front of a terminal with CIGA software and let them go to work with a mouse or trackball.

The mouse is a non-intuitive device which tends to be rejected by non-graphics users, until they try one. Actually, a physiologist recognizes the mouse concept immediately, for the optic nerve enters the brain adjacent to the ganglions which relay impulses from the hand; the necessity of hand/eye coordination in humans is no accident. Indeed, it is one of the reasons that paper is still useful, for it "feels right" to hold paper and write on it. But with the hand on a mouse, the computer display begins to approach the attractions of pencil on paper. And because of the computer's recursive powers, the utility of the mouse or computer drawing tablet exceeds what an artist can do with a pencil.

Within a small amount of time, attractive charts are being generated from columns of data by formally quite naive users. Pie charts are instantly transformed to bar graphs. Text can be culled from a word processor, or graphics readily inserted into a text document. Even color can be added, changed, and altered on some PCs. One of the side effects by beginners is an overuse of color, lines, and type – it is so easy to display and manipulate these things. Now that the barriers are down, quantities of graphics are produced. The same phenomenon appeared when word processors took hold.

The second input for desktop publishing is the laser printer, for they make almost perfect presentation copies – sometimes better than what is seen on the graphics screen. The output can be photo-offset or xerographically copied for further distribution, but for small quantities the laser printer can collate and duplicate by itself.

For absolute perfection, CIGA output (in the form of the PDL) can be brought or telecommunicated to a phototypesetting machine which makes photo-offset negatives directly. High-resolution, inexpensive color printers are now available, and will be common in the future. Multiple versions, or multiple copies of the same version can be produced by pressing a number. Networked machines can send copies to other machines, or remote printers, by the press of a button. A distribution list can have thousands of names, or sites and all the user has to do is type one command.

2. New Publishing Activities

The next generation of software will use expert systems techniques to aid the non-artist in producing better graphics, another form of accelerated positive feedback, with some de-stabilizing effects.

Already large files of public domain graphics can be produced which users can incorporate in their own work, just as artists use "clip art" for pasteups. Some of this is online. But, with scanners, any material can become computer clip art, including four-color screen illustrations from print. By manipulating the modulation transfer function of the scanner's optics, or electronically dithering the dots, the screen disappears and a new screen can be created for negative making or laser printing – in color. Anything in print can be copied, enhanced, distorted, re-used, forged, pirated, and counterfeited. New works can be created from old, or the old perfectly reproduced. And all of this by not terribly well-trained users. The price of this equipment is dropping quite rapidly. We discuss below the implications for evidence of fiduciary transactions as a side-effect of electronic publishing.

Other less criminal economic activity will result from widespread use of electronic publishing tools. Today we see newsletters of all types coming from laser-printer driven desktop publishing activities. New technical journals will be easier to establish. Short print runs can be economically handled by the laser printer itself. Typesetters, page layout artists and printers are unnecessary to get the information. And with technical people increasingly online, print distribution can be replaced by print on demand, and onsite.

3. Transfer of Information

An author today may input text (and graphics) directly from word processors and desktop microcomputers (hence "desktop publishing") to editors, publishers, or to colleagues remotely via telephone links. This has become common among many in the academic community, and is increasingly the preferred mode for periodicals, though there is a large lag between what the technology can do and general practice. Remote entry gives the author and artist much greater control over the ultimate output.

CIGA tools permit more than just text transfer. State-of-the-art desktop workstations can show precisely what the final printed or displayed result will look like, including type composition, page makeup and graphic details. Devices permit desktop proofing of full-color pages, galleys, etc. Remote processing of this order permits work to be spread over greater geographical areas. Collaborators and editors can work together without expensive and time-consuming travel.

Typesetting has now become trivial. Thousands of fonts are available, some as public domain software. Fonts are important for text, as is typesetting itself. 400 years of printing drew out the best ways of displaying text so it can be read faster, more accurately, and with less eyestrain. Justification (making the margin flush right and left), kerning (spacing letters so they look uniform in a justified line), ligatures (letters pushed together to improve readability), and a host of other printers' tricks are an important part of information transfer that now can be customized for the user.

Graphics make tables of numbers easier to understand. With the tables transmitted electronically, the reader can determine whether a pie or line graph is the better way to read the table. Raw data can be combined from different sources for new graphs. Suggestions – or mandates – can be built into the text as computer programmes for analyses. Color can be added to help distinguish detail. Automated tools permit incorporating the text, fonts, charts into personal notebooks, printed as if they are books.

This synergy of new publishing techniques – lower entry skills, CIGA-enhanced work, remote powerful workstations and output devices – ultimately promises delivery of presentation-quality, time-sensitive materials to their intended audiences quicker and cheaper than any system based on print publishing and distribution. This has profound implications for the rapid dissemination of scientific and engineering research results, for sales organisations, and industrial parts distribution. Technical literature increasingly rely on graphical interpretation of data, and access to raw data and sources is often necessary in science to verify research results; clarity in presentation often makes a large difference in acceptance of such information. Sales and manufacturing heavily use catalogues, parts lists and diagrams for distribution and inventory control, and indexes of firms and potential clients. These materials, not conventional literature or periodicals, comprise the bulk of the printing industry today.

Such new publishing concepts lead to what is called "hypertext", one of the most exciting concepts for information transfer and electronic publishing, and one of the most disconcerting. With hypertext, the utility of B-ISDN virtual memory space becomes clear. Hypertext permits the reader to point at a portion of text and get more information: footnotes, text from other sources, clarifications. Essentially it is a sophisticated database management system optimized for networking and information display. The term is Ted Nelson's, and the idea was developed in detail in the early 1970s by Doug Englebart. The technology was too crude then for implementation, but currently it is actively being explored. In fact, several electronic publishing aids include hypertext help files as prototypes.

Englebart gave an example in 1973 of how a hypertext handbook would work:

"The Handbook would include: principles, working hypothesis, practices, special-term glossaries, standards, goals, goal status, supportive arguments, techniques, observations, how-to-do items, etc. An active community would be constantly involved in dialogue bearing upon the contents of the last formal version of its Handbook – comments, errata, suggestions, challenges, counter examples, altered designs, improved arguments, new experimental techniques and data, etc., (...) flexible aids for 'on- line' navigation and view generation would be very important, as would the facility for automatic publication (...)."

But what if such a handbook drew from diverse sources of copy protected information, extracted, abstracted and re-written by an AI composing programme? Such software exists today; and its implications are discussed below in the chapter on intellectual property problems.

VII. PROBLEMS

Use of the computer to totally integrate the publishing chain, from the author to the reader or user, including the creation of paper prints from databanks, and especially hypertext, was anticipated in detail at the dawn of the computer age by Vannevar Bush in his well-known 1945 proposal for "Memex" – a microfilm store and digitally computer-driven database machine. These concepts were revived when time-sharing was invented in the early 1960s, variously then called "computer utilities" or "libraries of the future".

The problems of unconstrained positive feedback that we are dealing with today were immediately recognized at that time, but the primitive level of mainframe computer technology and particularly telecommunications hardware did not make these urgent issues. These issues are not new: ownership of information, author's rights, charging, veracity, and blurring of boundaries. Various proposals to revise domestic and international copyright and patent laws have repeatedly raised these same issues, but, again, none of the problems seemed real until quite recently.

The level of urgency has changed with the rapid introduction of the so-called desktop publishing technologies, and the arrival of highspeed digital telecommunications. Concepts such as hypertext, electronic mail with presentation graphics, the ability to scan and reproduce virtually anything on paper, and the direct extension of broadband networks as databases themselves all exacerbate these problems. Virtual memory space and direct memory access of one machine by another, especially if memory space crosses boundaries, and machines are owned by different entities, will be difficult for the legal system to digest.

Desktop publishing enhanced with CIGA and telecommunications technology raises a number of public policy issues related to standards, freedom of information, intellectual property, and transnational trade. These issues are not intuitively obvious to the people creating this new industry, nor have they been adequately addressed in the several (and disconnected) international fora concerned with different elements of the problem. Only three of these issues are discussed below:

- *i)*   Standards to promote (or inhibit) the use of electronic publishing and CIGA techniques;
- *ii)* Trade and potential employment effects;
- *iii)* Protection of intellectual property and prevention of fraud.

1. Standards

The standards being developed for presenting text and graphics, printing, binding and distribution, and hypertext databases are related to electronic mail (E-mail), facsimile (fax), ISDN, and B-ISDN telecommunications work. Yet, a dichotomy has grown between the graphics, publishing, and computer technical community and those industry groups which have developed similar, but markedly inferior standards for E-mail and Teletex. Though high-quality remote printing mixed with graphics is one of the goals of such standards as the CCITT's X.400, none of the E-mail proposals which have emanated from the telecommunications field have the capabilities of the page description languages described above.

Various software and devices used in desktop publishing – word processing, graphics, typesetting, page makeup, computer-aided design, database report generators – link together very poorly, if at all. This has inhibited the spread of desktop publishing/CIGA and has created islands of incompatible user communities, making interorganisational interchange more difficult. The result of the lack of attention by the telecommunications standards bodies to the critical areas described in this paper, is that firms are adopting and modifying proprietary products for remote presentation printing and electronic mail. Here we have a classic standardization case history: too early and innovation suffers, too late and we end up with costly incompatibilities. Still, some elements can be standardized early on. Character sets are one example. Unfortunately, lack of imagination and knowledge about character displays and fonts prevented the standardizers of all of the videotext/teletext systems from incorporating a utilitarian graphics subset as the next step.

The current trend seems to be the establishment of several different distinct display communications modes, systems, and standards:

i) Interorganisation linkages based on a not very flexible enhancement of Telex or facsimile, or both using the public-switched telecommunications networks;

ii) Narrowly defined, but highly utilitarian presentation modes for graphics communications in integrated communities;

iii) Data access systems with narrow linkages via electronic mail or plain text terminal; and,

iv) Hybrids controlled by a user community with sufficient sophistication to link their proprietary systems into the public systems, but not vice versa.

Specialized hardware to allow microcomputer word processing/graphics outputs to be sent directly to CCITT No. 3 fax machines is an example of the latter. An orderly integration of these systems could save users unnecessary expense and permit a greater degree of communication. An extensible set of standards could enhance the application of hypertext, and mixed media, for example. But an integration which ignores market and user needs – such as the examples of videotext and teletex – will not be successful in the face of alternatives available to sophisticated customers. Perhaps what is missing is an overall view of the utility of desktop publishing, presentation graphics, its relationship to industrial productivity and competitiveness, and its linkages to allied interests – telecommunications, postal networks, education, etc.

2. Broadband ISDN[8]

The development of broadband ISDN standards is bound to have a impact on the way hypertext database ideas grow. Essentially B-ISDN can be considered as a gigantic relational distributed database mechanism, based on decades of computer science theory. Unlike narrowband ISDN, B-ISDN interfaces are constructed as database relations, with data bytes (called octets by the CCITT) framed as database tuples (rows), data domains, and database attributes (columns). Database and computer terminology in telecommunication contexts can be confusing, indicating how little ISDN and B-ISDN standards have in common. Pointer chains are inherent in B-ISDN, allowing for the construction of hierarchical index tables and use of hashing techniques. These techniques permit B-ISDN switching, bandwidth, and routing capabilities to be used as functional substitutes for relational database dynamic table structures, completing the merger between computer and telecommunication standards.

Standardization for hypertext communications could emerge by coordinating broadband communications developments, such as the LAN fibre distributed data interface (FDDI) proposed by ANSI, proprietary standards for peer-to-peer CPU communications and for LAN-based distributed data management systems, and CCITT B-ISDN work.

Treated as a new form of basic infrastructure, hypertext – and hypermedia, including full-motion video – could have a major productive impact on all industry. For this to happen, negative feedback concepts have to be applied by public policy makers. This includes standardization for universal access and flexible implementation by innovators and entrepreneurs. More likely will be positive feedback loops which de-stabilize older information industries and rigid implementations which will slow hypermedia penetrations.

3. Trade Issues

Remote access and duplication of graphic materials will permit new industries to develop across national boundaries, stressing current international agreements relating to labour movement, trade, and information flows, as well as intellectual property. Publishing firms can shift labour inputs to less-developed countries and still maintain close control over production. CIGA software is currently being used between artists and advertising agencies working simultaneously on page makeup while separated by oceans. But that is just a trivial mechanism for such software.

The point of creation and of publication becomes blurred in electronic publishing. There is no real point of publication, and creation is too elusive to pinpoint or document. The product is similarly vague, since in dealing with computers one is concerned with processes not products.

These definitional problems may have impact on trade treaties which specify origin of product. There is no "product" until the information is used, perused, or becomes an input into some process. And even then, input could be into another ongoing process, such as a personalized or tailored information retrieval system, a robotic factory, a dynamic hypertext "handbook" (as in the above example), or into another network crossing even more boundaries.

Trade laws have never had to deal with processes of this type before. One of the issues to be dealt with in trade, as well as intellectual property protection, is that information is not the same as other forms of material property, for a number of reasons. The most basic have to do with conventional paradigms and shibboleths about supply and demand. Digitized information has extremely low or zero incremental costs for duplication. Furthermore, for electronically-based information, the information resource is not depleted after use. Information is not a package that can be weighed, measured, or easily valued; software is not what comes on a floppy disk or tape; data is not what is transmitted on a telecommunications line or is printed out.

To make matters worse, software can define hardware (the code is the machine), can be embedded on a chip, or become part of a vast communication switching architecture – quite invisible to humans and to smaller parts of the total machine. So with electronics we make machinery and writings fungible, confusing patents, copyrights and trade secrets; we replace people with code, code with output, and contextual information with data pointers. If a government presses too hard in one direction for some goal, the stored-programme can be made to move another way, somewhat like an amoeba, or a handful of silly putty.

4. Intellectual Property[9]

The cost of information production may be quite large, but producers need to be compensated. Governments may want to value electronic publishing activities based on these costs. But the economics of information use will not be that easy to pinpoint for trade or copyright policy.

One illuminating example is what can happen with electronic mail: with CIGA techniques, typeset displays, and animated graphics, is a powerful form of publishing with potential impacts beyond anything which paper could yield. It also has some potential powerful impacts on piracy. After product creation, transmission appears deceptively simple: all you do is type the name or names of the recipients (or their numbers), and instantly the message or creation is on its way to your recipient.

Now suppose the message you have captured, and perhaps manipulated, includes some item or article just read or derived from your electronic publisher's machine. To display that article, replete with graphics and perhaps matrices of data (which we assume you have properly paid for), your computer has to store it in some sort of a memory-buffer – our buckets of bits. There is no difference between this memory and the rest of memory which stores the programme for accessing and displaying this article. And for the same reasons that the computer can emulate any machine process, there is no way to prevent such a memory buffer from being activated.

The law of geometric increase is the critical publishing problem[10]. If you send the article not to one, but just two correspondents, and then they each send a copy to two others, ... and if each recipient retransmits the article, say, every 15 minutes (only a stroke of a key on the computer terminal) to two others, it does not take long before the whole world sees it (2 to the 32nd power is 4.29 billion; coincidentally, the same as the address space for a 32-bit central processor).

The ability to protect or set a value on intellectual creations which transcend boundaries via digital networks is very difficult due to the ease of replication of digitized materials. The very concept of intellectual property on such networks runs into definitional problems, because of the way text and graphics can be manipulated, merged, enhanced, and stored. CIGA can be used to counterfeit and pirate graphic products with unprecedented speed and accuracy. Complications abound: pages no longer have to be static, but may include animated graphics, or raw data so a user may manipulate or combine items from numerous sources.

General agreement on the basic principles of copyright appears in the two international conventions – the Universal Copyright Convention and the Berne Convention on Copyright. These copyright fundamentals give authors and writers:

"(...) the right to ownership in their works. They are entitled to protection agains unauthorized use of their work as well as a share in any earnings from its use by the public (...). But more than that, the rewards that copyright assures the individual creator (...) provides a stimulus to creativity from which all society benefits. In promulgating copyright laws, legislators have recognized the needs of society for access to knowledge. They have therefore attempted to find a balance between the essentially conflicting needs of society for knowledge and learning and the rights of the individual creator[11]".

Similar words are in the preamble to almost every national copyright law, proposed revision, and survey of problems created by the computer. The fundamentals are not an issue, but questions brought on by the stored-programme computer are virtually unresolvable in the context of these principles. Along with the new paradigm of electronic publishing and digital networks, we need a new model of how to compensate producers and disseminate information without making all users criminals.

The basic questions for computer-based creations are no different from that for print, but the answers are quite elusive. These are:

  i) What types of subject matter are to be protected? How will this be recognized in the digital form of a relational database, particularly if the database uses relational concepts?

ii) Is the right to be conferred upon some form of registration? How can or should this be done with networked distribution which eliminates the common standards of what constitutes publication? How would laws that require deposits be harmonized with reality?

iii) How long should protection last? How will this be determined in an electronic environment when there is no specified publication date? How does one pinpoint publication in a dynamically varying relational database; are database pointers to be copyrighted?

iv) How can publication be resolved where data bases overlap, are created independently, are based on standardized formats or indexing rules, and in virtual mode prove to be identical, though in real mode cannot be identified at all?

v) Is whatever right applied only against imitators, or should it be a full monopoly that affects independent creators of the same idea? How would this be enforced against machine creations? What arguments could be used to prove plagiarism or infringements? What is the meaning of an idea as expressed in terms of relational database constructs? What is expression? How much can be derivative? What is derivative?

How will these definitions work where the intellectual property is in the form of a chip (firmware), neither a "writing," nor a programme, but a data management system which access a set of specialized statistical and materials database for automated mask manufacture.

Sui generis legislation which pretends that a mask is something other than a special form of database does not help, for microchips are functional outputs of software engineering; "silicon foundries" are the names of place that produce chips, for they are the modern equivalent of iron-mongers factories. Circuit database output is engraved on semiconductor materials, much as the manipulation of a chemical database may be stored on magnetic media or fanfold paper. That these tiny outputs may themselves control other programmes or processes, or be a process, is consistent with computer fundamentals; so may the output from stock quotation services or news wires be made to control other processes: an automated stock trading procedure, for example.

Across national boundaries, these questions are likely to be interpreted differently by different national courts, no matter what the treaties state. Such variances in interpretation do little to protect property rights. That these are not trivial questions can be understood in terms of trade in intellectual property, as expressed by W.R. Cornish in his treatise, which addresses problems of print media[12]:

"(...) the growth of trade competition (...) has brought ever-increasing advantages to those in the van of innovation. Intellectual property rights, which help to sustain the lead of those with technical know-how, with successful marketing schemes, with new fetishes for pop culture, have come to foster immense commercial returns(...). But in some of these fields particularly, success has been accompanied by advances in copying techniques which make piracy possible on a scale that is just as new. The resources of existing legal techniques are under considerable strain(...).

The obvious purpose of intellectual property is to give protection against rival enterprises which would otherwise sell goods or provide services in direct competition. In international trade these rights have acquired a separate significance. In many cases, by adopting the appropriate legal technique, goods (...) can be prevented from moving from one territory to another, a barrier of private rights can be set up against imports or exports which is as effective as an embargo or tariff imposed by a state(...)."

But with electronic publishing, such remedies will not only be impossible, but any government attempting to enforce legal barriers to information movement will look ridiculous in the eyes of its citizens.

a) Copying

The characteristics of electronic publishing simply do not fit those of copyrights for several reasons. The most important in terms of computers is that the definition of copying is too vague, for all digital machines copy in order to communicate. Digital logic devices are essentially repeaters re-generating perfect copies many times within the system. Communications is the way the logic devices work (they cannot do binary arithmetic without communicating), and virtual networking is inherent. Textual information, through database relations, domains, and pointers, may have no original, no duplicate, no terminal output; instead all "copies" are originals generated from a computer store. And every copy may be unique, prepared on-demand to specific requirements.

All data which enters the machine – to be specific, say the data is alphanumeric text, binary encoded – must be stored, however temporary, in a "register" or some kind of buffer. This is a "copy". All processing, manipulation, further telecommunication or re-transmission of digitized information, instructions, and results of machine decisions must be delayed for some tiny time slice for the digital computer to perform its binary arithmetical and Boolean processes; store and delay is the essence of the CPU. But it cannot be localized just to one CPU, or one node, or one terminal on a network of processors.

What makes the concepts of copyright protection archaic is the way digital processors move encoded text or graphics data between locations. Data is copied from one buffer-register to another, copied from the buffers to the processnits, copied from input buffers to output buffers, copied from registers to central memory, and copied from temporary memory to storage or some other processor (which may be far distant – the machine does not know these things).

In copying, text in the register or memory may or may not be destroyed or altered, depending on register architecture and how the instructions are written. So in telecommunicating text on computer networks, the switching store-and-forward machines cannot be considered as mere neutral transmitter-repeaters (as on telegraph lines) but as duplicators extraordinaire, all linked together in a gigantic system of distributed intelligence. On a B-ISDN system this copying becomes apparent.

One can imagine all this copying of bits as a tiny bucket brigade, emptying some holes and filling others until some result is achieved. The result may be a display of letters on a screen, or on paper, or perhaps the result is not displayed at all, but stored on some physical medium somewhere on the (virtual) network. Or the bits in the buckets may enter an intermediate suspended state, waiting for something else (perhaps unknown at the time) to happen. Trillions of bits may pass through the buckets in a register-buffer until a certain pattern tips one special bucket which rings a bell. This pattern itself may be generated only after the bits were stored in the bucket (waiting for something to happen), and may have been generated by the passage of other bits, unknown at the time of original storage. The network of buckets and bits, therefore is recursive, and can define its own programme.

The pattern might fit the human message "war declared someplace", or some such. Or instead of ringing a bell, it might tip a bucket which means "sell stock". Or more usefully, it might fill a distant bucket in some other machine or machines which says, in effect, "the stock is sold", and simultaneously fill a set of bit buckets yet elsewhere enriching your bank account according to a table of currency and stock rates which continually vary in yet another set of bit buckets, and debiting another set of buckets in someone else's machine.

This is only a rough scenario of what active electronically encoded, networked, and perhaps proprietary information can be made to do. The point is that "reading" of computerized text does not infer that a human must be involved; however, any reading using digital computers does imply that copying is involved, and copying many times over. There is simply no parallel to the kind of text readings with which we have become familiar in normal print media. There is no way for an originator of electronic information on an open network to have control over what mode of "reading" or copying, or performance may take place somewhere down the line. Basic to this concept is the fundamental mathematics attributed to Godel which made the stored-programme digital computer possible in the first instance, that it is impossible to know in advance all of the potential results of a programme.

The nature of the computer process is such that at any one time there may be multiple copies of a text residing in various parts of the machine, or spread far and wide over a multi-machine network. More complicated, the text may not exist at all in any continuous, human comprehensible fashion, but be instantaneously reassembled by a series of database pointers; this is the way a microcomputer reassembles text with its file allocation table (FAT), and the way "erased" text can be retrieved after a mistaken delete command. The concept of a FAT yields numerous copyright problems when extended over a network; on B-ISDN each frame matrix is such a set of FAT pointers.

Some of the copies may be intended to be transitory, and some copies may stay around for a long time until some other programme or data needs its memory space and overwrites it. But there is no guarantee of its erasure at any particular slice of time.

The entire process so far described may seem trivial, for moving just a few bits or a few thousand at a time; in the early days of batch processing, it was trivial as far as copyright issues were concerned. But with modern solid-state electronics photo-engraved on tiny pieces of silicon, with optoelectronic transmission systems, and with the potential of superconductive switching, the digital computer has entered a different age: even microcomputers moves these bits some tens of millions of times each second. A PC's temporary memory can be configured to hold bits equal to several tens of millions of characters, and billions will be economically feasible by the end of the decade. With ISDN, this memory could be filled in less than a minute, and with B-ISDN a few seconds will move entire encyclopedia within seconds.

In this paper we are concerned primarily with the fruits of electronic publishing – text and graphics – but it should be recognized that the computer also contains programmes which are basically encoded lists of instructions telling the processors what to do with the text, graphics and data. Intellectual property protection for programmes is beyond this papers' scope, however it must be noted that by definition, there is no difference between the binary numbers which represent the data and the binary numbers which represents the instructions. Only the context counts. A line in memory may be data in one instant, and the same data may become instructions in the next. This also complicates copyright rules, since it often is humanly impossible to determine what is happening at any time inside of the machine or network.

Solutions for the problem of compensating creators of intellectual property, preventing abuse, and encouraging the "arts and sciences" must be found outside of any concepts of what is a copy and what is not. These will not be easy until new models for publishing are created.

b) Piracy and Counterfeiting

Users may create new materials from old with CIGA equipment. Veracity may be questioned, and property rights in differing jurisdictions impinged by these novel techniques.

Yet, these tools are too useful and powerful to forbid just because they cross ancient legal boundaries. Control of such tools at the current level of computer penetration and knowledge would be an impossible task causing injury to other industrial areas, and calling the legitimacy of the state into question.

The counterfeiting problem can be condensed into a set of issues: the verification of originals, duplicates, and extracts. CIGA technology will obsolete virtually all existing forms of paper-based fiduciary and legal documentation; yet computer-based documentation can also provide new ways of unique identification. Unfortunately, the tools for creating absolutely unique IDs cross over into cryptology – a technology which is severely restricted for civilian use by many governments on grounds of national security.

However, some compromise will eventually be necessary between national security for defensive purposes and national security for economic and legal purposes. Effective international control of pirated product goes far beyond that of intellectual property. New, highly productive, and affordable CIGA devices give pirates the ability to make virtually perfect copies of anything printed, embossed, in color, and with holograms. Computerized graphics enhances reverse engineering, whether chips, or complex designs for currency. Real objects can be mapped by digitized input into vectorized computer-aided design (CAD) software or screened color photographs for plate-making. High-resolution scanners are based on studio-quality color television cameras; and commercial manufacture of high-definition video equipment will bring the cost for even better equipment within a pirate's budget.

Under CIGA control of a computer-integrated manufacturing (CIM) process, the expression of an idea and its creation begin to merge. Like the paradox of semiconductor chip protection laws, a CAD drawing is for practical purposes more than just a design – it is a database. This database can be used in CAD/CAM devices to manufacture the product. For functional, copyrightable three-dimensional products, sculpting from the CAD database is within the CIGA's capability. Experimental three-dimension holograms have been produced which create visual "models" directly from CAD data tables, bypassing the need for real models. What is copyright and what is patent under such circumstances?

With CIGA databases an idea can be copyrighted and a writing can be patented; this goes much beyond the arguments about whether the "look and feel" of software is protectable. Are we creating new forms of industrial monopoly rights which will require new forms of antitrust to prevent abuses in the future? Will the computer as a robot generate protected ideas to confound humans with their archaic laws?

Counterfeiting, and its allied piratical activities may be amenable to solutions – using negative feedback to stabilize the system – as long as the solutions do not cross into other gray areas, such as bootlegging for information dissemination, and endemic copying for utilitarian reasons. Control of counterfeiting will depend on both the will and ability to use police methods to inspect goods sold on the open market, cooperation of the manufacturers of counterfeitable goods in the form of registration, and a internationally enforceable and workable system of authentication.

A copyright protection system would have, as a minimum, some form of statistical sampling and cryptographic identification scheme which could be embedded in a product in a unique fashion to prevent mere duplication. It is not enough to make a complex ID, such as a hologram, for any design can be duplicated or made to appear legitimate.

An anti-counterfeiting system must give sufficient evidence of a product's illegitimacy by disclosing an impossible number, a normally invisible unregistered mark, or some such to a police inspection. This mark is not difficult to devise, but the registry system could be politically complex and administratively difficult. Fast, transactional computer networking would be a great aid in this respect. Currency and fiduciary items would benefit immensely if their serial numbers were not consecutive, but randomly issued with a special kind of "check" code that statistically would inhibit counterfeiters. Again this would be enhanced by a centrally controlled authentication system.

An anti-piracy system needs to go further, since enforcement would be enhanced if a pirated product could be traced to the source copy. A combination of the anti-counterfeit ID code, coupled with a unique set of IDs for master items, programmes, etc., could help distinguish between master and copy. Furthermore, a properly maintained, online, authentication system could establish priority, and sequence of legitimate and illegitimate changes. Unfortunately, many nations' copyright laws do not permit registration, which would be a political barrier to implementation of such systems.

VIII.   THE COMPLEXITY OF CIGA – A REVIEW AND EXAMPLE

Intellectual property issues exemplify the non-linear dynamics of electronic publishing. In a non-linear system, positive feedback can (and usually) leads to catastrophe. Negative feedback is almost impossible to programme, since the system cannot be modelled. There are no easy answers, but many routes to collapse. It is not sufficient to simply modify copyright laws and treaties to "include" the new technologies, for the new technologies work in an altogether different manner and do different things than print media. "Performing" rights, "copy" rights, "authors" rights all become meaningless when dealing with information on computers and computer networks. Computer central processors know nothing about performances, displays, copies, and authors, especially when information accesses typically span several processing generations. Even the assumption that data will be displayed to humans is tenuous, since machine-to-machine information transfer may be common.

The non-linear dynamics of CIGA graphics may be shown by the several different implications of copying. Some may be detrimental, and some beneficial. As one can see, feedback may be positive (stable or catastrophic), or negative. The various types of copying may be categorized as:

i)   Copying in order to use a creation. This is positive feedback, and stable. Such copying may range from creating a copy as part of a computer system so it can be read by a human, so the information may be messaged for computational or other purposes (including literary), so it can be readily sorted and filed, or so that multiple persons can work with the information. Though stable, a slight change in the use of the copying system may cause instabilities, to wit;

ii)   Piracy, whereby a creation is duplicated for sale without authorization or proper compensation to the originator or owner, and sold to the public in competition with authorized copies. The original packaging or trade mark is not duplicated, though it may be similar. Positive feedback, but unstable for intellectual property protection;

iii)   Counterfeiting – a pirated duplication intended to appear to be an original in all respects. An example of negative feedback, that is inherently unstable from a property point of view;

iv)   Bootlegging, usually the unauthorized recording of a performance; a corollary definition would be the "unauthorized" use of an active process within another process. Similar characteristics to piracy and counterfeiting, but negative feedback with some useful, stabilizing quantities, however illegal it may be.

There are many variations of copying, and many gray legal and moral areas in copying. Clearly ii) and iii) are unfair, immoral, destabilizing, and detrimental to the general public; in most jurisdictions these states are illegal, though possibly hard to enforce. Types i) and iv) may or may not have utility to the public welfare, are arguably illegal in some jurisdictions and not others, and may be very difficult to distinguish from clearly legitimate activities.

A fifth definition for copying has emerged in recent years: the utility and often necessity of using mathematical algorithms developed by others in order to make computer-related processes function. Here we are discussing an idea or even the representation of a natural process which may require immense investment to prove out. The fungibility of semiconductor chips with computer programmes and industrial process is one example of the use of algorithms confusing patent, copyright, and trade secret law. Copying, in this sense, has often been essential for invention, improvements, and expansion in the arts and sciences. There are widely divergent opinions on the desirability of reducing this activity.

IX. THE PLANNING PROCESS

The dynamic nature of the technologies described for electronic publishing and information dissemination, in particular, make quantification of the information revolution very difficult. Quantification is important to determine the initial boundary conditions for a model to assess the role of feedback and chaos but quantification of what?

Measuring the productivity, output, or impact of office, clerical, management and information workers has no useful analogies to the measurement of the productivity of workers who produce "things". It is not enough to count letters typed, graphics generated, or pages output from laser printers or xerographic machines. These are examples of positive feedback which neither lead to stabilization nor useful policy. Similarly, tabulating jobs, skills, income, and production levels of labour which type, typeset, draw, and print, and which produce the machinery for those tasks, tells us little about future trends. Transitional and future skills are not evident from this accounting.

To predict opportunities and problems of the future, we also need negative feedback information: how the new technologies will be used, what will be the interaction with the novel machinery, the existing talent and skill base, the transitional labour and industrial base, and what are the working models of the future for so-called information technologies. Not only is this difficult, it assumes we can invent the future as well as predict it. This leads to a second problem: the transitional time scale has been greatly foreshortened. Models which compare small changes may have been useful in the past for policy making, but are grossly misleading today when microcomputer technology has an obsolescence factor of 1 to 2 years.

There are corollaries to these two points. Some information industries resemble manufacturing, so that there is a surface appearance that productivity can be measured, and measured within short time frames and narrowly-defined skill bases. These "information" industries are fundamentally transaction based, thus workers may be measured in terms of how many transactions get processed. But the technologies of electronic publishing will eventually have a complex effect on transactional processing as well; the problem is that this is already happening quite rapidly.

Transactional processing – cheque writing, airline reservations, inventory control, auditing, etc. – will be altered because of intellectual re-orientation. For example, business letter writing is the means to some business end – orders, inquiries, contracts. Integrated factory automation or computer-aided design can automatically maintain inventory and substitute for "front-office" tasks such as writing order letters. Expert systems programmes may schedule a trip, automatically make reservations and issue tickets (or some functional substitute for tickets). Today we see many clerical transactional replacements because of electronic funds transfer.

It is the intellectual activities beyond transactional processing which form the crux of the information revolution. In the future, if we plot growth or decline in the transactional information industries, we will probably see a distinct singularity, or discontinuity in the 1980-90 time period. Plots of other factors, agricultural employment, urbanization, money flows, etc., often show such discontinuities during a certain time period. What has happened is the catastrophe effect; enough of a change had taken place, that the statistics finally noticed a change. This should not be interpreted, as it often is erroneously, that the change began at that point.

One prominent example is attempting to pinpoint the beginnings of the manufacturing or information revolution at the point that agricultural employment dipped below that of other sectors. The information revolution and the agricultural revolution coincided when the Pharaoh noticed that the morning star's position could be correlated with the Nile's flood tides. Farmers began using intensive information in the early 1800s when they applied sophisticated machinery to planting and harvesting; their information skills had to be commensurate with such applications – including reading, bookkeeping, and knowledge of mechanics. These were significant information revolutions; the Pharaohs, the monks of the middle ages who rotated crops, and the 19th Century farmers who used mechanical machinery were all participants in an information revolution, and were "information workers". They were agricultural workers too. And they participated in a singularity or discontinuity.

How do we measure productivity when such technological change completely re-orients industrial sectors? Have sheet-metal workers who bend metal for microcomputer cabinets moved from the manufacturing sector to the information sector? Conventional answers based on current views of work and industry are not particularly helpful in aiding governments in their industrial or labour policies. Virtually all jobs and industries will require complex mixes of skills and knowledge different from the past. It is more important to determine when a singularity takes place, than to continue measuring what is not measurable. The paradox of electronic publishing shows that new theories of labour and industry will be needed to help plan. These theories will have to account for negative and positive feedback, and the fact that changes are non-linear, and hence cannot be modelled in conventional ways.

Some questions are unanswerable and some irrelevant. This means that governmental decreed policy and infrastructure must be very flexible and forgiving. Broadband fibre technologies, as noted, fits this description. Incremental, competitive forces will cause the adoption of electronic publishing and related technologies by firms and industries. Small amounts of productivity changes (which can be measured) will leverage larger changes – discontinuities – in industrial structure (which cannot be measured). This – the so-called butterfly effect – is the crux of chaos theory.

For example, from 1900 to today, transport in industrialized countries gradually moved from dominant common-carrier railroad and water transportation to a private/common carrier mix of air, automotive, water, rail, and no-transport (due to telecommunications and data processing). At every step of change, one could measure and model some index to show why linear change took place – it might have been strictly cost, or some measure of physical satisfaction. (These measurements often continue beyond a point where the model makes sense.) Now land use and transport are forever altered – in a non-linear way. How would one compare a transport productivity index today to that of 1900, when all of industry works in radically different ways?

Similar models may be developed for the incremental impacts of electronic publishing technologies, today. At some point the models reach a point of non-linearity, chaos enters, and the models will fail. The difference is that the non-linear changes will not take 87 years. While linear models may be marginally useful for very short-term labour policies, they cannot be used to discern major shifts, and are often misleading in that respect – some non-linear examples: CAD/CAM is rapidly replacing drafting. Engineers can do their own technical drawings. But mere counting of drawings created means nothing in the computer age. The drawings are databases by any definition; databases are inventory lists; and computerized inventory lists can be order forms and manufacturing templates. Hence changing drafting to computerized input, changes an entire industrial process. Do we count the number of drawings or objects produced by the engineer-driven CAD/CAM drawing?

In the (linear) short-term, we can state that CAD permits X number of engineers to directly affect Y number of widgets produced. Z number of drafting and machining jobs may be redundant. In the long-term, CAD permits X number of engineers to interact with the manufacturing sector in a unique way. Widgets are changed, not necessarily cheaper or more expensive, but different. Just as the "bread-basket" of 1900 makes it impossible to compare the value of today's money (1988), the future incremental measures of productivity will be not comparable with those of today.

Electronic publishing offers its own non-linear example: at first, word processing was adopted as a strict cost-effective tool to replace typewriters, just as electric typewriters replace manual devices. More pages could be typed with each incremental tool change. This is still the mode for change in most sectors. But in a few sectors it has been recognized that the computer-cum-word- processor is a different animal: the PC can compute and communicate; can type, correct, and draw pictures; it can merge facsimile with image enhancement; it is a filing cabinet and a library, substituting for printing, xerography, and the post office; it can connect concepts, and record ideas.

The communicating PC is a "workstation", doing synergistically far more than any incremental improvement on typewriters, teletypes, and automatic data processing would be able to do separately. But it doesn't stop at the workstation; the network means that "transactions" can be linked to other processes; so, for example, when my "mail" contains certain information, I do not necessary read it, but it is automatically "filed" through a series of pointers for some future reference, if need be. Therefore, in modern work environments, the question of whether to type or use a personal computer is no longer even raised. But this assumes the workers understand the tools and the process. Admittedly, such environments are only beginning to gain ground.

What is critical here is that the time span between the introduction of the first PCs, and their widespread application has been very short in some sectors, particularly in research institutions. We would be foolish to measure productivity in research by common measures of paper output, or "problems solved". In such cases, we might show immense productivity gains, for the electronic machinery is very good at generating paper, or enumerating things which can be programmed. This is nonsense, however. What we are doing in research is joining concepts. It is no accident that news, ideas, and research on superconductivity or broadband ISDN have spread so quickly. The computer networks have become part of the infrastructure, and it is more than messages which are passed along.

Similarly, there will be synergistic effects in all "idea handling" industries affected by electronic communication tools.

X. CONCLUSIONS

Tools are now available to permit the copying and alteration of virtually anything, from any digitized process to currency and fiduciary documents. This calls for a response to:

   i)   Determine whether a document is authentic;
   ii) Shift away from paper documents for legal and fiduciary purposes; and,
   iii) Establish an international regime for authentication, since a national regime will be unworkable where national sovereignty cannot be extended.

New forms of labour mobility will attach to information and service-related skills which use computers and communications. These, too, will cross national boundaries. Tracking these changes will be difficult since the fundamental job may itself be altered in the process.

Powerful techniques, in the form of global relational databases using broadband communications, will permit wider access to distributed information. How copyright and patent restrictions are interpreted may inhibit or encourage the spread of these techniques. Alternatively, dysfunctional application of copy rights may drive the use of these techniques underground, giving advantages to those who use them in spite of restrictions.

Standards are critical to utilitarian interfaces, but it does not necessarily follow that governments should participate or not participate in standards making or enforcement. The market tends to fill standards vacuums where needed. Governments could make an effort to better inform official standards bodies of market forces and directions, and work in interdisciplinary areas, so that whatever official workings take place are more efficient.

Where governments tend to be involved, in the provision of infrastructure such as telecommunications facilities, it would enhance their activities to become more aware of the interinvolvement of technologies. Broadband digital networks is one such area which will have an immense impact on electronic publishing, and could therefore have an impact on economic activities related to information dissemination.

Predicting and planning for the future is not only difficult, it is impossible in any fine-tuned way. Chaos theory tells us that in non-linear systems – which is what electronics has done to publishing – the slightest perturbation can have gross consequences as systems evolve. Feedback is what drives these perturbations, and mostly it is positive feedback which lets things get out of control. Negative feedback is more useful in stabilizing systems, but this is a paradox, since you need to know the future to make it work, and the future is not quite knowable. One way for public policy to handle this conundrum is to ease the way for a flexible infrastructure capable of handling diverse needs and readily changeable – that would be a form of workable negative feedback itself.

GLOSSARY

ASCII: American Standard Code for Information Interchange
B-ISDN: Broadband ISDN
Byte: 8 bits or an octet
CAD: Computer-aided design
CIGA: Computer-integrated graphic arts
CIM: Computer Integrated Manufacturing
Gigabit: Million million bits
ISDN: Integrated Services Digital Network
Megabit: Million bits
PDL: Page Description Languages

NOTES AND REFERENCES

1. For a more detailed explanation, see Anania, L. and Solomon, R., "Open Networks", *Telecommunications Magazine*, Dec. 1987.
2. Even well-modeled physical systems exhibit this factor. See Gleick, J., "Chaos: Making a New Science," Viking, 1987. This is not the place for an extended discussion of chaos theory, which among other things explains how snowflakes work and has presented us with fractal geometry and other insights. A simple explanation is that of the "butterfly effect": – a single butterfly flapping its wings in Tokyo will eventually affect the weather in Paris. No matter how well-defined a (weather) pattern can be stated, it takes very little change in its non-linear system dynamics to iterate to a level where an unpredictable effect is manifest. Chaos theory shows why the general weather pattern for a season can be predicted, but 48 hours out there is no sure way to know whether it will rain or be sunny. Similar dynamics take place in industrial policy planning and market forecasting.
3. For feedback in general, see Norbert Weiner's classic text, *Cybernetics*, MIT Press, 1949.
4. For a discussion of paradigm changes and long-wave industrial cycles in a closely related area, see Solomon, R.J., *Changing the Nature of Telecommunications Networks*, S Intermedia, May 1986.
5. In general, see: Hofstadter, *Gödel, Escher, Bach*, Vintage, 1980; Weizenbaum, J., *Computer Power and Human Reason*, W.H. Freeman, 1976.
6. Schreiber, *et al.*, paper in preparation for Feb. 1988, SMPTE meeting.
7. Solomon, R.J., "Open Network Architectures and Broadband ISDN: The Joker in the Regulatory Deck," in proceedings of the International Council for Computer Communications, Sept. 14-17, Dallas, 1987.
8. Ref. 5.
9. On Intellectual property, see: Cornish, W.R., *Intellectual Property*, London, Sweet & Maxwell, 1981. *University of Pittsburgh Law Review*, Symposium on "The Future of Software Protection", Summer 1986. Ploman, E. W. and Clark Hamilton, L., *Copyright: Intellectual Property in the Information Age*, London, Routledge & Kegan Paul, 1980. Pool, I.de S. and Solomon, R. J., "Transborder Data Flows: Requirements for International Co-operation", *in Policy Implications of Data Network Developments in the OECD Area*, OECD, 1980, pp. 79-139. Pool, I. and Solomon, R.J., "Intellectual Property and Transborder Data Flows," *Stanford Journal of International Law*, Summer 1980. Solomon, R. J., "Evolving Computer Infrastructure and its Effects on Corporate and Political Boundaries", OECD, *ICCP(86)10*, 19 Feb. 1986. "Computers and the Concept of Intellectual Property", in Martin Greenberger, *Electronic Publishing Plus, White Plains: Knowledge Industries*, 1985. "Electronic Printing Innovations Affect Counterfeiting, Copyright, and Int'l Trade", *International Networks newsletter*, March 15, 1986. "Computers & Highspeed Telecommunications: The Old Copyright Rules May No Longer Apply to Intellectual Property", *International Networks newsletter*,

February 1984. "New Technologies Hoist 'Jolly Roger' Over Intellectual Property Worldwide", *International Networks newsletter*, February 1985. "Intellectual Property and the New Computer-Based Media", August 1984, Consultant's report for the Office of Technology Assessment, US Congress, Washington, DC. "International Database Issues: A Case Study of NLM's Medlars", in Anne Branscomb, (ed.), *Toward a Law of Global Networks*, Longmans, 1986; and Yurow, J., "The New Electronic Technologies and International Intellectual Property Issues", Jan. 18, 1985, Consultant's report for the Office of Technology Assessment, US Congress, Washington, DC.

10. This writer, in a paper co-authored with the late Ithiel de Sola Pool, first described this in a different context for the OECD ten years ago in a discussion of transborder data flows.

11. UNESCO, *The ABC of Copyright*, 1981.

12. Cornish, W.R., *Intellectual Property*, London, Sweet & Maxwell, 1981.

POLICY OPTIONS FOR PROMOTING GROWTH THROUGH INFORMATION TECHNOLOGY

by

Erik Arnold and Ken Guy
Science Policy Research Unit
University of Sussex, United Kingdom

TABLE OF CONTENTS

I. THE IMPORTANCE OF INFORMATION TECHNOLOGY (IT) 135

    1. Introduction 135
    2. Defining IT 136
    3. Long Waves, IT and Industrial Restructuring 136

II. GROWTH CASES IN IT 144

    1. Introduction – About Convergence in IT 144
    2. IT in the Economy 146
    3. Household Technology 153
    4. Convergence and Infrastructure 158

III. IT AND RELATIVE GROWTH IN MANUFACTURING AND SERVICES 164

    1. Introduction 164
    2. Arguments for the "New Service Economy" 164
    3. The Changing Boundary between Manufacturing and Services 166
    4. The Interdependence of Manufacturing and Services 167
    5. The Effects of IT 168

IV. OBSTACLES TO IT-BASED GROWTH 170

    1. Introduction 170
    2. Learning 170
    3. Social/Institutional 171
    4. Supply-side 172
    5. Demand-side 172
    6. Education and Training 174
    7. Innovation Policy 174
    8. Trade Barriers 175
    9. Infrastructure 175

V.   POLICIES AND POLICY OPTIONS 176

    1. Introduction 176
    2. IT Policy 177
    3. Demand-side Actions 179
    4. Standardization 179
    5. Supply-side Actions 180
    6. National Actions 185

VI. POLICY IMPLICATIONS 188

    1. Introduction 188
    2. Costs and Benefits of Different Approaches 189
        a) Demand-side actions 189
        b) Supply-side actions 191
        c) Bridging 194
    3. Strategy 195
    4. Conclusions 199

BIBLIOGRAPHY 200

134

I. THE IMPORTANCE OF INFORMATION TECHNOLOGY (IT)

1. Introduction

Information Technology (IT) is arguably the most *pervasive* technology of our time. It not only comprises a major, growing branch of economic activity in its own right – a branch which has been a major "driver" of economic growth in the post-War period – but also generates a flow of product and process innovations in other branches. These encompass both rationalising (productivity-enhancing) innovations and growth-promoting ones which enable new types of economic activity. Their impact spans manufacturing, services and government (including defence).

More broadly, IT enables structural changes to take place in the economy. Rapid growth in IT sectors alters the relative size of industrial branches. Improved computational capabilities allow larger organisational entities to be managed and permit management to span more complex portfolios. Improved communications capabilities permit centralised control of multinational corporations. Thus, IT helps firms grow larger, more complex and to operate globally – tending to undermine the power of individual nation-states and to increase the need for new forms of international organisation on the side of government. Further, the growing opportunities for information-handling generated by IT permits these to develop into separate industrial sectors. New service sectors thus appear, leading some economic activity (classically, the writing of computer software) to be reclassified from "manufacturing" to "services".

The crucial characteristic of IT, of course, is that it is concerned with information – that is, with control and communication. That IT addresses these two ubiquitous functions of human activity (including, especially, economic activity) explains its pervasiveness. Unlike most innovations, which address single activities or industries (a new board game, a new chemical process, a new machine for making a product), IT addresses functions involved in all such activities. (We can easily imagine control and communication functions in our three examples to which IT is applicable: monitoring, storing, sensing, counting, calculating, actuating, etc.)

Our contemporary concern is with electronic IT. The mechanical feedback loops and control mechanisms of classical mechanisation played a great role in the last century and the period up to World War II. The distinctive features of IT in the latter half of the 20th century can only be obtained by electronic means. Among these features are:

- *Flexibility*: A separation between hardware and software allows general-purpose machines (computers, televisions, flexible manufacturing systems, telecommunications networks) to be built and flexibly applied across different uses. (This hardware-software dichotomy was, of course, anticipated in limited mechanical forms by the Jacquard-controlled loom, player pianos or pianolas, mechanical record-players and so forth.);

- *Productivity*: A dramatic reduction in the cost of information processing allows new levels of optimisation in all kinds of productive activity – control to marketing research;
- *Integration*: Processing and communications combine to integrate the control functions in any enterprise;
- *Knowledge*: Continuing the trend of conventional mechanisation towards the capture of knowledge (skill, know-how – including in modern 'expert systems' technology judgemental or heuristic forms of knowledge) in the design of equipment, and its separation from its traditional person-embodied form, IT promotes the formalisation, analysis and improvement of knowledge in disembodied form. This separates it from the control mechanisms of specific machines and generalises it via software, leading ultimately to the goal of artificial intelligence (Braverman, 1974; Kraft, 1977; Weizenbaum, 1976).

2. Defining IT

Freeman and Soete (1985) have reviewed efforts to define IT, and identified four approaches.

The first regards IT as a technological continuation of the trends which gave rise to the "automation debate" in the 1950s, and emphasizes process innovations using electronics: factory automation; office automation.

The second regards "IT industries" as major new branches of the economy, leading to macroeconomic growth. This approach emphasizes IT industry's role as the provider of new products and services.

The third stresses the growth of information-based occupations and the corresponding shift in the functional composition of employment. Freeman and Soete describe this as the "information society" approach.

Finally, the fourth and most comprehensive definition focuses on IT as a new kind of technology, encompassing both products and processes and promoting substantial shifts in the structure of the economy. Freeman and Soete themselves define IT as:

"A new techno-economic paradigm affecting the management and control of production and service systems throughout the economy, based on an inter-connected set of radical innovations in electronic computers, software engineering, control systems, integrated circuits and telecommunications, which have drastically reduced the cost of storing, processing, communicating and disseminating information. It comprises a set of firms and industries supplying new equipment and software, but its development and applications are not limited to this specialised IT sector (Freeman and Soete, 1985)."

Such a broad definition is required in order to perceive the economy-wide implications of IT *qua* new technology, capturing the relevant multiplier effects across the economy, and to deal with the growing convergence between the individual technologies encompassed within IT.

3. Long Waves, IT and Industrial Restructuring

A number of writers (Schumpeter, 1947; Freeman, Clark and Soete, 1982; Mensch, 1979; Coombs, 1981; etc.) have linked the *pervasiveness* of certain types of technology with very long cycles or periods in economic development – the so-called

Figure 1. **A SIMPLE SCHEMATIC OF THE KONDRATIEV WAVES**

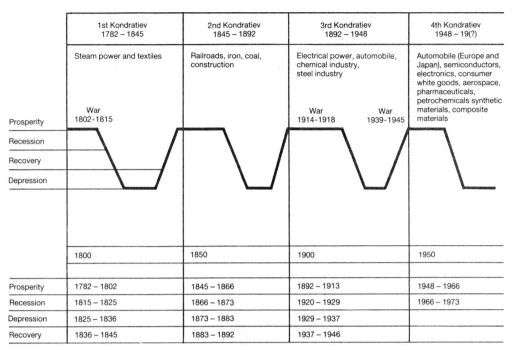

	1st Kondratiev 1782 – 1845	2nd Kondratiev 1845 – 1892	3rd Kondratiev 1892 – 1948	4th Kondratiev 1948 – 19(?)
	Steam power and textiles	Railroads, iron, coal, construction	Electrical power, automobile, chemical industry, steel industry	Automobile (Europe and Japan), semiconductors, electronics, consumer white goods, aerospace, pharmaceuticals, petrochemicals synthetic materials, composite materials

Prosperity	War 1802-1815		War 1914-1918 / War 1939-1945	
Recession				
Recovery				
Depression				

	1800	1850	1900	1950

Prosperity	1782 – 1802	1845 – 1866	1892 – 1913	1948 – 1966
Recession	1815 – 1825	1866 – 1873	1920 – 1929	1966 – 1973
Depression	1825 – 1836	1873 – 1883	1929 – 1937	
Recovery	1836 – 1845	1883 – 1892	1937 – 1946	

This diagram shows simply fluctuations over time and does not attempt to indicate the relative magnitudes of the economic upswings and downswings for the different Kondratievs. In practice, of course, the base line will rise from left to right as the average level of world economic activity has risen considerably during the period covered.

Source: R. Rothwell, 1982.

"Kondratiev long waves". Rothwell and Zegfeld (1982) have mapped these in schematic form (Figure 1). It is argued that the growth of new industries based on such pervasive new technologies and the diffusion of the products of these industries through the other branches of the economy provides at least one important set of causal mechanisms underlying the Kondratiev long waves. Electronics (IT) is generally viewed as the most important Kondratiev technology in the post-War period.

The mechanism through which Kondratiev technologies pervade the economy resembles the classical product cycle or industry life cycle. Freeman, Clark and Soete (1982), who describe major Kondratiev technologies in all their ramifications as "new technology systems" have laid out a schema for the transition from one wave to the next (Table 1; Freeman, Clark and Soete, 1985) which bears a close resemblance to more orthodox product cycle models (Figure 2; Abernethy and Utterback, cited from Rothwell and Zegveld, 1985). In each case, movement from many smaller labour- and skill-intensive production units towards fewer, large, capital-intensive ones involves transition from job-creation and skill shortage to

137

Table 1. **A simplified schematic representation of new technological systems**

	Previous Kondratiev	"Main carrier" Kondratiev		
		Recovery and boom	Stagflation	Depression
Research, invention	Basic inventions and basic science coupled to technical exploitation. Key patents, many prototypes. Early basic innovations	Intensive applied R&D for new products and applications, and for back-up to trouble shooting from production experience. Families of related basic innovations	Continuing high levels of research and inventive activity with emphasis shifting to cost-saving. Basic process as well as improvement inventions are sought	R&D investment becomes less attractive. Despite the fact that firms try to maintain their level of research it becomes increasingly difficult to do so with the slackening of their sales. At the same time the volume of sales required to amortize the cost of R&D is steadily increasing. Basic process innovations still attractive to management but may meet with social resistance
Design	Imaginative leaps. Rapid changes. No standardization, competing design philosophies. Some disasters	Still big new developments but increasing role of standardization and regulation	Technical change still rapid but increasing emphasis on cost and standard components	Routine "model" type changes and minor improvements of cumulative importance
Production	One-off experimental and moving to small batch. Close link with R&D and design. Negligible scale economies	Move to larger batches and where applicable flow processes and mass production. Economies of scale begin to be important	Major economies of scale affecting labour and capital but especially labour. Larger firms	The slowdown in output and productivity growth leads to over-production and excess capacity in some of the modern industries. These structural problems are "cumulative and self-reinforcing" with repercussions for the economy at large, and lead to a further decline of economic activity

138

Investment	High risk speculative, small scale. Some inventor-entrepreneurs. Some large firms. Fairly labour-intensive. Problems of venture capital	Bunching of heavy investment in build-up of new capacity. Band-wagon effects. Large and small firms attracted by high profits and new opportunities	Initially continuing heavy investment but shifting to rationalization. Continuing rapid growth, but increasingly large sums required to finance R&D and rising capital costs. Rising capital intensity	Relatively low levels of investment. Underutilization of the capital stock in some of the most modern sectors of the economy; low profit margins and the general 'pessimistic mood' with regard to expectations lead entrepreneurs to be very (over)cautious in relation to new investment opportunities. Investment which will take place will be primarily directed towards rationalization. Search for new investment opportunities abroad
Market structure and demand	Innovator monopolies. Strong consumer resistance and ignorance. Some new small firms to promote basic innovations	Intense technological competition for better design and performance. Falling prices. Big fashion effects. Many new entrants in early build-up	Growing concentration. Intense technological competition and some price competition. Strong pressure to export and exploit scale economies	Even stronger trend to oligopoly or monopoly structure. Bankruptcies and mergers
Labour	Small-scale employment generating effects. High proportion of skilled labour, managers and technicians. Training and learning on the job and in R&D	Major employment generating effects as production expands. New training and education facilities set up and expand rapidly. New skills in short supply. Rapid increase in pay	Employment growth slows down, and as capital intensity rises, some jobs become increasingly routine	Employment growth comes to a halt. Unemployment rising. In addition to the continuing labour displacement effects of rationalisation investments, employment suffers (in the first instance) from the general recessional and depressional tendencies in the economy at large
Employment effects on other industries and services	Negligible, but imaginative engineers, managers and inventors are thinking about them and planning and investing accordingly	Substantial secondary effects, mainly employment generating but gradually swinging to displacement	Labour displacement effects, as new technology now firmly established and strongly cost-reducing	Continuing labour displacement as new technology penetrates remaining industries and services

Source: Freeman, Clark and Soete, 1985.

Figure 2. **REINDUSTRIALISATION AND TECHNOLOGY**

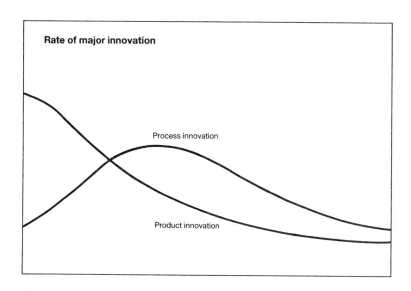

	Fluid pattern	**Transitional pattern**	**Specific pattern**
Competitive emphasis on	Functional product performance	Product variation	Cost reduction
Innovation stimulated by	Information on users' needs and users' technical inputs	Opportunities created by expanding internal technical capability	Pressure to reduce cost and improve quality
Predominant type of innovation	Frequent major changes in products	Major process changes required by rising volume	Incremental for product and process, with cumulative improvement in productivity and quality
Product line	Diverse, often including custom designs	Includes at least one product design stable enough to have significant production volume	Mostly undifferentiated standard products
Production processes	Flexible and inefficient; major changes easily accommodated	Becoming more rigid, with changes occurring in major steps	Efficient, capital-intensive, and rigid; cost of change is high
Equipment	General-purpose, requiring highly skilled labour	Some subprocesses automated, creating "islands of automation"	Special-purpose, mostly automatic with labour tasks mainly monitoring and control
Materials	Inputs are limited to generally-available materials	Specialised materials may be demanded from some suppliers	Specialised materials will be demanded; if not available, vertical integration will be extensive
Plant	Small-scale, located near users or sources of technology	General-purpose with specialised sections	Large-scale, highly specific to particular products
Organisational control is	Informal and entrepreneurial	Through liaison relationships, project and task groups	Through emphasis on structure, goals, and rules

Source: Abernathy and Utterback, 1978.

Table 2. **Employment levels in the US information technology industries employees**[1]

	1972	1982	Percent change 1972-1982
Manufacturing[2]			
Computers	145	351	+142
Office equipment	34	51	+50
Radio and television receiving sets	87	63	−28
Telephone and telegraph equipment	134	146	+9
Radio and television communications equipment	319	454	+42
Electronic components	336	528	+57
Totals, manufacturing	1 055	1 593	
Services			
Telephone and telegraph	949	1 131	+11
Computing[3]	149	360	+141
Radio and television broadcast[4]	68	81	+19
Cable television[5]	40	52	+30
Totals, services	1 206	1 624	

1. In thousands.
2. Estimates provided by the US Department of Commerce, Bureau of Industrial Economics.
3. Figures are for 1974 and 1983. *Source:* US Industrial Outlook, 1984.
4. Figures are for 1979 and 1983. *Source:* Federal Communication Commission in telephone interview with OTA staff, May 1984.
5. Figures are for 1981 and 1982. Ibid (FCC).
Source: OTA, 1985.

rationalisation and job losses. A contribution to economic growth which is large in the early part of the cycle declines and eventually becomes negative with maturity.

The employment growth achieved within the electronics and computing industries, regarded as the "drivers" of the current Kondratiev, is spectacular. Table 2 (OTA, 1985) shows this growth in the US IT industries during 1972-82. Table 3 (OTA, 1985), covering the shorter period 1978-82, shows the acuteness of the difference in the growth of IT and industry as a whole. The most notable indicator is, again, employment, with the IT industries enjoying 11.8 per cent growth compared with -7.8 per cent for the composite of industrial branches surveyed by *Business Week* in compiling this table. This contrast is all the more remarkable for occurring at a time when growth in the long post-War boom was levelling off (Table 4; Freeman, Clark and Soete, 1982). At this time, a Dutch study indicated that three quarters of Dutch value-added was realised in industries in the saturating and declining phases of the product cycle – a picture not untypical of other OECD countries (Rothwell and Zegveld, 1982). The phenomenon of strong relative growth in IT industries is also by no means confined to the USA (Table 5, OECD, 1987).

Clearly, such differences in growth rates help account for the phenomenon of *industrial restructuring*, altering the relative size and importance of different branches within the economy. In an hypothesised economy where all branches produced consumer goods, such restructuring would result whenever product innovation led to the creation of a new branch of industry. However, in the real economy, other more complex interactions take place between branches. Table 6 sketches in schematic form the relationships between the "driver" branches (electronics), existing mature branches and new IT sub-branches. Growth in electronics

Table 3. **Comparison of the US information technology industry with composite industry performance, 1978-82**

	1978	1979	1980	1981	1982	Percent change	
Sales	1 085 291	1 277 764	1 421 551	1 586 510		40	Composite
(millions of dollars)	131 872	149 783	174 449	193 921	218 862	66	Infotech
Profits	59 578	72 505	73 493	81 757	63 365	6.4	Composite
(millions of dollars)	12 780	13 821	15 474	16 056		36.4	Infotech
Profits/sales	5.5	5.7	5.2	5.1	4.2		Composite
(per cent)	9.7	9.2	8.9	8.3	7.9		Infotech
Employees	15 133	15 542	15 498	15 045	13 959	−7.8	Composite
(thousands)	2 952	3 099	3 226	3 252	3 301	11.8	Infotech
R&D	20 610	24 674	28 984	33 285	37 179	81	Composite
(millions of dollars)	4 961	5 885	7 221	8 531	10 473	111	Infotech
R&D $/sales	1.9	1.9	2.0	2.1	2.5		Composite
(per cent)	3.8	3.9	4.1	4.4	4.8		Infotech
R&D $/profits	34.6	34.0	39.4	40.7	59.0		Composite
(per cent)	38.8	42.6	46.7	53.1	60.1		Infotech
R&D $/employee	1 362	1 588	1 870	2 212	2 667		Composite
	1 680	1 899	2 238	2 623	3 173		Infotech
R&D expenditures per employee Infotech/Composite (per cent)	123	120	121	119	120		

Business Week "Scoreboard" Numbers Notes:

1. This is a sample of R&D spending in information technology by US corporations. It is based on total R&D expenditures for those companies that are publicly held, have annual revenues over $35 million dollars, and R&D expenses of $1 million or 1 per cent of revenue. Only that spending by companies whose primary business is information technology (electronics, computers, office equipment, computer services and peripherals, semiconductors, and telecommunications) is included.
2. Sales, R&D spending, and R&D spending per employee figures have been adjusted to reflect the numbers from Western Electric and other AT&T subsidiaries that are not included in the "Scoreboard" numbers. This adjustment involves:

    a) Addition of revenues received from Western Electric to the total operating revenues figures in the AT&T Annual Reports for the years covered;
    b) Use of the total AT&T spending figures for R&D which include spending by Western Electric and other AT&T subsidiaries as provided in 'Business Week' for the years 1980-82 and as estimated from a chart in the 1983 AT&T Annual Report for the years 1978 and 1979;
    c) Use of total AT&T employment figures provided in Forbes each May for the years 1976-82.
3. Employment numbers for all sectors have been calculated from the R&D spending per employee and the R&D spending figures provided in *Business Week* and may reflect rounding errors.

Source: OTA, 1985.

Table 4. **Average annual growth rates of gross domestic product**

	1870-1913	1913-50	1950-60	1960-70	1970-80	1973-80
France	1.7	1.0	4.7	5.6	3.5	2.8
Germany	2.8	1.3	8.1	4.8	2.8	2.4
Italy	1.5	1.4	5.1	5.3	3.1	2.8
Japan	2.5	1.8	8.6	10.3	4.7	3.2
UK	1.9	1.3	2.7	2.6	1.8	1.0
USA	4.1	2.8	3.2	4.2	2.9	2.1

Source: Freeman, Clark and Soete, 1982.

Table 5. **Production of information technology based goods and services as a percentage of GDP**

		IT Based Services	IT Based Goods	Total %
Belgium	1975	12.76	1.76	14.52
	1983	16.08	1.82	17.90
Finland	1970	12.94	3.43	16.37
	1975	15.18	4.17	19.35
	1980	16.79	4.16	20.95
France	1962	15.80	2.70	18.50
	1973	16.40	2.70	19.10
Germany[1]	1970			14.00
	1980			16.90
Japan	1960	6.72	1.69	8.41
	1970	14.52	4.30	18.82
Norway	1975	11.30	4.50	15.80
	1980	10.20	4.00	14.20
Sweden	1970	15.10	·1.83	16.93
	1975	15.46	2.34	17.80
	1980	16.70	2.30	19.00
United Kingdom	1963	13.98	2.06	16.04
	1972	19.55	3.46	23.01
	1980	22.20	3.70	25.90
United States	1958	17.44	2.19	19.63
	1967	20.79	3.05	23.84
Average Quinquennial Changes		+1.69	+0.40	+2.09
		(2.38)	(0.82)	(3.20)

1. The figures for Germany have been calculated by the DIW in Berlin. They are based on a different statistical basis and are not directly comparable with the results of the other countries included in this table.
Source: OECD, *ICCP Report No. 11*, "Trends in the Information Economy".

results from product innovation in consumer goods (e.g. television, electronic watches, etc.), capital goods (especially computers), and intermediate goods (such as electronic components and controls).

Some consumer goods (television) generate net growth because they provide new consumption opportunities (though there are few pure cases: television has substitution effects with theatre and cinema). Other new electronic consumer goods simply displace existing branches (electronic watches displaced mechanical ones).

Product innovations in electronic capital goods become process innovations in user industries, with mixed effects on employment. In established manufacturing industry, new computers often lead to rationalisation, but they also generate new growth opportunities – especially in information-based industries (such as market research and various database services). There is a secondary effect, as activities are transferred from manufacturing to the new service industries – market research might be a case in point.

Finally, intermediate goods move from the new branch, both to other branches and to established ones. Where they provide substitutes for existing goods (for example, electronic controls displacing mechanical or electro-mechanical ones) labour will be displaced from

Table 6.   **ELECTRONICS AS THE «DRIVER» SECTOR**

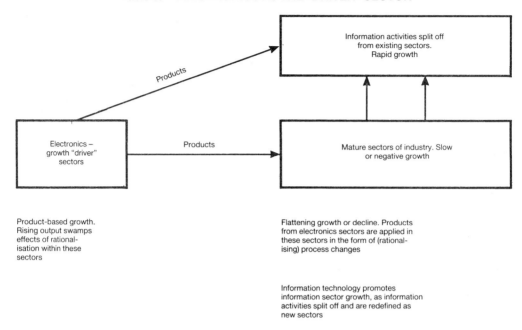

Product-based growth. Rising output swamps effects of rationalisation within these sectors

Flattening growth or decline. Products from electronics sectors are applied in these sectors in the form of (rationalising) process changes

Information technology promotes information sector growth, as information activities split off and are redefined as new sectors

mature industries. However, the same controls will also increase the usefulness of mature products, extending their sales lifetimes.

The analytical problems of convincingly separating the electronics-generated shifts in branch structure and output from those associated with existing pre-electronic trajectories have not been overcome. Clearly, it is much easier to document cases where new electronics technology has led to job displacement in existing industry than to identify and aggregate the growth-promoting effects of electronics in those same industries (for a more extensive discussion, see SPRU *Women and Technology Studies*, 1982). Nonetheless, policymakers are increasingly pinning hopes of future economic development and growth on new business opportunities in the IT sectors.

II.   GROWTH CASES IN IT

1.   Introduction – About Convergence in IT

The enormous power of IT to "shrink" the world we live in so that, in certain respects, it resembles a "global village" depends on the phenomenon of convergence – crudely, IT's ability to connect everything to everything else. In a technical sense, convergence involves the

Figure 3. **ELECTRONICS AND THE ORGANISATION OF PRODUCTION**

Pre-electronic organisation of factory production

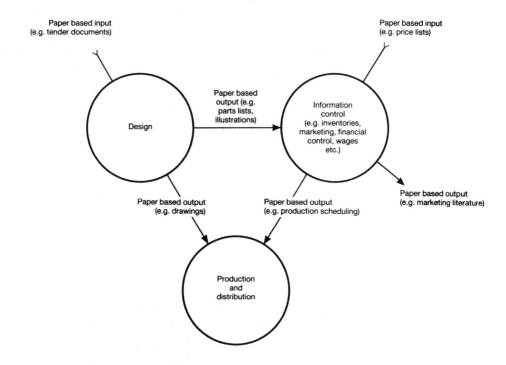

The move to the single system automated factory

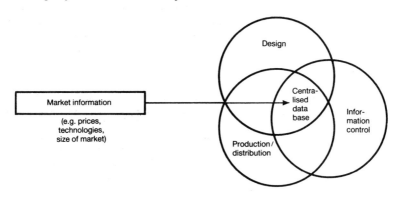

Source: Kaplinsky, 1982.

145

ability to use a single technology across areas which used to be regarded as quite separate: notably, data processing, word processing and telecommunications. Microprocessors, for example, perform crucial roles in all three areas.

Some people (Kaplinsky, 1982; NEDO, 1987) argue that convergence implies the reintegration of the functions of the entrepreneur, which were split up into different parts at the start of the Industrial Revolution. Kaplinsky gives the example of Computer-Integrated Manufacturing (CIM) (Figure 3), where the technologies of Computer-Aided Design (CAD), Computer-Aided Manufacturing (CAM) and Management Information Systems (MIS) such as Manufacturing Requirements Planning (MRP) converge to create a gigantic computer system controlling the enterprise. This system covers the same range of functions as that spanned by the inventor-entrepreneur of the 19th century. But convergence actually goes beyond this, to allow new combinations of factors of production, new product and process opportunities and therefore new lifestyles. The discussion of new products for the home, below, exemplifies this wider aspect of convergence.

Particularly since convergence is bound up with networking, developments in telecommunications (with associated regulation) have a crucial importance for convergence-based economic growth. Compatibility of standards is needed, both to permit international networking and to allow producers and users to reap economies of scale – in turn permitting cheapening and new product and service innovations, especially for the home. Government action (or *in*action) relating to telecommunications and standards will strongly influence growth opportunities.

2. IT in the Economy

A considerable amount of literature exists which catalogues economic applications of IT and their implications (for a review, see Braun and Senker, 1982). In a path-breaking analysis in 1978, McLean and Rush classified microelectronics applications into new and old product and market types (Table 7). This provided a way to differentiate between rationalising and growth-promoting applications. More recent work (also involving Rush) listed key IT applications by economic sector and estimated the relative importance of different IT applications (Tables 8 and 9). Each IT category used in these tables corresponds with an area in which new businesses and industries have become established and grown.

Surveys by Northcott *et al.* (1984) of microelectronics adoption in Britain, France and Germany indicate the degree of IT adoption in ten manufacturing sectors (Table 10). As would be expected, microelectronics-based product innovation occurs primarily in the

Table 7. **Some applications of microelectronics by product and market type**

Product Type	Market Type	
	New	Old
New	Pocket Calculators	Electronic watches Electronic cash registers
Old	Computers	Washing machines Cars

Source: McLean and Rush, 1978.

146

Table 8. Key applications of IT by economic sectors

Agriculture, Forestry, Fisheries:
- Remote sensing (to identify patterns in pest control, migration, and weather);
- Farm management aids (including the use of artificial intelligence/expert systems (for achieving optimum yields);
- Communications systems for large farm operations/remote operations;
- Advanced portable instrumentation (for moisture analysis, blood tests, etc.);
- Viewdata and other databases (for access to market and other data);
- Simple robotics, and automatic/remote control systems (for operations such as tractor work, milking, poultry management, sheep shearing, picking and harvesting).

Primary Extractive Sector:
- Remote sensing (for identification of likely deposits);
- Expert systems (for prospecting and extraction management);
- Advanced process monitoring and control;
- IT-based management and distribution systems;
- Integrated mining systems (combining extraction and finishing operations under hierarchical control);
- Remote and automated extraction from hostile areas (deep sea robotics).

Construction:
- Computer-aided design (architecture) and prefabrication;
- IT-based management and distribution systems;
- IT-enhanced power tools, surveying equipment;
- Simple robotic construction machinery.

Manufacturing:
- Computer-aided planning/scheduling/management;
- Automated stockholding/warehousing;
- Computer-aided design and draughting;
- Automated handling and manipulation;
- Automated manufacturing monitoring and control;
- Automated testing and quality control;
- Automated packaging and dispatch;
- Integrated, inter-site communications (via local area networks and wide area systems).

Service Sectors:
- Office automated technologies, combining processing (text, voice, image), storage/retrieval and communications in both integrated and stand-alone equipment (operating within local and wide area networks);
- Automated operations in fields like banking via automated telling machinery (ATM) and in retailing via electronic point of sale equipment (EPOS);
- Electronic funds transfer/point of sale linkages between banks and retailers;
- Expert systems/artificial intelligence-based database search and retrieval systems, providing new forms of library-type services;
- Electronic mail;
- Viewdata (including interactive systems);
- Advanced telecommunications equipment (message forwarding, cellular radio type local/mobile communications, satellites);
- Home computer-based service access (financial services, teleshopping, electronic mail/fax terminals).

Source: SPRU, 1985.

Table 9. **IT applications by economic sector**[1]

System Type	Sector						
	1	2	3	4	5	6	7[2]
Integrated text & data processing	+	+	+	++	++	+++	+++
Transaction clearing	+	+	+	+	+++	+++	+
Online enquiry systems	+	+	+	++	+++	++	+++
Management information systems	+	+++	++	+++	+++	++	++
Professional problem solving	++	+++	++	++	+	++	+
Professional databases	+	++	++	++	+	+	++
Electronic mail & teleconferencing	+	++	+	++	++	++	++
Material planning stock control, scheduling systems	++	++	++	+++	+++	+	+
CAD and draughting	+	++	+++	+++	+	+	+
Computer-aided manufacturing		+	++	+++			
Computer-aided fault diagnostic systems	++	+++	+	+++	+ +		
Remote sensing devices	++	+++	+++	+	++ +		

1. + = Moderate significance; ++ = High significance; +++ = Very high significance of IT equipment.
2. 1 = agriculture, etc.; 2 = extractive; 3 = construction; 4 = manufacturing; 5 = goods services; 6 = information services; 7 = people services.
Source: SPRU-Irg, 1984.

engineering sectors. Process adoption is more widely spread, though slower in the traditional textiles and clothing sectors. Job losses due to microelectronics occur throughout manufacturing, especially in engineering and process industries (Table 11). Gains are concentrated in "electrical engineering". Unfortunately, this broad category straddles dramatic job losses where electronic components displace electromechanical ones (for example in telephone switching equipment or typewriters) and other electronic equipment (such as computers) where significant job gains arise.

Most process users were employing microelectronics to substitute for mechanical and electro-mechanical controls in classical machine automation. Fewer were yet involved in the more distinctively electronic application of CAD or robotics (Table 12) implying continuing large scope for further adoption (and job losses) in these areas. Adoption difficulties centred, above all, on skills shortage (Table 13).

Figure 4 attempts to locate the development of key IT innovations in time. However, lists such as this give a rather static picture; they do not capture the "trajectories" of technologies in time. Treated in isolation, they suggest ways to replace old technologies and to rationalise: replacing paint sprayers with robots, typewriters with word processors and so on. But, in the long run, reintegrating functions that were long ago separated in the industrial division of labour is likely to be more important. More than merely providing a technology for "islands of automation", IT offers the possibility to integrate functions into a *system* of production.

The example of Computer-Integrated Manufacturing (CIM) involves a system tying together design (via CAD), Computer-Aided Manufacturing (CAM) and managerial/administrative functions. This not only increases the effectiveness of the firm by automating and integrating existing activities, but also allows the knowledge on which the firm bases its competitive advantage to be systematised and captured within computers. (This need not involve the use of expert systems, but is increasingly likely to do so in the future.) Links with

148

Table 10. **Extent of use of microelectronics by industry (weighted)[1]**

	Food	Chem. metal[2]	Metal goods[2]	Mech. eng.	Elec. eng.	Vehicles	Textiles	Clothing	Paper print	Other	Total
BASE											
Britain	3.320	3.252	4.164	5.467	3.258	1.863	2.927	3.771	3.571	6.213	37.806
Germany	4.100	5.426	2.307	5.056	4.512	2.700	1.812	3.227	2.750	8.291	40.181
France	4.917	3.253	5.586	5.117	2.043	.537	2.280	4.046	3.588	6.727	38.110
PRODUCT USERS											
Britain	0	0	1	28	50	14	0	0	0	3	10
Germany	0	7	5	42	42	9	1	0	6	3	13
France	0	1	4	23	28	23	0	0	1	4	6
PROCESS USERS											
Britain	60	51	40	45	51	33	30	27	62	36	43
Germany	46	52	43	59	54	39	40	32	77	37	47
France	39	43	38	31	33	58	34	23	50	28	35
ALL USERS											
Britain	60	51	40	54	73	33	30	27	62	37	47
Germany	46	53	44	67	66	41	41	32	80	38	51
France	39	43	38	45	49	59	35	23	50	31	38
NON-USERS											
Britain	40	49	60	46	27	67	70	73	38	63	53
Germany	54	47	56	33	34	59	59	68	20	62	49
France	61	57	62	55	51	41	65	77	50	69	62
TOTAL	100	100	100	100	100	100	100	100	100	100	100

1. Weighted for percentages of all manufacturing establishments.
2. For French figures metals are included under metal goods instead of under chemicals
Source: Northcott *et al*, 1984.

Table 11. Changes in employment due to use of microelectronics in past two years: all users by industry.

	INDUSTRY										
	Food drink	Chem. metal[1]	Metal goods[1]	Mech. eng.	Elec. eng.	Vehicles	Textiles	Clothing	Paper print	Other	Total
BASE											
Britain	94	92	54	119	116	68	42	34	70	87	776
Germany	86	161	48	161	152	56	36	37	68	138	943
France	71	56	127	103	79	46	26	40	68	109	726
SAMPLE ESTABLISHMENTS											
Percentages of establishments with:											
increase in jobs											
Britain	10	3	11	7	22	7	2	0	6	5	8
Germany	8	8	10	12	21	5	11	0	6	7	10
France	3	4	5	9	14	4	0	7	3	5	6
No change in jobs											
Britain	64	63	61	64	51	57	76	82	64	78	64
Germany	69	73	67	63	61	84	72	89	75	65	69
France	75	75	68	78	61	67	58	77	69	78	71
Decrease in jobs											
Britain	23	25	22	21	20	22	17	9	24	13	20
Germany	21	17	23	23	16	5	17	8	16	25	19
France	13	5	13	8	11	13	35	10	12	9	11
ALL MANUFACTURING ESTABLISHMENTS (weighted)											
Percentage change in jobs:											
establishments with increase											
Britain	+1	0	+5	+1	+7	+1	+1	0	+5	+2	+6
Germany	+3	+3	+10	+4	+4	0	0	0	+9	+10	+4
France	+2	+4	+13	+9	+8	+1	0	+31	+5	+2	+9
Establishments with decrease											
Britain	-5	-4	-2	-7	-6	-1	-2	-3	-3	-7	-5
Germany	-5	-3	-7	-10	-8	-3	-10	-7	-17	-6	-5
France	-11	-7	-10	-10	-7	-6	-18	-4	-6	-1	-9
All establishments											
Britain	+1	-1	0	-1	0	0	0	0	-1	-1	-1
Germany	0	0	-1	-1	0	0	-1	-1	-2	-1	-2
France	-1	0	-1	0	0	-1	-7	+2	-1	0	-1
Change in total jobs ('000)											
Britain	-6	-8	+1	-8	0	-5	-1	-1	-2	-3	-34
Germany	-1	-3	-2	-10	-2	-2	-1	-1	-4	-4	-30
France	-3	-1	-3	+1	+1	-1	-4	+2	-1	0	-12

1. For French figures metals are included under metal goods instead of under chemicals.
Source: Northcott et al., 1985.

Table 12. **Type of microelectronics based equipment used:**
Process users

Percentages of sample establishments

	Britain	Germany	France
BASE	737	900	686
TYPE OF EQUIPMENT USED			
CAD work stations	17	29	25
CNC machine tools	29	44	38
PLC (programmable logic controllers)	39	59	56
Machine controllers	21	34	29
Process controllers	23	26	22
Pick-and-place machines	8	9	22
Robots	5	8	12

Source: Northcott *et al.*, 1985.

Table 13. **Type of microelectronics based equipment used:**
Process users (weighted)

	Percentages of all the manufacturing establishments with process applications			Percentages of all manufacturing establishments		
	UK	Germany	France	UK	Germany	France
BASE	16.386	19.083	13.416	37.806	40.181	38.110
TYPE OF EQUIPMENT USED						
CAD work stations	13	17	15	6	8	5
CNC machine tools	23	36	31	10	17	11
PLCs (programmable logic controllers)	29	41	40	13	19	14
Machine controllers	16	27	29	7	13	10
Process controllers	15	17	17	7	8	6
Pick-and-place machines	4	5	13	2	2	5
Robots	2	3	7	1	1	2

Source: Northcott *et al.*, 1985.

customers and suppliers will become increasingly "informatised". In the factory of the future, the sub-systems will be highly integrated, with high-capacity Local-Area Networks (LANs) providing the interconnections between them. Similar sorts of trajectory are likely for organisations whose central tasks are concerned with information and financial flows, rather than manufacturing.

In general, we anticipate shifts towards systems integration in most areas of the formal economy. This will occur for the following reasons:

– Systems integration enables greater productivity improvements than are available from stand-alone equipment (by reducing delays in reprocessing and transmitting information between various stages of production);

Figure 4.   **SOME KEY EVENTS IN THE CONVERGENCE OF INFORMATION TECHNOLOGY**

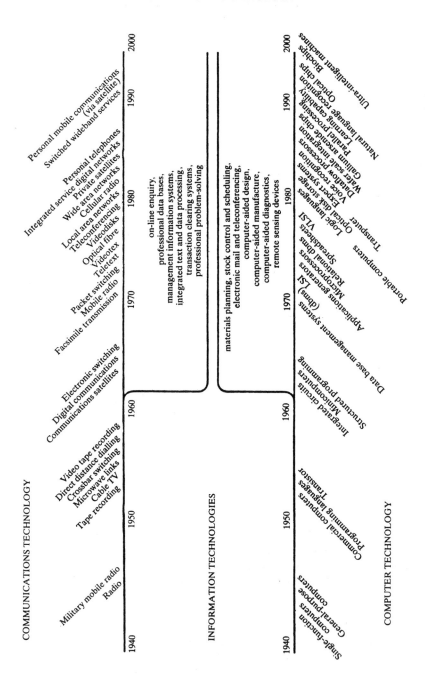

- It enables more monitoring of product and process performance and hence quicker analysis of problems and opportunities;
- It enables more complex problems and greater quantities of information to be handled;
- It enables great variety, flexibility and rapid response.

Most organisations are responsive to these benefits.

Integration of IT equipment requires effective communication. This depends on the availability of networks. LANs suffice within single-site organisations, but communication between organisations and sites demands a telecommunications infrastructure. Many organisations have been reluctant to install LANs. High-volume networking through the telecommunications grid will depend on the development of ISDN (Integrated Services Digital Network) or better facilities at a national level. Since ISDN is unlikely to be widely available for at least a decade, IT-based integration will be correspondingly limited until the end of the century.

Data communications standards are crucial ingredients in this integration. Important efforts are being undertaken – especially in the International Standards Organisation (ISO) with the Open Systems Interconnect (OSI) – to achieve standardization. However, the complexity of commercial and national interests make this a slow process. More specialised initiatives such as General Motors Manufacturing Automation Protocol (MAP) are able to make faster progress but in narrower domains.

Another key issue is packaging: the process of assembling discrete items together into integrated systems. Without packaging, the major benefits of IT cannot be realised. The packaging operation can be undertaken in various ways, even if end-users themselves shy away from the complexities of the task. Major IT firms are pursuing strategies which involve delivering *systems* solutions, and are establishing divisions centred on packaged factory, office, banking and other automation systems. Such solutions can involve establishing *de facto* standards, which disadvantage smaller producers – and potentially users, who are not consulted about standardization. Especially in those OECD Member states where domestic firms are less powerful in the IT industries, therefore, there is a strong perceived need for state action on standards.

3. Household Technology

IT applications in the home are argued to have a peculiar economic importance, because producer markets tend to saturate and because the large number of consumers in the potential domestic markets lead to attractive scale economies (Figure 5).

Developments in household technology have usually lagged behind technological change in the formal economy. However, the applications in which households use new technologies may be very different from their formal-economy counterparts. These differences are partly caused by the different motivations and financial constraints of households, compared with business organisations. Innovations in the household use of technology transferred from industry may be developed by households themselves, or may derive from service industries. But the convergence of different types of device around similar types of electronic control, monitoring and display (which is prevalent in industry) is also reflected in domestic appliances. Liquid crystal displays and keyboard-type controls are already used in a remarkably wide range of consumer goods. The trend towards integration of functions is likely to be a major factor. A great deal of effort is being put into developping Interactive Home System (IHS), based on LAN technology modified for the home. Mechanical and

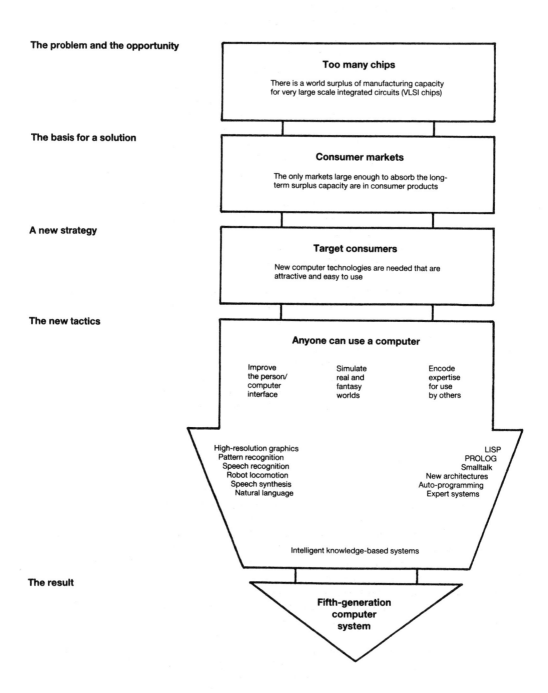

Figure 5. **FIFTH GENERATION OBJECTIVES**

The problem and the opportunity

Too many chips

There is a world surplus of manufacturing capacity for very large scale integrated circuits (VLSI chips)

The basis for a solution

Consumer markets

The only markets large enough to absorb the long-term surplus capacity are in consumer products

A new strategy

Target consumers

New computer technologies are needed that are attractive and easy to use

The new tactics

Anyone can use a computer

Improve the person/ computer interface

Simulate real and fantasy worlds

Encode expertise for use by others

High-resolution graphics
Pattern recognition
Speech recognition
Robot locomotion
Speech synthesis
Natural language

LISP
PROLOG
Smalltalk
New architectures
Auto-programming
Expert systems

Intelligent knowledge-based systems

The result

Fifth-generation computer system

154

electro-mechanical controls on many household – as on many industrial – goods are being replaced with electronics. Many of the new functions provided are "gimmicky", but a number of apparently more durable trends are also evident (Table 14).

We can place household innovations on a rough continuum. As Table 14 suggests, many current innovations relate to improving controls and displays. However, radically new functionality is also likely to be added to domestic equipment: reduced energy consumption through more sophisticated control; feature-enhanced telephones incorporating answering machines and telefax; televisions combined with printers. Radically new functions are often associated with a change in the "core" equipment involved – as in the case of the digital watch, the compact disc (CD) record player and new digitalised audio, video and communications equipment. Finally, IT allows novel "core" activities to develop in households, or at the very least a revolution in the way activities are carried out. Current examples are home computers, videotex and video tape recorders. Future examples will probably include active solar heating systems and IHS. Over time it will be possible for an increasing number of more radical innovations to appear – provided the requisite infrastructure is in place, especially in telecommunications.

There is evidence for a long-term shift in household consumption from the purchase of services to purchases of goods to satisfy equivalent needs. (That is, shifts to buying goods such as washing machines, private cars and television are shifts away from services such as laundries, public transport, cinema and theatre.) This shift relates partly to the falling price of goods compared with equivalent services and partly to the greater convenience of "self-service". Some new service demand is, of course, generated by the growing purchases of

Table 14. **Trends in IT applications to household technology**

On the basis of current developments, domestic equipment over coming decades is likely to be increasingly:

- *Remote controlled* (e.g. infra-red switches), leading to *multiremote* (multiple devices operated by same controller), and
  distance or telecontrol (e.g. controllable by telephoned instructions, as are telephone answering machines now, in a fairly primitive way).
- *"User-friendly"* (voice control; menu-type displays for control; more informative output displays, voice synthesised messages).
- *Programmable* (offering increased options to fit current user requirements, and automatic control which takes into account, for example, energy tariffs, the weight and nature of the food or clothing being processed, etc.).
- *"Informed"* (memory to recall previous programming and data inputs – e.g. weight of dieter on successive days – and ability to interface with other devices to optimise performance, and with external information sources to achieve desired outcomes).
- *Portable* (smaller, more personal, devices; devices permitting greater mobility; devices for cooking, washing, etc., for single people and for fitting into small spaces, etc.; cordless devices for convenience of use);
- *Safety featured* (warning indicators, automatic fail-safe controls).
- *Breakdown featured* (easier repair, diagnostics; auto-diagnostics).
- *Power conserving* (more energy-efficient devices, ability to take account of environmental temperatures and energy tariffs).
- *Integrating* different items of equipment around common monitoring and control systems (moving toward IHS).

Source: SPRU-Irg, 1985.

goods – but this is for services which are *complementary* to the goods involved. So, there are fewer jobs for railway workers and more for car mechanics: fewer laundresses and more washing machine repairmen. (The replacement of "feminine" service work by "masculine", technology-related employment is a frequent pattern; see SPRU, *Women and Technology Studies*, 1982.) There is also a shift from goods-handling services towards information-handling services – fewer postal workers and more telecommunications workers.

In principle, IT also makes it possible for services to be less "mass-produced" and more closely tailored to users' needs. SPRU and the Innovation Research Group at Brighton Polytechnic recently made an assessment of the likely developments in household equipment in coming years. Tables 15 to 17 show the results of this exercise, attempting to indicate the

Table 15. **Developments in "white goods[1]"**

	KITCHEN AND HOUSEHOLD GOODS	PERSONAL CARE AND LEISURE GOODS
C. 1980		Baby alarms
	Timers on ovens, washing machines	Dolls and toys with voice and other sound synthesis
	Integrated washer/dryers	Electronic board games
		Video-games
	Specialised ovens	
	Frostfree freezers	Cordless baby alarms
	Cordless irons, cleaners	Digital thermometers, sphygamometers
	Self-setting microwaves	Voice- and digital-output weighing machines, with memory
	Multi-power cleaners	
	Programmable tea and coffee makers	
C. 1990		
	Advanced knitting and sewing machines	
	Mains control of washers	Exercise machines with displays, memory, programmed tests, etc.
	Multi-function fridges	
	Mains control of cookers	Robotic toys
	Infra-red taps	
	Remote monitoring of details of operating status of major white goods	Electronic masseur
		Biofeedback devices
C. 2000		
	Remote (e.g. telephone) control of detailed operations of white goods	IT incorporated in chairs, beds, baths, etc.

1. The chart above indicates the approximate period at which these items of consumer electronics are likely to be widely retailed and in use, not the date of invention: indeed most of them have already been developed at least as experimental models.
Source: SPRU-Irg, 1985.

Table 16. **Developments in "brown goods"**

	RADIO/AUDIO	TV/VIDEO
C. 1980	Personal stereos	Teletext, Videotext Portable colour TV
	CD players	Videocamera, Videorecorder
	Digital Cassette Players	Personal TV ("Watchman") Camcorders
	Digital Cassette Recorders	Split-screen TV
C. 1990	Radio Data Broadcasts	"Stored TV"
	Narrowband Traffic Services	Stereo sound TV Peritelevision
	Digital Radio	Electronic still cameras
	Radiotext	Flat TV Widescreen/Videoprojectors
C. 2000	Advanced Digital Radio	Digital VTR High Definition TV Fully Digital TV TV Printers

Source: SPRU-Irg, 1985.

likely pattern of widespread diffusion into households (as distinct from dates of invention or innovation). As Figures 6 and 7 indicate, convergence is a central feature of future developments, both in computer-communications equipment and in home energy systems.

Clearly, much integration or "convergence" in the home is a simple aggregation of equipment: the radio and telephone are put into the same housing, but no functions are shared. However, from here it is a short step to shared functionality – such as the sharing of a loudspeaker or a keypad between telephone and radio. The need for similar components to be incorporated into different pieces of home equipment naturally encourages integration in order to share components between different systems. (This argument should not be taken too far – sharing components can be inconvenient. Home computer users, for example, tend to buy a separate television or monitor, rather then spoil the whole family's viewing by trying to share the television screen with television broadcasts.) Rather than massive centralisation of functionality in home electronic equipment, the SPRU/Irg team envisioned a combination of central and 'distributed' intelligence, according to the functions involved. A home LAN connected to the telecommunications system provides an important "spine" to which electronics and controls can be connected as appropriate.

IHS is likely to evolve from modest beginnings. Two crucial influences will be: the ease with which early, limited systems can be upgraded to carry more data; and the opportunities for interlinking independently-purchased pieces of equipment with the IHS system. Both factors point to a need for forward-looking decisions about standards. Japanese electronics manufacturers' choice of the MSX standard and NTT's plans for the Integrated Network System (recabling Japan with broadband telecommunications) are important examples, though they are probably far from the last word on this matter.

A sudden transition to a single form of IHS seems unlikely. Different IHS applications areas involve different data transmission and processing needs, some of which could be met

157

Table 17. **Household services**

	TELEPHONY	COMPUTER/ COMMUNICATIONS	COMPUTERS
C. 1980	Answering machines	Videotext	Home computers
	Memory phones	Multi-standard modems	Floppy discs
			Dot-matrix printers
	Remote-access answering machines	Bulletin Boards	
	Cordless phones		
	Milti-line households	MIDI interface to synthesisers	Early teleshopping, telebanking
	Telephone alarms	Computer hobbyist networking	Video digitisers
			Laser printers
C. 1990			
	Home cellular phones	Home videotext systems	Laser cards
			Laser disc storage
	Electronic mail		Special-purpose domestic robotics
	Telephone interrogation of domestic equipment	Teleworking	Portable terminals with large capacity
		Sophisticated teleshopping	
			Computer control of equipment
	Electronic messaging systems	Networking	
C. 2000		Sophisticated tele-services	
		General purpose portable computer-communicator	

Source: SPRU-1rg, 1985.

through mains signalling, others of which require broadband communications. Applications areas may be technically clustered according to their communications characteristics, leading to fully-integrated IHS only in the long term (Figure 8).

4. Convergence and Infrastructure

A pivotal factor in the way that technologies for the factory, office and home develop is the development of communications infrastructure. All major telecommunications authorities are committed to digitalisation. With this has come the possibility of using computers to manage information flows in the telecommunications network, and the prospect of a wide range of services being carried quickly and efficiently – be the data involved voice, image or text. Figure 9 illustrates the range of telecommunications services that are appearing. Convergent IT can be used to bring together all these divergent applications.

The prospect of continued digitalisation of telecommunications and the support this gives to convergence has promoted the idea of the ISDN as the appropriate goal for the medium

Figure 6. CONVERGENT COMPUTER-COMMUNICATIONS TECHNOLOGIES IN THE HOME

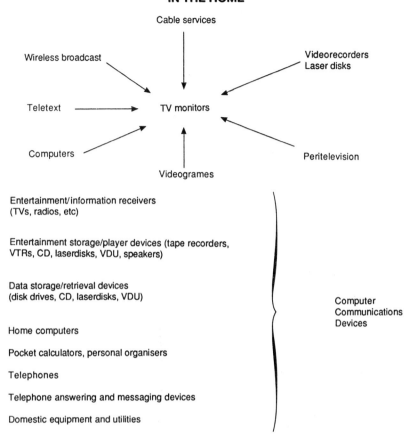

Cable services

Wireless broadcast

Videorecorders
Laser disks

Teletext → TV monitors

Computers

Peritelevision

Videogrames

Entertainment/information receivers
(TVs, radios, etc)

Entertainment storage/player devices (tape recorders, VTRs, CD, laserdisks, VDU, speakers)

Data storage/retrieval devices
(disk drives, CD, laserdisks, VDU)

Home computers

Pocket calculators, personal organisers

Telephones

Telephone answering and messaging devices

Domestic equipment and utilities

Computer
Communications
Devices

Source: Spru-Irg, 1985.

term in telecommunications infrastructure. While the timescale for ISDN is relatively lengthy – twenty years or more before full implementation in many countries – it is not clear that it provides a satisfactory model compared with wideband alternatives, such as Japan's Integrated Network System (INS). As Figure 10 shows, the choice of ISDN builds in a bandwidth bottleneck, impeding the use of the network for broadband services. The built-in limitation of ISDN to the 64 kilobits per second which can be carried via existing twisted copper wire pairs is likely permanently to disadvantage ISDN users, as compared with broadband network users. An Integrated Broadband Network (IBN) is an inherently more "robust" (in the sense of Gardner and Rotherwell, 1986) design than ISDN, because it builds into its design the possibilities of "stretching" into new service and product possibilities, while ISDN constrains future developments. Nevertheless, initial implementation costs for IBN are dramatically greater than for ISDN.

Figure 7. **CONVERGENCE IN HOME ENERGY SYSTEMS**

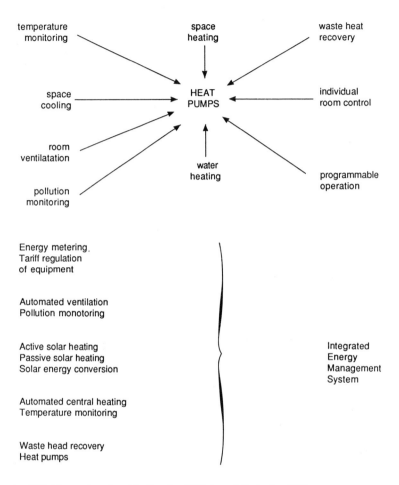

Source: Spru-Irg, 1985 (diagram based on John Douglas, *EPRI-Journal,* September 1985).

Figure 8. **THE NETWORKING OF HOUSEHOLD FUNCTIONS**

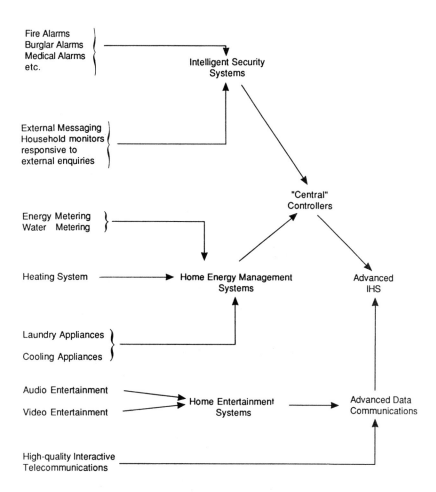

Source: Spru-Irg, 1985.

Figure 9. **THE EVOLUTION OF DIVERSE TELECOMMUNICATIONS SERVICES**

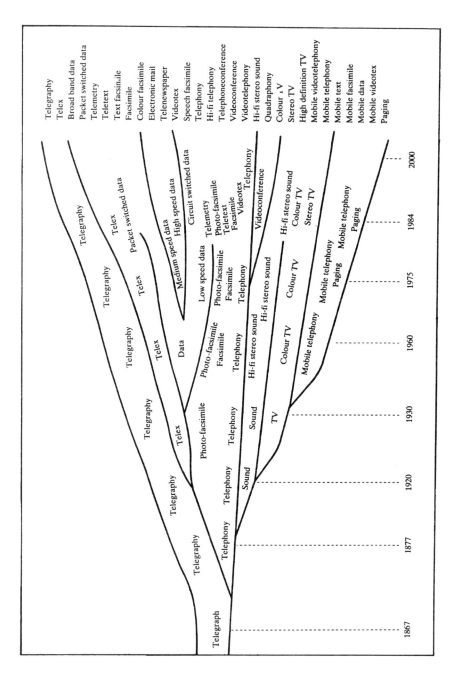

Source : *Electronic Times,* 2nd May 1985 (article by C. Partridge).

Figure 10. **TRANSMISSION RATE AND DURATION FEATURES OF TELECOMMUNICATIONS**

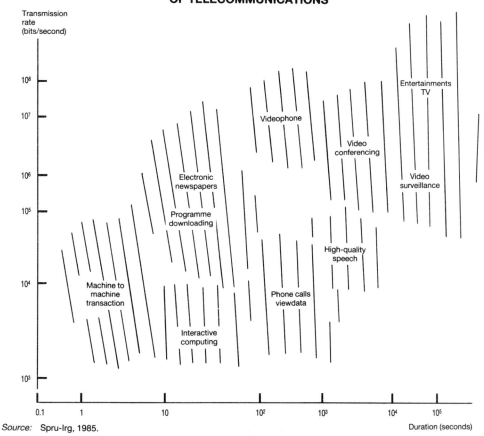

Source: Spru-Irg, 1985.

Figure 10 *(continued)* **Services to be handled by ISDN systems**

	TELEPHONE	DATA	TEXT	IMAGE
Current Services	Telephony Mobile/cellular telephones	Low-speed data Packet-switching	Telex Teletex Electronic mail	Viewdata/videotex Low-speed facsimile
Emerging Services	Leased circuits Information retrieval (voice analysis & synthesis) Digitised voice Teleconferences	Leased circuits Circuit-switching EFT Information retrieval Telemetry Alarms	Leased circuits Information retrieval	Surveillance/security Slow-scan video communications
Services requiring Wideband System	High-quality sound, music	High-speed computer communications (data transfer, online CAD, etc.)	Quality teletex Bulk text transmission	Quality videotex Videophone Videoconferencing Cable TV

Source: SPRU-Irg, 1985, drawing on W. Stallings, 1984, "The Integrated Services Digital Network", Figure 4, *Datamation* (December).

III. IT AND RELATIVE GROWTH IN MANUFACTURING AND SERVICES

1. Introduction

Like others, Stonier has argued that information "has upstaged land, labour and capital as the most important input into modern productive systems". Information reduces the requirements for new materials and energy. It spawns entirely new industries. It is sold in its own right, and it is the raw material for the fastest growing sector of the economy – the "knowledge industry" (Stonier, 1983).

However, the production of information is itself susceptible to rationalisation. *Two* opposing forces are at work. Stonier is correct in identifying information, and correspondingly IT, as a source of new economic activity, but it also reduces the size of existing activities through rationalisation. The idea that we move from an era of manufacturing into one of services is a dangerous simplification. While there is real growth in services, a great deal of activity is being *reclassified* from 'manufacturing' to services simply by being undertaken by specialists in new service-industry firms instead of being done within firms in manufacturing. The *boundary* between manufacturing and services is shifting, but the two remain interdependent. IT largely has the effect of speeding-up this reclassification process; it is doing little to de-couple manufacturing and service activities.

2. Arguments for the "New Service Economy"

In the 1960s and 1970s, a common view emerged of services as the growth sector of the economy. Implicitly, this was seen as a by-product of the natural trajectory of economic development – from "primary" industry based on exploitation of natural resources through "secondary" industry transforming those resources through manufacturing activities to "tertiary" activity which used manufactured output to provide services. In effect, this is an extension of Engel's law, arguing that as people get richer their needs become more sophisticated and their expenditure shifts towards services.

Miles (1987) contrasts this view of "post-industrial society" with an opposing analysis, which typically emerges from economic as opposed to the more sociological approach of the post-industrialists. This contrasting view holds that the increasing economic importance of services results from lower productivity growth in services than in manufacturing (see Guy, 1987, for empirical evidence). As a result, in a period of continued macroeconomic growth, jobs lost through rationalisation in manufacturing have been soaked up by the service sectors.

Both Skolke (1976) and Gershuny (1977) have pointed out that slow productivity growth in service sectors implies rising prices for services compared with goods. This should lead to substitution of goods for services, where this is practicable. Gershuny (1983) provided

Figure 11. **SUBSTITUTION OF GOODS FOR SERVICES**

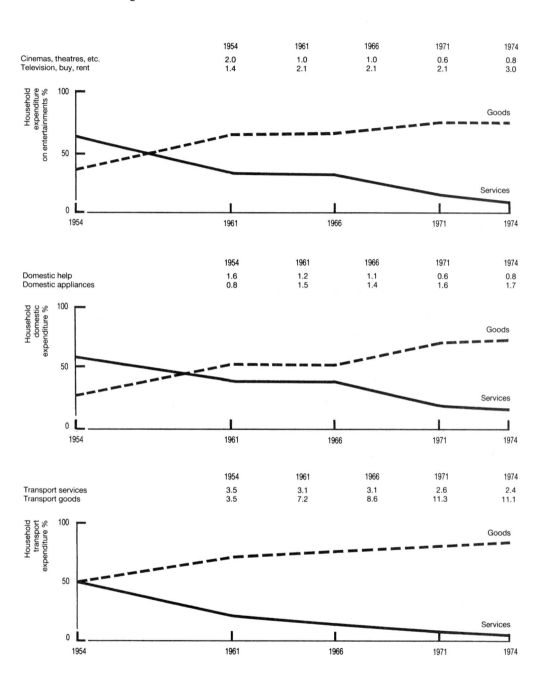

	1954	1961	1966	1971	1974
Cinemas, theatres, etc.	2.0	1.0	1.0	0.6	0.8
Television, buy, rent	1.4	2.1	2.1	2.1	3.0

	1954	1961	1966	1971	1974
Domestic help	1.6	1.2	1.1	0.6	0.8
Domestic appliances	0.8	1.5	1.4	1.6	1.7

	1954	1961	1966	1971	1974
Transport services	3.5	3.1	3.1	2.6	2.4
Transport goods	3.5	7.2	8.6	11.3	11.1

Source: Gershuny, 1983.

considerable evidence that such a substitution has in fact been taking place, as Figure 11 indicates.

Miles (1987) sums up the causes of shifts in services employment:

1. Shifts in the goals of consumer expenditure;
2. The impact of productivity differentials on employment generated to meet demand levels;
3. The effects of productivity differentials on relative prices and thus on demand for goods or services;
4. Changing demand for producer services in the course of economic development;
5. The institutional demand for public services.

Growth in producer services depends on improvements in quality and packaging of services, the innovation of new services which involve scale economies and which are therefore not economically produced by the individual user organisation, and improvements in services productivity. IT provides important opportunities to enhance all three aspects.

3. The Changing Boundary between Manufacturing and Services

While goods (or, actually, the use of domestic capital equipment to enable "self-service") are substituting for services in the home, in industry the flow of activity is in the reverse direction: from "in-house" activity to sub-contracting. The statistical consequence of this change in industry is that activities – ranging from catering to electron-plating, from legal advice to information management – are transferred from industrial SICs to service categories. That is, certain activities are being *reclassified*, but they are still being performed. In many cases, they are performed more efficiently. Specialist service providers can reap economies of scale and specialisation which are not available to those who produce equivalent services within manufacturing companies.

Many services (catering, security, window-cleaning) cannot be traded internationally. Others – and especially information services – can be so traded. At the national level, however, producer service growth is closely bound up with, and complements manufacturing growth. As Table 18 shows, services have not grown as a share of world trade in recent years.

Table 18. **World trade in goods and services**

	Percentage of 1983 total world trade	Average annual growth 1968-83[1]
Manufactured goods	49	11
Other goods (oil, minerals, commodities)	33	11¾
Services (transport, travel, financial services, consultancy, etc.)	18½	11½

1. In current dollar prices.
2. Excluding government transactions.
Source: From "Services in the UK Economy", *Bank of England Quarterly Bulletin*, September 1985 (quoting IMF data).

4. The Interdependence of Manufacturing and Services

The occupational structure of the economy has shifted dramatically towards service employment, as Table 19 shows. In this period, reductions in production employment were matched by increases in white-ccll r, "service" occupations. (Later, in the 1980s slump, the economy was no longer able to s stain this combined level of employment.) Gershuny's analysis shows that only about one quarter of the employment shift was related to the growth of new service industries, while three quarters was attributable to the shift in the occupational structure in all industries towards white-collar workers. That is to say that "service" employment growth was more to do with the imbalance in productiv ty between the shopfloor and the office than with growing service opportunities. Continuing IT innovation is likely to lead to more rationalisation in white-collar work, but also to growing service opportunities. Occupational shifts will contribute less and new services will contribute more to the growing share of white-collar work in total emp'oyment in future. As a result, we have the paradox that traditional knowledge workers' jobs will continue to be rationalised away while new knowledge-based branches expand the opportunities for knowledge-based entrepreneurship and work.

Table 19. **Occupational change by sector**

	Admin, Prof, Tech and Clerical		Other White Collar		Manual Workers	
	1968-73	1974-78	1968-73	1974-78	1968-73	1974-78
	%		%		%	
Primary	0.4	0.5	0.1	0.1	3.4	2.7
Manufacturing	8.1	8.2	2.1	1.9	25.7	22.5
Utilities	1.6	2.1	0.3	0.2	5.8	4.9
Services	24.4	31.1	15.9	16.2	12.2	9.6
All Sectors	34.5	41.9	18.4	18.3	47.1	39.8

Source: Gershuny.

Within IT-based services, there is a tendency towards concentration in the higher skilled, white collar jobs. Table 20 shows the case of computer services employment in the United Kingdom, with operations and data preparation jobs declining in both absolute and relative terms. Selling, programming and systems analysis took up most of the share lost by these lowlier jobs. This is consistent with the pattern of deskilling in computer services discussed by Kraft (1977), and based on exactly the same principles of division of labour, standardization and mass-production as those employed in manufacturing industry (Braverman, 1974). New software technologies such as expert systems involve increasing reliance on high-level skills of consultants and experts, rather than creating lower-skilled work (Johnson, 1984).

But software is also the classic case of a complementary good in IT. Hardware companies make general-purpose computers, in order to realise economies of scale. By and large, if it were necessary to build different hardware for each application computers would be beyond the financial means of almost everyone. Software writers complete the engineering task by transforming general-purpose machines into special-purpose ones – able to undertake

167

Table 20.   **Computer services employment**[1]

	1978		1984[2]	
	Numbers	%	Numbers	%
Consultancy	2 345	10.5	3 703	11.6
Programming/Systems Analysis	7 081	31.8	11 617	36.4
Operations & Data Preparation	6 921	31.1	5 911	18.5
Administration	2 854	12.8	4 207	13.2
Selling and Others	3 063	13.8	6 510	20.4
Total	22 264	100.0	31 948	100.0

1. Changes in the BSO enquiry coverage in 1982 mean that 1978 and 1984 data are not directly comparable. Relative proportions, however, are reasonably illustrative of actual changes.
2. In 1978 about 1 100 additional personnel were employed part-time (5 per cent of total) and in 1984 about 1 900 (6 per cent of total).
Source: NEDO, from BSO Business Monitor SDQ 9.

particular tasks. Without hardware, the software is utterly pointless. The classification of "software" in national statistics as a service activity separate from hardware manufacture is – in engineering terms – a nonsense. In historical terms it is similarly strange: no-one would have dreamt of calling the manufacturers of mechanical controls for automatic lathes "service workers"; but their counterparts in the software industry are indeed labelled in this way. This point applies more generally to information-based services. All are hardware- and infrastructure-dependent.

5.   The Effects of IT

As in other sectors, in services, IT provides both a source of rationalisation of traditional activities and the basis for new ones. It provides important opportunities to reduce the productivity anomaly between blue- and white-collar work. For example, one effect of the innovation of word processing was to focus attention on office productivity. Stewart (1979), among many others at the end of the 1970s, claimed that while the productivity of manual workers rose between 1960 and 1970 by more than 80 per cent the productivity of office workers rose 4 per cent in the same period. While these kinds of figures conceal real problems in measuring office output, they are generally agreed to point in the right direction. A key thrust of the selling effort in the late 1970s and early 1980s wave of office equipment sales exploiting the "convergence between data and word processing" was to reduce this productivity imbalance (see Table 21).

One of the many important parallels between the opportunities afforded by IT in manufacturing and services is the inherent *flexibility* of IT-controlled production. Mass-produced information services (newspapers, television, broadcast videotex) provide a standard product to consumers. (Some degree of quasi-flexibility is being introduced by the extreme cheapening allowed by IT – for example, the purchaser of a CD-based database would only tend to use a fraction of the database, and would effectively "discard" the rest.) Like flexible production automation, however, interactive information services provide user-tailored outputs.

Probably the growing importance of IT in services is now making it possible to *begin* to disconnect producer services and manufacturing. For example, software has become an

Table 21. **Technological change in office activities**

Office Functions	Technologies
External Communications	From: external mail (postal services); telephony; telegraphy; telex To: the above plus electronic mail; new telephone services (PBXs, messaging, etc.); telefax; viewdata, teletext
Internal Communications	From: memo slips, telephony To: the above plus electronic mail; new telephone services; electronic bulletin boards
Data Storage and Retrieval	From: filing cabinets; libraries; microfiche; tape storage of (mainly numerical) data on mainframe computers for restricted access to large data files (payrolls, etc.); press cutting services To: the above plus storage of all forms of data (text, numbers, graphics; and now digitalised voice and video) on new media (hard and floppy discs, CD and videodisc) for distributed or local use by terminals and microcomputers, and accessed by user-friendly database management systems; on-line databases for news items, bibliographies, etc.
Information Processing	From: calculators; statistical modelling on mainframes; systematic and intuitive use of human skills and intellectual techniques To: the above plus an array of microcomputer-based techniques such as spreadsheets, "idea processors", interactive graphical systems for data inspection, and "expert systems" of various degrees of sophistication; overhead transparencies and slides
Information Presentation	From: typewriters and electronic typewriters; conventional printing; hand-drawn graphics (using transfers and other means of standardization) To: word-processing (eventually with direct voice input); desktop publishing; computer graphics derived from spreadsheets or graphics/CAD packages; videotapes; "videoslides"
Meetings	From: conventional meetings and conferences To: the above plus telephone conferences; video-based teleconferences; computer conferencing
Activity Management	From: diaries, wallcharts, secretaries' memories To: diary programmers on PCs which act as alarms and reminders; programmers to help scheduling and task ordering

Source: NEDO, from BSO Business Monitor SDQ 9.

internationally-traded commodity, and this is true not only of standard packages (like operating systems or spreadsheets) but also of custom software. Latterly, it has become possible to have custom software written by telecommunicating a specification to a contractor off-shore and receiving code and documentation in return "down the wire". Payment can then be effected electronically, so that conventional paper- and travel-based activities are omitted entirely. However, the importance of this type of development must not be exaggerated – information services form, as yet, only a small fraction of all services.

The future of the industrial structure in OECD countries is often posed as a choice between manufacture and services, this is actually a false choice. Manufacturing and services are *complementary*: IT plays a vital role in industrial competitiveness in both the secondary and the tertiary sectors. While in many areas of personal consumption goods are substituting for services, the opposite trend is occurring in intermediate goods and services, with producer services substituting for in-house production.

IT-based rationalisation in traditional work is difficult to avoid. It is enforced by the competitive process, and it is being accomplished within the established technological trajectories in IT. Policy efforts need to be aimed at smoothing transition and minimising its social costs.

The opportunities for policy to affect IT-based growth in a positive way are much greater. The key is to minimise the constraints placed on opportunities for entrepreneurship, so as to minimise growth opportunities. Growth can be induced by infrastructural investment which is:

- *Ahead* of demand; and
- Of *robust design*, so as not to design bottlenecks into the process of economic development.

The choice of broadband communications networks as against ISDN must be a key element of such a policy.

IV. OBSTACLES TO IT-BASED GROWTH

1. Introduction

Constraining factors on IT adoption are broadly similar across primary, secondary and tertiary sectors, as well as among domestic consumers. Obstacles to adoption of IT include: the learning processes involved in taking up any new technology; social and cultural barriers; institutional objections; supply- and demand-side factors, some of which are structural; education and training; innovation policy; trade barriers; and infrastructure.

2. Learning

Almost all new technologies bring problems of *learning*, since by definition they bring users into contact with the unfamiliar. Wasson states the case for consumer goods.

Any new offering can pose the problem of one or more of three kinds of learning:

i) Learning of a new sequence of motor habits (as in changing over from a three-speed to a four-speed, or from a wringer to an automatic washer);

ii) Learning to perceive new benefits as valuable and thus worth paying for (as in learning to appreciate the cornering qualities offered by the small sports car);

iii) Learning to perceive one's role in the use of the product as of less importance (as in the acceptance of automatic transmission) (Wasson, 1968:41).

This kind of learning is a corollary of consumers' need to be *educated* about new technology and product opportunities; few domestic consumers can second-guess producers' technological opportunities and progress.

The learning processes among producers are not all that different (with the key exception of the 'von Hippel' industries discussed below). Governments have in fact recognised these learning needs in many countries and launched publicity programmes describing the benefits of new IT-based technologies like CAD to industrial users. Often, demonstrations have been funded to allow the accumulation and transfer of experience, reducing the perceived risks of new technology adoption. The learning process also tends to involve creating new pools of skilled manpower, giving rise to training needs (see Swords-Isherwood and Senker, 1980, for a wide-ranging review).

3. Social/Institutional

Many changes brought about by the pervasiveness of IT pose challenges to existing institutions. IT will promote major social and institutional changes for at least the next two decades. The institutions able to adapt flexibly will survive and flourish. Those which ignore, or are unable to cope with change, will wither away.

New technology, like almost all change, sparks resistance in society – not all of which is economically logical. The power of IT to rationalise certain types of production sparked a wave of cautious resistance in the late 1970s. Perhaps surprisingly, while unemployment in most OECD countries has grown dramatically in the 1980s, concern with the job-destroying potential of IT has declined. Nonetheless, IT's perceived impact on jobs remains one factor impeding IT diffusion. A number of options exist to mitigate this – from reductions in working hours to guaranteed retraining and/or employment for people whose jobs are lost via this type of technological change.

The challenge to *companies* is, perhaps, the most widely recognised, and is the subject of much government policy. IT brings new process, product, marketing and distribution opportunities, as well as displacing many existing ones. While resistance to technological change from unionised workforces has been much discussed in recent years, many commentators expect growing resistance from middle managers, who become marginalised as major parts of their work (which frequently consists of information processing tasks) are automated. Managers need to be aware of the opportunities and to have the skills to exploit them. This implies that education, re-education, training and re-training need to take place to allow people to institute and cope with change.

The *integration* of different corporate functions through IT enables new organisational forms to evolve. However, established corporate structures are very slow to change. For example, the introduction of CAD allows closer links between design and production, yet in our studies of CAD/CAM in the United Kingdom between 1982 and the present, we have only found one case where this occurred (Arnold and Senker, 1982 ; Arnold, 1983; work in progress at Science Policy Research Unit, 1986-87). This is one of many cases where IT appears to threaten the role and position of middle managers.

New IT-based technologies such as CAD and Flexible Manufacturing Systems (FMS) are very difficult to cost-justify, especially when the technology is immature and there is limited experience available on which to base cost-benefit calculations. (For example, FMS installations often cost several million pounds and have a payback of around ten years, as opposed to firms normal payback standard of 2-3 years for most types of process improvement.) In many countries, these types of pioneering investments have been state-aided in order to generate a body of experience and "pump-prime" the investment process at the national level.

Trades unions need to respond to changing industrial structures and new technological opportunities. Since the end of the 1970s, many have expanded their role in training their members to deal with new technology. Some unions have found that their membership is largely confined to older, declining industries and that their constituency is tending to disappear. Increasingly, both employers and employees are seeking flexible, decentralised,

171

individual work arrangements which pose new problems of representation (particularly in the case of teleworkers). Liberalisation of state monopolies such as telecommunications speeds the transition from unionised to non-unionised work. Union representation in many of the new IT industries is minimal. As a result, industrial restructuring poses a major challenge to the union movement.

The *professions*, too, face challenges from IT – especially since most professional work has a high information content. In many cases, restrictive professional codes constrain existing providers from selling IT-based services. The use of expert systems provides a particularly keen challenge. In the short term, expert systems appear to have a useful role to play as 'smart assistants' to professionals. Early experience with expert systems oriented towards professional knowledge domains indicates that they are useful in the hands of experienced professionals, but that they do not allow lay people to substitute for professionals. However, this may change as large new systems are built covering wide knowledge domains, as opposed to the very narrow sub-specialisms which can be addressed with current technology. As with manufacturing industry, the capture of the know-how embodied in professional work and its embodiment into technology (hardware or software) provides opportunities for scale economies, increased productivity and – by implication – reduced exclusivity of professions.

For *government*, the advent of IT poses all the industry policy problems of restructuring. It re-opens debates about centralisation *versus* regionalisation. It provides scope for enormous increases in administrative efficiency – and for massive invasions of citizens' privacy. The scope for oppressive control of citizens' activities is enormously increased by improvements in monitoring and information processing technologies. The opportunities range from tight control of government parties' political opponents to reducing the size of the black economy.

4. Supply-side

The industrial structure of any economy is a key determinant of its ability to exploit and develop IT. Many countries recognise this and follow deliberate "restructuring" policies, aimed at replacing declining industrial activities with enterprise in the newer, fast-growing industries.

A related issue is the social choice made by some countries (notably the USA, UK and France) to devote as much as half of the national scientific and technological effort to military ends. As a result, scientific manpower is diverted away from sectors where competitive markets hold sway and into areas where national preference tends to take precedence over economic efficiency.

IT accounted for just under 20 per cent of the US DoD's spending in fiscal 1987 (Guy and Arnold, 1987), indicating that IT forms a very substantial ingredient in modern defence systems. As recent DoD programmes such as VHSIC have shown, military and civilian IT products require different skill and production bases. Allocation of a high share of national activity to military efforts may therefore impact civil competitiveness.

5. Demand-side

Users with strong knowledge of IT opportunities and who are able to make stringent demands on suppliers are a vital ingredient of economies making strong use of IT. Such users play a double role – both in stimulating the supply side and in demonstrating opportunities and adoption benefits on the demand side. Von Hippel has defined a whole class of industries where such users play a vital role in generating innovations. In few places has the process been taken so far as in the case of NTT's Den Den family.

NTTs typical research project for telephone switching equipment involves its own Electrical Communications Laboratory (ECL) and the Den Den family companies – Fujutsu, Oki, Hitachi and NEC. The project passes through five stages:

Stage 1   NTT specification of technical standards following close consultation with NTT supplier firms.

Stage 2   The design of prototypes by each of the four firms (in accordance with uniform specifications set forth by ECL).

Stage 3   Field testing of new switching systems.

Stage 4   Development of commercial switching equipment.

Stage 5   NTT procurement order for each firm and installation of new equipment. (Okitmoto and Hayase, 1985).

ECL orchestrates the research process, while the companies compete to supply the best prototype designs. Their shares of procurement reflect NTT's judgement about their contribution to the research process. Once a prototype is approved, design information is transferred from the designing firm to the others in the Den Den family, each of which receives a smaller share of procurement orders. In this way, the best project reaps an immediate reward in terms of a larger share of procurement, while the laggards are dragged up to the leader's technological level through technology transfer. Not dissimilar processes are involved in US DoD procurement.

The principle of leading-edge applies as much to government as to private enterprise. It is important to note, however, that leading-edge users have a second role, in addition to stimulating technical excellence. Typically, the most effective leading-edge user strategies involve relatively high volumes of procurement at an early stage in the product/technology life cycle. This drags suppliers down production experience curves, cheapening the new product – both generating competitive advantage and stimulating adoption through the price mechanism.

Leading-edge users can play a vital role in promoting technology diffusion by imposing *standards*. The best-known case in IT is perhaps General Motors' Manufacturing Automation Protocol (MAP) – a standard for electronic shop-floor communications in the field of CAM. GM is a massive purchaser of computers and Computer Numerical Control (CNC) production equipment. Few other users are in a similarly powerful position. As a result, GM has been able to *impose* the MAP on its suppliers, which include the largest firms of the IT industry such as IBM and DEC, by making the incorporation of MAP into the products it buys a condition of purchases. MAP has been enthusiastically endorsed by users and suppliers in both North America and Europe. One of its key attractions is that it is *user-defined*, tending to remove CIM communications from the sphere of *de facto* standardization by the dominant suppliers, especially IBM.

Similarly, the "interoperability agreement" reached by the twelve major European IT suppliers promoted multi-vendor solutions by using OSI as a basis for designing next-generation systems components which could be interconnected. This is intended to reduce suppliers' ability to "lock users in" to their own product offerings, preventing them shopping around and introducing an element of monopoly pricing into computer supply through enforcement of these idiosyncratic standards. Such standardization processes speed IT diffusion by reducing the scope for monopoly pricing and reducing investment risks.

6. Education and Training

Education and training needs are dramatically increased by IT, both at the individual and at the social level. Research by IBM in the USA has led to the conclusion that, in computer science, knowledge becomes obsolescent 2.7 years after graduation unless it is up-dated. The changing mix of skills – reflecting the general shift from labour - to knowledge-intensity – is illustrated in Table 22, which shows employment by occupational category in the electronics industry for Great Britain in 1978 and 1984. The table indicates a clear shift away from "shop floor" occupations and towards scientific and technical work.

However, the electronics sector is only a leading indicator of electronics-related skills shortages elsewhere in the economy. A 1985 CBI/MSC survey (cited in NEDO, 1987) of 1 300 United Kingdom firms showed that one in eight expected output to be limited by shortage of skilled labour in the next four months. Shortages were most noteworthy in electrical industrial goods and electronic consumer goods, with 61 and 50 per cent of firms respectively reporting shortages.

Skill implications of IT in engineering have been analysed more extensively elsewhere, in a programme of research which spanned the United Kingdom engineering industry (Swords-Isherwood and Senker, 1980; Arnold and Senker, 1982; Brady and Senker, 1982). The need for new skills arises at all levels in the industry, implying a need for changes in curricula, education and training provision throughout the system – not merely in the scientific and technological categories most obviously affected.

Table 22. **Employment changes in electronics industry, 1978-84**

Occupational category	1978		1984	
	Numbers	%	Numbers	%
Managerial staff	20 513	5.2	21 505	6.4
Scientists and engeniors	20 914	5.3	34 512	10.3
Technicians, including draughtspersons	44 464	11.2	44 802	13.4
Administrative and professional staff	28 761	7.3	31 633	9.7
Clerks, office machine operators, secretaries and typists	51 282	13.0	39 860	11.9
Supervisors including foremen	21 353	5.4	15 854	4.7
Craftsmen	29 019	7.3	22 632	6.8
Operators and other employees	179 325	45.3	123 258	36.9
Total employment	395 631	100	334 056	100

Source: EITB statutory returns.

7. Innovation Policy

Technology has become an important arena for international competition – conducted at the level of nation-states, as well as between companies. A key question for policymakers has become: Can we afford *not* to take part in the international race to subsidise and exploit IT R&D? This may raise fundamental idealogical problems, not least in the many OECD countries whose governments in principle are against state intervention in certain cases.

174

However, the choice facing policymakers is not simply one of *whether* to join the international IT R&D support race, but *how*. Most countries cannot afford to support all candidate technologies or to intervene at all stages, from research through development to marketing. Policymakers are therefore forced to devise selective strategies – which may, again, be political anathema. The strategic choices made by IT policymakers in a number of OECD countries are repor ed in Arnold and Guy (1986).

A key success-factor f r government policymakers appears to be a climate which permits long term policy formulati n and implementation. We have described elsewhere the roles of the United States military-industrial complex and what we called the Japanese "bureaucratic-industrial complex" n creating and sustaining technological and industrial advantage (Arnold and Guy, 1986; Arnold, 1987; Guy and Arnold, 1987). United States and Japanese policymakers work in close partnership with industry over long periods of time, largely outside the usual party-political processes and unaffected by changes in the part of government. Policymakers in other "stop-go" environments are considerably disadvantaged. Not only are resources for industrial and innovation policy only intermittently available in such countries, but they tend to lack a *forum* where a long-run consensus can be established within industry and between industry and government about likely economic development patterns and the policies (industrial, infrastructural, educational) which are needed to support them.

8. Trade Barriers

Trade barriers form an important obstacle to IT diffusion. For example, high EEC tariffs on semiconductor components allow higher prices to be maintained within the European Common Market than outside, reducing the attractiveness of electronics-based innovation. For largely historical reasons (products which were formerly electro-mechanical have now become electronic), EEC tariffs on electronic equipment are lower than those for components, encouraging "off-shore" assembly and importing. This, in turn, leads to political tension and the imposition of minimum "local content" rules on certain products, notably television (and cars). Community companies are competitively disadvantaged by the tariffs, making it harder for them to compete in finished goods. Both the absolutely high tariff rates and the historical paradox in the rate structure impede IT diffusion and exploitation in the Community.

Elsewhere tariffs and other types of government policy – whether explicitly stated in law or enshrined in bureaucratic practice – have pernicious effects in constraining free trade in electronics. Examples range from the explicit "buy American" policy to implicit national preference in government procurement, which is almost universally practised.

National standards can also be exploited to play a significant role in *impeding* technology diffusion, negating their potential to enlarge and unify markets, so encouraging diffusion. This has been of key importance in telecommunications markets in many countries.

9. Infrastructure

If our arguments about the key role of telecommunications in IT convergence are correct, the provision of a wideband telecommunications infrastructure is a crucial precondition for IT-based economic development and growth in OECD countries. The investment costs are massive. Most attention focuses on the switching and trunk transmission technologies and investment needed to realise ISDN or IBN systems. Since trunk connections are already wideband (in order to generate economies of scale in long-distance transmission), they are inherently flexible between ISDN and IBN. However, the cost of local connections is likely to be more significant. Barron and Curnow (1978) claimed that 85 per cent of the marginal cost of adding a connection to a telecommunicaitons network consists of making the local connection between the local exchange and the new telephone subscriber. The investment cost of replacing existing copper wires with broadband cable (fibre optics) would therefore be very substantial in relation to the installed value of entire telecommunication networks.

Techniques are available for reducing this cost. One Japanese idea involves using high-quality, expensive glass fibre from the telephone exchange to each street, then using high-loss (but low-cost) plastic fibre for the connection from the street to the user's equipment. While this would dramatically reduce materials costs, it would have little impact on labour cost. Some governments, concerned to find projects to form the basis of Keynsian-style public works programmes, might not regard this wholly as a disadvantage.

V. POLICIES AND POLICY OPTIONS

1. Introduction

Strategy is necessary for government to cope with the implications of the microelectronics revolution. This revolution is one feature of a continuous process of industrial transformation and restructuring – the very basis of economic "progress": Schumpeter's "gale of creative destruction (1928)". It is not possible to opt out of it without also opting out of the world economy.

Some countries' industrial structures are "wrong" – they do not favour exploitation of comparative advantages or technologies which produce high living standards. This generates a need for adjustment. Often, the 'inappropriateness' of existing industrial structures impedes change:

- The existing capital stock is relevant to old, not new, industries;
- Skills, training and geography impede movement into new industrial branches;
- Infrastructure, such as telecommunications, does not meet the requirements of new industy.

Market mechanisms do exist which will "correct" inappropriate industrial structures, but they are slow and they can lead to dramatic reductions in real wages and other costs to society.

The pervasiveness of electronics technology and its ability to alter patterns of competition and comparative advantage lead countries which successfully exploit it to *restructure* their economies. Like the railways in the nineteenth century, which were equally pervasive in their economic effects, electronics has involved state intervention from its very early days. This has been particularly clear in the major period of growth in electronics-related industry, after World War II. Even in the slump of the first half of the 1980s, the United States experienced the creation of millions of jobs in electronics (Soete, 1985). Far fewer jobs were created in countries which performed relatively weakly in the new industry.

The "small country squeeze" discussed by Stankiewitz (1981) makes the issue of industrial restructuring particularly important for smaller OECD countries, not least those which rely heavily on primary sectors and therefore run a particular risk of "de-industrialisation" if only a small number of their existing industrial sectors cease to be viable.

176

But pressures for restructuring policy are strong in all industrial economies, hence convergence among state policies to promote electronics leads to a "swarming" in policy efforts around the new technology. As the 1982 assessors of the USA's Very-High-Speed Integrated Circuits (VHSIC) programme pointed out:

> "Many countries desire a strong semiconductor industry but do not have the internal market demand necessary to adequately support a native industry. Most government supported semiconductor programs are based on the assumption of substantial sales to other countries – usually countries with their own government plan. The prospects of substantial success are unlikely, particularly when seen in the context of previously weak or nonexistent national capacity (Committee on Assessment of the DoD Very-High-Speed Integrated Circuits Program, 1982)."

In fact, this policy convergence (together with the increasing quantity of R&D effort which must be concentrated in one place to reach "critical mass" in some of the more mature electronics technologies) has promoted a trend toward intervention through establishing collaborative R&D projects. This is happening not only at the state level, but internationally, especially in Europe. Examples include Eureka and the EEC's ESPRIT and RACE programmes.

2. IT Policy

As was indicated in Chapter 1, the electronics industries began to be seen as a policy problem in many OECD countries – primarily those in Europe – during the late 1970s. The predominant concern was with *micro*electronics and its implications for employment, the quality of working life and society at large. Initially, there was a sense of shock at the possibilities, often extrapolated from the employment effects of chip technology in the electromechanical industries. Eventually, it was realised that these effects were not typical of the whole economy (Braun and Senker, 1982). This realisation, and the rather deterministic notion that since microelectronics would inevitably ravage employment it would be better to adopt the technology whole-heartedly and share in such competitive benefits as it brought than to suffer *both* technological unemployment and reduced competitiveness, began to alter the policy debate by about 1980. The problem of electronics began to be seen as one of *industrial structure* and company competitiveness within that structure, rather than solely an issue of the social implications of microelectronics. In France, this wider problematic issue was theorised and discussed in policy debate as the *"filière électronique"*. In the United Kingdom, in a more atheoretical way, the term "Information Technology" (IT) came into use. Both terms provided slogans for government policy. Dutch policymakers placed particular emphasis on the role of state action in promoting national restructuring towards IT. In Japan and the United States, where policymakers tend not to indulge in the European penchant for despair, the issue of competition began to come to a head within industry itself, as Japanese firms provided a realistic challenge to US dominance (for a more detailed discussion, see Arnold and Guy, 1986).

As the central problems in electronics came to be seen as ones of competition and structure, so worldwide attention focused on the Japanese announcement of the "Fifth Generation Computer Project" in 1981. This was not only a technologically daring move by a country hitherto considered technologically imitative, but it also threatened to change the "rules of the game" in large parts of the electronics industry. Perhaps most significantly, it focused attention on the possibilities for creating national advantage by establishing new industrial branches.

The worldwide strategic targeting of electronics has important implications. It means that economic development is less than the positive-sum game based on the exploitation of "comparative advantage" which is implied by conventional trade theory and closer to a zero-sum game, since many countries target the same growth sector. It creates ratchet effects in the funding of intervention measures (such as research). Since it is expensive to participate in this type of game, small countries and less developed countries (LDCs) have difficulty in keeping up and need to develop survival strategies, such as specialisation and international co-operation.

The range of policies pursued to generate national advantage in electronics and related industries is very large. Table 23 summarises some of the more important categories of direct support, assigning them to three major categories: demand-side; bridging; and supply-side. To these must be added the macroeconomic weapons at the disposal of policymakers. These range from manipulating the fiscal climate to specific supports for increments to company R&D, such as the tax exemptions introduced by the USA. Other policies can be 'twisted' to favour electronics: most notably regional development supports.

Table 23.   **IT POLICY OPTIONS**

	Supply Side	Bridging	Demand Side
Weak intervention / Cheap	1. Research: often collaborative	1. Coupling supply and demand side policies. Strategy formulation	1. Information dissemination
			2. Demonstration projects
	2. Innovation policy: may be mission oriented	2. Standardization, to strengthen supply side and enable adoption	3. Adoption / innovation incentives
			4. Technological capability development
Strong intervention / Expensive	3. Industrial policy: subsidy to "national champions"	3. Infrastructure, e.g. telecommuni-cations	5. Procurement

Source: Eric Arnold and Ken Guy.

178

3. Demand-side Actions

Demand-side actions have one or both of two purposes:

– To improve the efficiency of non-electronics branches by promoting the use of electronics;
– To stimulate demand for nationally-made electronics products, to the benefit of producing firms.

For countries trying to "catch-up" in producing electronic equipment, these two objectives conflict. Insistence on national supply means that electronics adopters outside IT are offered access to technology which lags behind the "state of the art". But subsidising IT adopters' access to the best internationally available technology makes it still more difficult for national suppliers to catch up.

Demand-side actions in IT typically include the use of monetary incentives to encourage adoption, such as subsidies for investment in new types of computer system eg. CAD. Related activities include the funding of demonstration projects. Government information about IT has been disseminated in many OECD countries in order to demystify the new technology. Education and training may also be extended through special courses, new IT training centres or broadcasts in order to provide IT skills and encourage take-up.

Some government actions on the demand side take note of the need (which arises whenever technology is transferred) for those acquiring technology to be already conversant with its important aspects – otherwise they are unable to negotiate about it or to exploit it when it is transferred. This aspect has been emphasized in, for example, Dutch and Swedish IT programmes, where explicit commitments have been made to maintain a minimal national research competence in IT technologies which are unlikely to be exploited by national suppliers. Where, of course, national supply does occur, governments are able to stimulate local activity through selective procurement.

4. Standardization

Standardization provides a vital bridge between demand- and supply-side actions. Agreed standards speed the diffusion of IT by removing important elements of uncertainty from adopters' investment decisions and by increasing the benefits available through interworking of the different information technologies. On the supply-side, standards are an important competitive weapon which can be used to "lock in" users to particular architectures and, equally, to "lock out" undesirable competitors. Hence, government's role in standards-setting may be a crucial determinant of national competitiveness in IT.

Governments have used the standards definition process to help forge technical communities. AT&T's UNIX operating system has played this role for the European Commission's Multi-Annual Programme in Data Processing and in the succeeding ESPRIT programme. It plays the same role in the UK Alvey programme and the Japanese Sigma software project: namely, it establishes both a technical paradigm and a means for communication and exchange within the community.

General Motors' Manufacturing Automation Protocol (MAP) and the International Standards Organisation's Open Systems Interconnection (OSI) standards for information interchange primarily serve the interests of users, who can exploit them to avoid "lock in" to *de facto* standards, by providing a way for companies to compete by offering improved systems components without necessarily delivering complete systems. Barriers to entry are reduced, and users can themselves choose more advantageous combinations of price and quality characteristics in building up their systems.

5. Supply-side Actions

Supply-side policies for IT divide between relatively traditional forms of state *industrial policy* and *innovation policy*. Industrial policy mechanisms are similar to those used widely in other industries, notably: nationalisation or subsidy intended to place substantial state resources at the disposal of an ailing and under-capitalised national competitor: industrial reorganisation through compulsory mergers and acquisitions; and the designation of "national champions", to benefit from a broad range of state aids (usually including procurement) in order to secure a national stake in a particular sector. In mainframe computers, ICL (UK) and Bull (France) have fallen into all three categories, while Siemens (F.R. Germany) is in the third. Japan appears unique in designating *six* national champions (Fujitsu, Oki, NEC, Hitachi, Mitsubishi and Toshiba) in computers – partly as a result of government inability to merge the industry into three major companies during the 1970s.

Naturally, where national industry is strong, there is no case for such policies. In the more mature IT sectors (such as mainframes, public telecommunications switching, semiconductor chips and the sectors which depend on them – software, CAD and so on) static economies of scale and the dynamic economies of the "experience curve" combine with high and rising threshold R&D requirements to entrench the positions of strong competitors. A key success-factor in such "experience curve" industries is to attain scale *early* in the life of the technology involved. Astute management of this scale, through company policies of growth and innovation, provide *structural* competitive advantage. US government innovation policy has played a crucial role in doing this for certain key players (notably government funding and procurement in relation to IBM during the 1950s and certain semiconductor firms in the 1960s). Very large domestic markets also provide a crucial advantage in achieving scale. But the role of entrepreneurship is crucial. For example, IBM's decision in the 1960s to "bet the company" on developing the 360 range of computers was the crucial factor in transforming it from one among several potential US winners in the computer industry to the dominant force in mainframes worldwide.

Attempts to use the brute force of state funding to counter the structurally disadvantaged position of national champions in the maturer IT sectors have tended to give way to a greater concern with R&D support in recent years. That is, *industrial policy* has tended to give way to *innovation policy*. There are several reasons for this:

- The scope of GATT, and the international acceptability of the free trade ideology which underpins the GATT, has been growing, so that the tools of industrial policy have increasingly become internationally illegal;
- The transfer of certain national powers to the centre within the EEC has played a similar role in outlawing some European industry policy practices;
- As IT sectors have matured, so entry barriers (i.e. the structural advantages enjoyed by successful competitors) have tended to grow in absolute terms, making industry policy more expensive year by year;
- World recession and increasing policy concern about high levels of government spending have prompted a search for cheaper policy options. In very crude terms, the cost per intervention must follow the rule of thumb relating the investment cost of research to that of production: if research costs one unit, then development and engineering costs ten and scaling up to production costs 100. Innovation policy, it follows, is cheaper than industry policy.

US policy for IT (and for other "high" technologies) is strongly *mission-oriented*. National technology leadership is seen as a crucial plank in defence strategy. For example, the perceived threat from large numbers of comparatively simple Soviet fighter aircraft is countered with smaller numbers of more complex, high-technology machines. The Department of Defense (DoD) spends large sums on financing university- and industry-sector R&D in the United States. The case of the microelectronics industry itself is a well-known example, with R&D contracts complementing state demand from the Minuteman/Apollo programme. This combination of research contracts with procurement has been used repeatedly to define the path of technological development. Recent cases include:

- The VHSIC Program, intended to "correct" the US semiconductor and systems industries' emphasis on civilian markets at the expense of military needs for signal processing equipment;
- The Strategic Computer Program (SCP), aimed at applying artificial intelligence (which has been funded by the DoD since the 1960s – a crucial factor in explaining the advanced state of development of AI industry in the USA compared with elsewhere in the world) to military systems;
- The recently-sanctioned Defense Semiconductor Initiative (DSI), including a proposal to constitute a collaborative fabrication facility to manufacture leading-edge 16M DRAMs.

Apart from the latter, these DoD interventions have proceeded by specifying products or systems which have a military mission, but which require research and development effort because they exceed the state-of-the-art at the beginning of the programme. Procurement then follows, as the next step in fulfilling the military mission so defined – with the virtuous industrial effects already described. DSI differs in that the product goals are non-military in the first instance – a strong civilian industry is the desired end-point – but military orders for end-products are also intended.

There is no particular reason why this type of mission-oriented, "coupled" technology programme should necessarily be restricted to the military sphere. However, in practice the military character of the project has provided shelter from accusations of improper state intervention, simplifying the political justification of state intervention. DSI effectively casts aside this shelter.

The Japanese Fifth Generation Project has inspired a worldwide wave of policy imitation. While policy recipies vary from country to country, most include the ingredient of *collaborative research*. Two factors suggest that this results from more than mere fashion among policymakers. First, it is a central feature of private-sector actions such as the Microelectronics and Computer Technology Corporation (MCC) in Austin, Texas, Stanford University's Center for Integrated Systems and the European Computer Industry Research Centre (ECRC) operated by ICL, Bull and Siemens. Second, it reinforces the trend to the formation of *strategic alliances* among IT companies.

As Sigurdson (1985) points out, the 5G Project is itself the latest form developed in a long tradition of Engineering Research Associations (ERAs), pioneered in the UK. Figure 12 sketches out some of the collaborative research structures employed in various places over the years. The early, largely anglo-saxon, models employed in countries including the UK and Canada involve the idea of technology generation in a central institute followed by outward technology transfer to relevant companies. This form is founded in the post-War 'technology push' thinking which has characterised technology policy in the anglo-saxon world, based on the idea that there is a linear progression from new discoveries in basic science to innovation and commercial success in industry. This model does not readily allow for information flows and feedback from the market or the demand side.

The traditional Japanese variation of the UK ERA model limits participation to selected, strong companies and replaces the permanent, central research institution with a division of

Figure 12.   **COLLABORATIVE RESEARCH STRUCTURES IN IT**

Alvey/Esprit Model

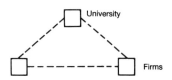

- Joint research and/or labour division
- No co-location
- Joint research agenda
- Few firms (usually)
- No career path/research institution

UK ERA Model

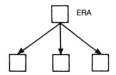

- Central research
- Lowest common denominator and contract research
- Many firms
- Research career path/institution

Anglo-Saxon Research Institute Model

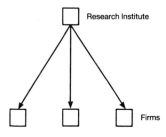

- Central research
- Scientific/centrally determined research agenda
- Many firms
- Research career path/institution

Japanese ERA Model (pre-ICOT)

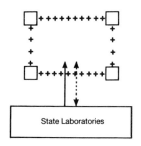

- Division of research labour
- No co-location
- Few firms
- Joint research agenda, agreed with state research laboratories
- Inputs/personnel loans from state laboratories
- No career path

Key:

– – – – –	Collaboration
⟶	Disembodied information transfer about technology
◄·····►	Loan personnel
++++++	Division of research labour

182

Figure 12.   (cont'd)

ICOT/[MCC MKI] Model

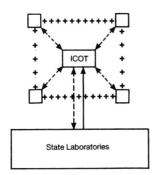

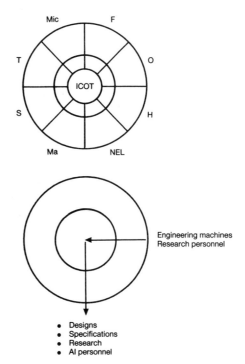

State Laboratories

- Central, collaborative research
- Engineering division + labour
- Few firms
- Fixed-life research institution
- But no career path
- Joint research agenda, agreed with state research laboratories
- Inputs/personnel loans from state laboratories

Engineering machines
Research personnel

- Designs
- Specifications
- Research
- AI personnel

labour in research among participating companies. Researchers are tutored and assisted by government laboratories, but technology transfer problems are minimised because those who develop technology are to a large extent the same people as those who will subsequently use it.

The European Strategic Programme of Research in Information Technology (ESPRIT) orchestrated by the EEC Commission and the UK's similar Alvey Project have evolved a variant on this Japanese model. Here, companies and universities collaborate on research projects without setting up a central R&D facility and, generally, without research inputs from government institutes. The ESPRIT strategy is revised annually by representatives of the "Round-Table Companies" – the twelve major European IT firms which are the programme's major beneficiaries. Alvey's strategy was formulated at the start of the programme in 1983-84 and implemented by a board of directors, principally seconded from industry to government.

The 5G Project uses yet another model, combining characteristics of the anglo-saxon, centralised ERA and the decentralised Japanese version. Arguably, this reflects a shift to higher basic science and systems development contents in a Japanese ERA, raising the importance of shared research facilities. The central laboratory is a place where secondees come together to develop technology and from which they transfer results both 'on the hoof' when they return to their companies and through specifying machinery to be built by the collaborating companies. Government research laboratories' knowledge is also made available through the secondment mechanism. The eight participating firms and ICOT can be seen together as a *system* (Figure 13) for technology development and transfer involving characteristic flows of personnel and technology. While many outside observers doubt ICOT's ability to reach its stated technical goals, it clearly provides a massive education and training effort in the new artificial-intelligence-based computing paradigm for the key firms of the Japanese IT industry (Arnold and Guy, 1986).

While 5G-inspired projects have tended to rely on co-operation as a means to reach apparent R&D thresholds, the transportability of the Japanese model of co-operative research effort between cultures and countries has often been effortlessly assumed, though in practice there are national and regional variations in the style of co-operation undertaken. White points out that "it has yet to be demonstrated that collaborative ventures, even when undertaken by firms for purely commercial motives, are an efficient way of doing R&D. In effect, the innovation literature is virtually unanimous in stressing the importance of tight integration between the R&D, marketing and commercial functions within firms as a factor in the success or failure of development efforts".

Figure 13. **THE TRAINING ROLE OF ICOT**

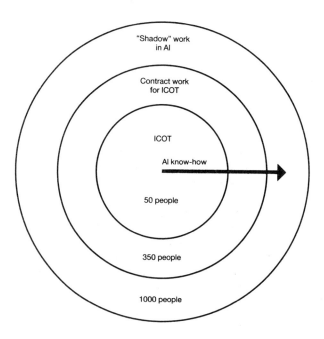

Source: Eric Arnold and Ken Guy, 1986.

However, there is considerable support in the innovation literature for the idea that university-industry links are important in successful innovation (for example, Illinois Institute of Technology, 1968; Rothwell *et al.*, 1974; a recent concise review of relevant literature can be found in Rothwell and Zegveld, 1985, Chapter 2). Conversely, unsuccessful innovators studied tend to have poor or non-existent links with universities. The same studies highlight the importance of co-operative producer-user links in successful innovation. These links are especially important in the design of innovative *systems*, and this is an *a priori* reason for expecting such links to be especially important in IT.

6. National Actions

Table 24 summarises major IT initiatives in the countries discussed. The USA has a long history of IT policy, with interventions in semiconductors in the 1950s, integrated circuits (in connection with the Apollo and Minuteman programmes) and computer-aided design (CAD) in the 1960s, artificial intelligence (AI) and software in the 1970s, and all of these during the 1980s. Government support has underpinned US leadership during the entire post-War period, and the need to link technological development with the industrial capability to satisfy procurement needs has meant that the military has played a *developmental* role in fostering the growth of electronics within the "military-industrial complex". In contrast, US civil policy has been concerned with the *regulation* of industry (e.g. anti-trust) rather than development. A crucial feature in the 1980s has been the emergence of *private-sector IT policy*, in the form of industry-university co-operations (such as those listed in Table 1), especially the Semiconductor Research Corporation (SRC), and the Microelectronics and Computer Technology Corporation (MCC). These address the need for a national "fightback" against the perceived Japanese challenge in electronics. However, they also allow US competitors to pool R&D in their struggle with IBM and AT&T – notably at the MCC, from which both these giants are excluded on anti-trust grounds.

Japanese IT policy also has a long history, with ERAs promoting "catch-up" with US levels of technology over the past quarter century. NTT has played a vital role for the so-called Den Den family firms which supply its equipment needs (Okimoto and Havase, 1985; Arnold and Guy, 1986). The Japanese state's role has been "more developmental than regulatory" (Bluementhal and Teubal, 1975), focusing on creating industrial power through repeated interventions over a long period of time in a select group of companies whose roots stretch back to the pre-war *zaibatsu*.

IBM has been a crucial target of Japanese computer policy, which can be seen as having four stages.

First, catching up with IBM. This involved MITI projects during the 1960s and 1970s: High Capacity Computer Development Programme, 1962-66: Super High Performance Electronic Computer System, 1966-71 – designed to master the technologies of mainframe computers in order to allow the major Japanese electronics companies to participate in the industry; the Mainframe Computer Project from 1971: Computer Peripherals Project 1972-80; and more recently the 4th Generation Operating System, Project.

Second, "Japanisation" of computer technology. This began with the Pattern Information Processing System Project (PIPS) and continues via the 5G Project. This work reorientated computer technology away from dependence on English language and western-style alphabetic-symbolic processing and towards Japanese language and scripts and the elimination of the difficulties at the person-machine interface which exist worldwide, but which are more pronounced in Japan than in the west because of the non-alphabetic character

185

Table 24. **Characteristics of IT interventions**

	Policy focus	Industry cycle	Selectivity	R&D co-operation
US				
Apollo/Minuteman	coupled	1	Y	N
CAD	coupled	1	Y	N
Strategic Computer Programme	coupled	1	Y	N
VHSIC	coupled	3/4	Y	some
Software Eng. Institute	N/A	3/4	N/A	N
SDI ("Star Wars")	coupled	1	Y	some
SRC	manpower	3/4	N/A	Y
CIS	manpower	3/4	N/A	Y
MCC	R&D	various	N	Y
Japan				
IBM-style computer progs.	catch-up	various	Y	nominal
Supercomputers	users in	2	Y	some
PIPS	push	1	Y	nominal
Fifth generation	push	1	Y	Y
VLSI	catch-up	3/4	Y	some
Optoelectronics	push	1/2	Y	nominal
New Function Elements	push	1	Y	some
Automatic Software	catch-up	3/4	N	N
Interoperable Databases	push	3/4	Y	some
SIGMA	catch-up	3/4	N	N
NTT actions *	coupled	various	Y	N[1]
UK				
Alvey	push/catch	various	N	Y
France				
PAFE	coupled	various	Y	some
Germany				
Informationstechnik	push/catch	various	some	some
Belgium				
Maystadt Plan	push/catch	various	some	some
Netherlands				
INSP	push/catch	various	some	some
Switzerland				
Impulse I/II	education	3/4	N	some
Canada				
No programmatic initiative	Traditional science push policies			
EC				
ESPRIT	push/catch	various	N	Y
Europe				
Eureka	push/catch	various	N	Y

1. Japanese and French programmes involve co-ordination and co-operation through government laboratories.
* NTT enforces transfer of technology between its suppliers, so that the most successful R&D available among these firms is used to underpin second-source manufacture.
Source: Arnold, 1987.

of Japanese writing. Fujitsu launched the first Japanese-language products in 1979, well ahead of IBM.

Third, full-frontal attack on IBM. NTT developed its "DIPS" family of computers in competition both with MITI's efforts in the 1960s and 1970s and with IBM machines. DIPS technology was commercialised by NEC, Hitachi and Fujitsu, which – together with OKI –belong to the Den Den family of companies. Mitsubishi and Toshiba produced computers which are not IBM-compatible and have tended to become minicomputer – rather than mainframe-makers. The dangers of encroaching too closely on IBM territory were underlined by the "Japscam" episode in 1983, when employees of Hitachi were caught (or entrapped according to interpretation of events) stealing IBM software secrets. This setback has necessitated larger efforts to develop proprietary, non-IBM Japanese operating systems for Japanese mainframe computers. It has dashed many Japanese hopes to "out-IBM" within the architectural and communications standards defined by the American giant, increasing the importance of 5G for the future of Japanese computing. In the wake of Japscam, enthusiasm for UNIX has increased in Japan, and this operating system forms the core of the new Sigma software engineering initiative.

Fourth, market enlargement outside the ambit of IBM. This in turn has four elements:

- Artificial Intelligence;
- Non-Roman script approaches;
- Supercomputers;
- New markets in developing countries.

By competing in new ways, Japanese companies can avoid direct conflict with IBM's power.

Particularly since the *1980s Vision*, Japan has been trying to raise the proportion of funding going to science as opposed to technology, thereby coming into line with other OECD countries. In moving from "catch-up" to innovation, the national need for science increases. Crudely, in "catch-up" development, much of the science needed is a special form of "know-how", which involves applying scientific manpower to technological problems. Other science is already available in the form of *information*. It can be identified and used because technologists in other countries have already identified and used it. In contrast, once at the scientific and technological frontiers, the need for *new* information rises dramatically in order to suggest technological opportunities and to break bottlenecks. At that point it is no longer so possible to "piggyback" on others science: Japan has stepped into an era in which there is no textbook.

The EEC is of comparable economic size to the USA, but is far less significant in IT than the USA or Japan. Policy has focused on breaking down internal barriers which prevent exploitation of a common European market as a base from which to attack world markets. The ESPRIT (European Strategic Programme of Research in IT) programme of co-operative R&D is an important plank in this strategy, and is being followed by an intervention in telecommunications (RACE). The extent to which EEC initiatives are beginning to form aspects of industrial policy and to establish something like a "EuroMITI" for IT represents a new departure.

The medium-sized European countries – France, the UK and the Federal Republic of Germany – follow strategically confused policies. Luke-warm support for ESPRIT coexists with policies aimed at creating solely national advantage. French policy has involved nationalisation and reorganisation within the IT industry as well as the promotion of R&D, and is the most developmental of the three. The UK has retreated from this type of industrial intervention since the 1960s, fielding a range of innovation subsidies and the 'Alvey' programme of government subsidy to university/industry R&D co-operations. German IT policy involves a mixture of broad innovation promotion and technology adoption measures with R&D subsidies aimed at strengthening areas of existing competence. All three countries have subsidised "national champions" in mainframe computing, and vacillate about the need to maintain a world-class presence in microelectronics, where barriers to participation may be even higher. Since most IT companies in these medium-sized economies operate behind the technological frontier, a great deal of R&D subsidy goes to "reinvent the wheel" and to catch-up activity. The inability of industry to attain the scale needed to fund continuing progress at the technological frontier tends to make the need for "catch-up" R&D support structural and permanent. As in the USA and Japan, co-operative R&D programmes reduce the inequalitites of access to new technologies between the medium-sized and the largest firms.

While the medium-sized countries struggle against the economics of participation in the "world-scale" sectors of the electronics industry, notably mainframe computers and mass-produced microelectronics, the small countries do not regard such participation as an option. (The exception is Holland, via Philips, but even there the major opportunity for participation in IT at the world level is seen as being through the EEC rather than nationally.) Policies stress general innovation-promotion measures, education, maintaining sufficient basic research to permit effective exploitation of imported technologies, and the pursuit of niche strategies focused in applications know-how. The small number of significant national IT companies operating in these countries means that policy is necessarily oriented towards their needs. Especially in Switzerland and Holland, these companies are deeply involved in the policy formulation process.

In the medium and small economies especially, a great deal of "new" IT policy is largely a repackaged version of existing initiatives. This is true, for example, of the British Alvey programme, the Dutch INSP and the Belgian Mavstadt Plan, each of which represents an important attempt to reorient an existing policy system towards the needs of the IT sector.

VI.   POLICY IMPLICATIONS

1.   Introduction

Governments have a wide range of policy options available to them in dealing with the implications of IT and economic growth. Here, these options are classified as "demand-side", "supply-side" and "bridging" actions. Each category has associated with it a range of costs and benefits. None is likely to be successful unless it forms part of a wider strategy. Each must build on existing strength and connect with available opportunities and so that other policy actions do not conflict with it.

The need for strategy is great – and is especially large for small countries which do not have the economic resources to "let a thousand flowers bloom". The difficulties of implementing such a strategy are considerable. Governments need to devise mechanisms for coupling the design of intervention mechanisms with consensus about industrial need. Often they must play the role of midwife in generating such consensus. Policymaking must be done in a state of critical tension between, on the one side, the tendency of state planning mechanisms to suppress industrial and market signals and, on the other side, the tendency of industry towards anarchy and away from strategies which cohere at the national level.

The major intellectual contribution to thought about strategy formulation and IT policy in the 1980s has come from France, with the concept of *filière* treating the economy as a network of interrelated branches, so that intervention in one can affect events in another. While the actual policies promulgated in France in the early 1980s have been less than successful, probably through the traditional French policy weakness of *dirigisme*, few other countries have undertaken policy initiatives in such a deliberately coherent way. The French approach provides an important exemple, and a first step along the road of desirable policy formulation methodology.

2. Costs and Benefits of Different Approaches

There is a broad range of policy options available sketched out in Table 23. Policymakers have the option to interlink actions. For example, the expansion of computer education in schools has been used in France, the UK and Canada as a way to stimulate demand for domestically-produced microcomputer hard- and software.

Consideration is not given here to macroeconomic measures. Naturally, these have an important role to play in facilitating growth in IT-related activities, as in others. Of particular importance is the general level of corporate and individual taxation (with implications for company location) and the particular treatment of R&D expenditure for tax purposes. The recent US example of exempting increments in R&D from corporation tax have produced dramatic increases in R&D expenditure. It is unlikely that *all* of this increase results from creative accounting. There is an extensive literature which associated R&D spending (especially *civil* R&D spending) with economic performance (see Pavitt, 1980 for an excellent review).

a) Demand-side Actions

Demand-side policy options range from relatively inexpensive measures which stimulate demand for IT-related goods and services in general, to more focussed (and generally more expensive) policies which generate demand for the products of particular produces – generally national ones.

Many European countries have followed option 1 (Table 23) – information provision. Here, a few million dollars can go a long way, especially where the enthusiasm of people in the media is co-opted. The best known example of this is perhaps the extensive influence of the BBC Horizon Programme "When the Chips are Down", made in 1977 and screened repeatedly through most of Europe during the policy debate about microelectronics in the late 1970s and early 1980s. Microelectronic awareness schemes (in countries including France, the UK, Netherlands, Belgium and Canada) encourage the multiplier effects of IT adoption, but tend to have perverse effects on the supply side. Countries where IT demand is relatively weak and needs stimulation tend (more or less by definition) to lack leading-edge customers for IT, and this is in turn associated with a weak supply industry. Demand-promoting measures tend to such in imports, further undermining national supply.

Demonstration projects are an extension of information provision policies. They are sometimes more useful for encouraging *industrial* IT take-up in that they provide potential adopters with something they can "touch and feel", and with people whose experience can be shared. Particularly where large capital investments are required, this can reduce the level of risk perceived by new adopters. As with category 1, perverse effects on the supply side may result. A good example is provided by the British Department of Industry's subsidy of machinery manufacturer Baker Perkins' first Computer Aided Design installation in 1977. This provided a demonstration of the use of US interactive graphics technology which was visited by thousands of British engineering managers, and which was cited by many as a factor influencing their adoption of CAD (Arnold and Senker, 1981). Predominantly, they chose US CAD systems, undermining the nascent UK CAD industry.

Where demonstration is expanded to more general adoption or innovation subsidy (category 3), greater influence can be exerted over the choice of suppliers. To continue the British CAD example, once the Department of Industry extended its CAD work from demonstration in the late 1970s to adoption subsidy in the early 1980s, it was able to influence supplier choice. It was not explicitly stated that subsidy would be given preferentially to adopters of British CAD equipment, but the predominant choice of national suppliers by the beneficiaries of the Department of Industry's CADCAM and CADMAT schemes suggests that this message was received by applicants for subsidy. Again, the corollary of (overtly or covertly) favouring national suppliers can be limitation of demand-side adoption multipliers through promoting use of technology which lags behind the leading edge. As this continual conflict between demand- and supply-side policy indicates, it is extraordinarily difficult to move forward from a position of technology lag into one of strength on the supply-side.

Measures to build national technological capability are an essential part of acheiving such movement. These measures may be very applied – such as the provision of free or subsidised consultancy services to organisations adopting IT, so as to help them learn ways to evaluate and apply unfamiliar technology. Examples are widespread in Europe (Belgium, Netherlands, the UK and elsewhere). An alternative is to build in a research element to adoption programmes as has been done in West German CAD adoption schemes and British office automation pilot projects. The risk here is that attempts to adopt semi-developed technology by non-professional researchers prevents achievement of either the adoption or research objectives.

Measures may also operate at the level of "basic" science. The Swedish National Board for Technical Development (STU) has built a particularly powerful model, based on strategic choice between areas of basic science through making judgements about their likely relevance to the present (and sensible future) structure of Swedish industry. As a result, STU supports two categories of research:

  i) Science and technology relevant to Swedish suppliers. This is generously funded and commercial results are expected;

  ii) Science and technology unlikely to provide a basis for Swedish supply, but which will be inwardly transferred. A lower level of research is funded to ensure sufficient national technology capability is available to make good judgements about how to import and exploit technology.

These two different levels and types of support need to be reflected in levels of support in higher education as well as research. Incorporating industrial-strategic thinking into research and education funding is alien to the style of many longer-established industrial countries, running counter to traditions of "academic freedom" which have long been (rightly) regarded as a social check on political extremism. Countries which are unable to support a truly independent, self-directed academic community in certain basic disciplines therefore run a political risk. But it is not clear that *all* – or even the greater part – of the higher education and research systems should be de-coupled from economic needs in the name of academic freedom.

190

Procurement policy is perhaps the most traditional demand-side measure. While selective procurement is increasingly seen as being at odds with the principles of the GATT, few governments are so naive as to allow their *statements* about open government procurement policies to accord with their *actions*. Early in the life cycle (as was the case with microelectronics) government procurement may comprise most or all of demand. Market signals are deliberately suppressed in the expectation of changing the characteristics of supply and demand. Later in the industry life cycle, procurement may become an expensive crutch for ailing national suppliers. One point of view is that this has become the case with the three "national champions" in European mainframe computing.

Procurement policies can be directed towards small and medium-sized enterprises (SMEs), helping these firms to find their footing (as has been done in US and UK defence spending by allocating a small fraction of the budget to small suppliers). These policies are probably at their most powerful when they are *coupled* with supply-side actions to promote the generation of a new technology. However, while this case, when procurement is equal for a time to the whole of demand, can be very powerful, it is also the most risky. Government action may turn out to be irrelevant to industrial needs. An important strand of thought about US defence policy states that the coincidence between military and civil needs in electronics during the 1960s has disappeared in the 1980s. As a result, DoD procurement has been transformed from a powerful and positive force in (implicit) US industrial policy to a negative one.

In general, demand-side actions bring important multipliers through accelerating the adoption of new productivity- and growth-enhancing technology. They can promote the development of more sophisticated customers, and this can bring benefits to national suppliers. More direct linkages between demand-side and other actions are potentially very powerful – but can also be very risky.

b) Supply-side Actions

In recent years, the thrust of supply-side action has moved toward *innovation* policy rather than *industry* policy. This has focused intervention in the area of R&D. An important benefit for some countries has been the relative inexpensiveness of this form of intervention. A long-established rule of thumb says that if research costs one unit of money, then development costs ten units and pilot production one hundred. Reorienting from *industry* to *research* and *innovation* policy therefore involves moving from the expensive to the relatively cheap portion of the product development cycle. It is possible that this movement is abetted by a growing need for developments in basic science and technology within the technological trajectory of IT.

Sigurdson argues that new ways to undertake R&D are needed because the character of technology itself is changing, and that this is reflected in:

i) Increased attention to events taking place at the frontiers of fundamental research;

ii) A high degree of intellectual codification and "academisation" – as opposed to the unsystematic empirical character of many traditional technologies;

The growing intellectual complexity which requires the co-operation of researchers with highly specialised scientific and technological backgrounds (Sigurdson, 1986).

This leads to closer links between industry and universities and, especially in the case of Japan, where academic links are difficult to forge, to greater focus on basic research. The changing pattern of industry-university links in the West and the growth of ERAs and basic

R&D laboratories in industry in Japan are both factors which support Sigurdson's argument. Elsewhere (Arnold, 1987), we have extended this argument to suggest that this growing need for basic science as an input heralds a new discontinuity as radical as that imposed by the development of the industrial R&D laboratory at the end of the nineteenth century. We suspect that new scale requirements are imposed by this in certain sectors of electronics (especially mainframe computers and performance-critical high-volume chips), but this hypothesis still needs serious empirical testing.

Following the perceived success of Japanese collaborative R&D projects and the shake-up in Western IT policy encouraged by the Fifth Generation Project announcement, there has been a tendency for intervention to operate through collaborative R&D projects (category 1 in Table 23). Since these tend to involve co-operation between competitors, they generally operate at the so-called *pre-competitive* stage in the innovation process. Here, basic technology is being developed, which can subsequently be exploited in different ways by different product developers. "Pre-competitive" R&D, however, is a rather nebulous concept. In practice, a great deal of what goes on under this heading is straightforward product development.

Collaborative R&D projects can become less mission-oriented than some more traditional government-funded technology development programmes, such as those of the US DoD. The market needs which they ultimately address are less certain than those of mission-oriented work, because the market involved tends to be commercial rather than a government market. Fewer planning and negotiation steps are required to translate mission-oriented goals into R&D work-programmes than is the case with pre-competitive collaborative research programmes (Table 25).

Table 25. **PLANNING STEPS IN MISSION-ORIENTED AND COLLABORATIVE RESEARCH**

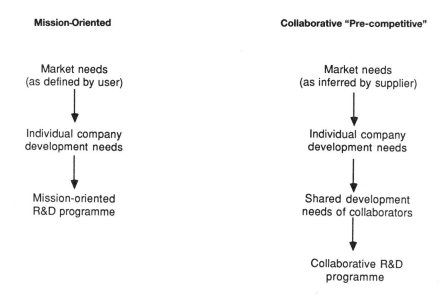

192

In principle, collaborative "catch-up" R & D programmes which aim to overcome lags in technology can be well-focused. Technology leaders have already shown what the targets are for developing technology and capability. True leading-edge collaborations – as the Fifth Generation Project was intended to be – lack this advantage of "having a textbook before them".

In practice, outside Japan, the collaborative R & D model remains an experiment. Interim evaluations of two major European collaborative programmes – ESPRIT (ESPRIT Review Board, 1985) and Alvey (SPRU, 1987) are cautiously positive but point out that the long-term nature of much of the research involved means that economic benefits will take time to appear. Collaborative research can provide a stepping-stone to other forms of partnership and to industrial reorganisation. This has been attempted by MITI in the past. Elsewhere, we suggest that industrial reorganisation is an important *agendum* of ESPRIT (Arnold and Guy, 1986).

The superimposition of a national (or European) framework on collaboration is a corollary of the fact that intervention funds are state funds in Europe. Private US initiatives (Semiconductor Research Corporation – SRC, and the Microelectronics and Computer Technology Corporation – MCC) have been exclusively national in character, too. This imposes costs on participant firms, whose interests might better be served by international partnerships. For example, ICL has an important strategic partnership with Fujitsu while also being a major participant in the ESPRIT and Alvey programmes.

Certain very broad collaborative R & D programmes appear to lack technological focus. This is especially true of the ESPRIT and Alvey programmes. However, ESPRIT has the major advantage that the principal European IT companies negotiate annually about ESPRIT strategy and workplans, so there is a continuous process interlinking state intervention and corporate needs. Alvey, on the other hand, had limited freedom to modify its strategy once the programme was under way because it lacked the resources to incorporate such a process. This may be an important weakness.

The historically most successful supply-side policy (category 2) has been that of the US DoD in the 1950s and 1960s. Here, formal collaboration was absent and contractors' missions were tightly defined by the Department. Arguably, the success of the entire US electronics industry was built upon the support of the DoD in developing technology and its simultaneously performing the role of launch customer via military procurement. This moved suppliers down experience curves, cheapened electronic products and set the character of the ensuing technical and economic trajectories. While the DoD has had to couple supply- and demand-side interventions in this way, MITI's catch-up policies have benefited from the fact that the character of demand has already been set by the USA. It is only now Japanese projects are at the leading edge of technology that a comparable need for coupling arises in Japan. The apparent loss of direction of the Fifth Generation Project (Arnold, 1987) may be partly explained by this lack.

The most traditional form of supply-side action in Europe (category 3) has been subsidy of national champions – both directly and by the indirect means of protection and procurement. Protection has been particularly important in telecommunications markets where PTTs have tended to be arms of the state. Generally, these policies reflect a belief that it is strategically necessary – for commercial or military reasons – to retain a national presence in certain sectors of the economy. US policies to impede outward technology transfer have encouraged European governments to protect their autarky in this way especially in France.

As electronics sectors have matured, so this form of intervention has grown more expensive in absolute terms. (This perception has encouraged EEC collaborations: ESPRIT and, especially, RACE.) The scale of resources required has led some countries to nationalise relevant companies (UK, France), with attendant controversy. However, only in the case of the French *Plan d'action pour la filière électronique* (PAFE) has this been part of a national *strategy*. In the event, PAFE seems to have foundered on the grandioseness of its aims and the size of the budget required. (We have elsewhere [Arnold and Guy, 1986] suggested that the collapse of PAFE led to the French proposal to establish the Eureka programme. This view is highly controversial.)

c) Bridging

Bridging activities couple together, or enable, demand- and supply-side events and actions. In Table 23 they are classified as: coupling; standardization; and infrastructure.

Coupling (category 1) encompasses the linking of technology development with procurement and the elimination of obstacles to IT adoption. The popular view of invention, innovation and marketing is of a linear process involving orderly progress from inspiration to wealth. As we have already indicated, during the 1960s and 1970s, attempts to study the innovation process centred on the relative importance of different parts of the sequence leading from invention to the market in determining success (for a more detailed account, see Rothwell and Zegveld, 1985). This debate was put to rest by Mowery and Rosenberg (1979), who showed that successful innovations *coupled* changes in supply-side opportunities with market demand. The policy implication is that interventions should achieve coupling by acting on both sides of a market or by relating actions on one side to events on the other.

This policy lesson is embodied in the US Department of Defense's (DoD) technology policy. The Department funds the innovation process *via* R&D subsidies and the adoption process through procurement. This has fostered industrial growth by pushing US industry down learning curves associated with commercialisable products. Microchips and computers are "dual use" technologies of this kind. In some cases, the commercial benefits have been reaped at one remove. The DoD did not fund the start-up firms of the early 1970s which now dominate the CAD industry worldwide, but it did pay to generate the technology at MIT, to underwrite its further development in user (aerospace) firms and thereby to generate a *cadre* of CAD-skilled manpower, some of whom became successful entrepreneurs (Arnold, 1984). In other cases, DoD policy – however well-coupled to the military demand side – appears to have been less than wholly successful. CNC machine tools are argued to be a case in point (OTA, 1985), though one may ask whether failure to translate technological capability acquired with DoD funds into commercially relevant products should be ascribed to poor policy intervention, bad firm strategy or a pernicious side-effect of the coddling of firms by the military establishment.

Eliminating obstacles to IT adoption allows demand to be coupled to supply. National needs vary, but key obstacles are likely to include lack of information, a need for data-protection legislation so that people feel confident about using IT, and – most especially – a lack of education and training. In many cases, therefore, the state has a beneficial role to play as an honest information broker.

Standardization (category 2) is a way to operate on the supply side by determining characteristics of demand. It can bring benefits to users by increasing competition and promoting IT equipment inter-operability, but it can also be used by suppliers as a weapon against users. In practice, state policymakers are rarely able to act early enough in the life cycle to set standards. They tend to *react* to *de facto* standards which have emerged from the supply side.

The overlap between standardization and infrastructure (category 3) is more fruitful. Where policymakers can back up their power to define standards with control over necessary infrastructure, their hand is immensely strengthened. Colour television standards are a case in point. Japan chose NTSC in order to use commonality with US standards as a way to exploit superior production economics on the US market. PAL and SECAM were subsequently used in Europe as forms of *defensive* standardization, reducing the importance of US and Japanese producers' scale and learning-curve advantages while introducing defensive non-tariff barriers to trade in television sets through technology licences. This was, of course, a two-edged sword. Increasing the defensibility of European markets reduced their usefulness as bases for export offensives.

Standardization on the basis of infrastructure-building can be used to seize the initiative. Borrus *et al.* (1985) argue that this is the case with the Japanese Integrated Network System (INS). "In essence, INS aims to put a digital, broadband infrastructure in place in anticipation of its uses while simultaneously developing those uses through model programmes and pilot projects targeted at business and residential users." This entails recabling Japan on a broadband standard, leap-frogging 64kbit/second ISDN, currently favoured by CCITT. The EEC has recognised the potency of this effort, and its implications for Japanese suppliers' competitiveness in IT. As a result, the European Commission and the member-states are working to implement RACE as a European equivalent to INS.

In our view, INS and RACE represent two of the most important current initiatives promoting IT-based growth. They smash through existing bottlenecks (whose origins are in nineteenth-century telephony) and open up immense new product and market opportunities. Suppliers and users with early access to broadband communications will inevitably define standards and products ahead of others, with resultant competitive advantage. Against the current trend towards deregulation in communications, the centralised definition and (at least initial) control of broadband communication networks offers a rare point of leverage for a policy intervention to provide a major "mid-life kick" to the electronics Kondratiev. The broadband message needs to be rapidly understood by policymakers in all OECD countries, in case some fail to benefit from this new growth spurt, exacerbating economic inequalities and disagreements between members.

3. Strategy

A thought-out national strategy is useful for at least three reasons. First, it helps to ensure that national actions all tend to pull or push the IT industry in the same direction. This avoids, or at least enables decisions to be taken about, situations like that which prevailed in the UK Computer-Aided Design (CAD) industry in the early 1980s when the Department of Industry sought simultaneously to support UK-owned CAD suppliers and subsidised imports of US CAD systems (Arnold, 1984). Second, it ensures consistency and clarity in the policies which shape the economic environment. If firms know what to expect (and, especially if they agree with it) they are far better placed to plan research and investment. Third, the process of explicit strategy formulation allows judgements to be made about feasible futures. An intellectual connection can be made between supply-side actions and the market, exposing limits on policy action and market opportunities. Research and investment thresholds can be related to market sizes. The benefits of infrastructural investments can be calculated at national level, rather than necessarily regarding infrastructural investment (such as the highly-acclaimed US ARPANET research communications network) as needing to generate short-run returns.

In realising these types of benefit, Japan and the USA have had additional advantages in that their IT policies are designed and implemented at a bureaucratic, rather than a governmental, level. This increases the continuity of policy between successive governments, in contrast to the "stop-go" environment of Europe. It also underscores the importance of bureaucratic symbiosis: there is consistency in the group of individuals who formulate policy on both sides of the boundary between industry and state bureaucracy.

These arguments would be applicable to most industries and to most industry policy. However, the particular case of IT imposes a further reason for formulating a strategy: convergence between the information technologies themselves. It is no longer sensible (if, indeed, it ever was) to treat individual branches of electronics as separate entities. Everything is now connected to everything else. Thus, telecommunications involves setting standards which foster or constrain computing and consumer electronics. Computing stretches from consumer electronics to defence. Strength in components can only be established on the basis of national strength in systems industries, such as computers, and so on. Changes at one point in the electronics industry enable or constrain changes elsewhere. These can be difficult to predict or to take into account without consultation and strategy analysis.

The most essential prerequisite for the formulation of an IT policy strategy is that it be seen as *legitimate* to do so. In many countries, this condition is only partly satisfied (Table 26). US interventions are legitimated by their "national security" role and as responses to government interventions abroad. Since the *Meiji* restoration in 1869, when Japan chose a path of accelerated economic development to ward off the risk of being colonised, the state has been seen as having a proper role to play in the economic development of the "nation-family", justifying a major role in industry. In contrast, in the European Community, the Commission has not so far been able to undertake a fully fledged IT industrial policy. It may be argued, however, that in the management of the ESPRIT and RACE initiatives, which are formally precompetitive R&D, the Commission has gone some way towards creating a strategic industrial approach in this sector.

Among medium-sized countries, France has a long tradition of state involvement in industrial planning while in Germany and the UK the role of the state is traditionally more limited. Industrial interventions are undertaken *ad hoc*, in practice, and the high prestige of

Table 26. **Legitimacy of government intervention in IT**

	Bases for legitimacy
USA	Military needs seen as supra-economic
	"Unfair" foreign government policies require US response
Japan	The state's responsibilities include economic development of the "national family"
UK	Varies. Major economic interventions now largely seen as illegitimate, but the state has a role to play in high-prestige science and technology
France	Strong role for the state through traditions of "dirigisme" and indicative planning
F.R. of Germany	Intervention is generally agreed to be illegitimate in principle, but is pragmatically undertaken in practice
Belgium	Varies. Intervention more acceptable on a regional than on a national basis
Canada	None
Netherlands	"Scandinavian" attitude: the state has a large role to play, but the limits of the role are contested
Switzerland	None

Source: Arnold, 1987.

science makes scientific and technological (as opposed to industrial) interventions relatively uncontentious.

The legitimacy of government intervention in the IT industry varies greatly among small countries. In Switzerland and Canada (both of which have experienced failed interventions in the past), intervention is seen as improper. The preferred mode of action is through education. In Holland and Belgium (especially at the regional level within Belgium), the state is seen as having a larger role to play.

Intervention in IT can reach one of several stages. The first step along the interventionist path involves blanket support; if measures must, reluctantly, be taken, they should at least be even-handed. Where there are several industrial actors, it is politically difficult to justify favouring some over others. Hence, support tends to be offered to all comers or, at the very least, all must be entitled to enter a competition for support. This is the worst of all possible worlds, making it hard to pursue policies which *develop* industrial capability over time. Blanket measures suppress signals about firm conduct and performance. The good, the bad and the downright ugly all receive their share of cake. As a result, the bad survive longer than they should and the good are underfed.

Military funding has the advantage that it can be more selective. Since its ostensible purpose is not economic there is fewer worries about distorting competition. Hence, military suppliers are nurtured over long periods of time, nursed from contract to contract and technology to technology in pursuit of a goal which is above reproach: national defence. This is the American Way. To some degree, it is also the British and French way, but with the difference that in Europe it is often more technologically defensive than aggressive.

Japanese traditions allow a broader range of interventionist measures than US ideology. A key benefit this brings is the idea that civil policy can properly be *selective* in offering support to industry. Thus, both US and Japanese IT policy involves strategic targeting – not only of specific industries, but also of particular firms. They imply that rather than seeing national strategy as tied up with nation-state-level actions there is a need to consider the *company* level more closely. In Europe, by contrast, Alvey and ESPRIT set out strategies and announced a competition, which everyone inside the appropriate border was entitled to enter.

Japanese strategy formulation is self-conscious and delicate. Relatively little money is spent on focused actions, but the process of deciding what the strategic priorities are and how to spend the money is enormously important. At its widest, this involves using the process of formulating "visions". More narrowly, it involves intensive consultation and extensive market research before embarking on new policy initiatives. Less information is suppressed by government in the process of taking decisions in Japan than elsewhere. As far as possible, government tries to hear what "the market" has to say. Once consensus is reached, the act of publishing policy reduces uncertainty in industry; there is agreement about the broad outlines of the future. Companies can act, knowing that they act on the best available information and believing that they know the dimensions of the canvas upon which they are to draw. The *feeling* of stepping into a future that is at least partly known is very important in permitting R&D resources to be allocated and in permitting bold investments to be made. The consensus mechanism reduces *perceived* risk, and not necessarily *objective* risk. As Keynes observed, investment is to do with "animal spirits" not sober calculation of risk (1936). But firms' willingness to invest on the basis of reduced perceived risk helps to make their investment assumptions into self-fulfilling prophecies.

Smaller developed countries have often to struggle with the problem that in several technologies they have only one company worth supporting. The need to strengthen what is, on the national level, already a monopoly (and therefore a "bad thing" in conventional economic terms and in national anti-trust law) runs against the grain.

197

A major weakness in the debates to date about the relative importance of science and technology and of push and pull in the innovation process has been that the problem has been analysed in a *static* framework. Observers outside the US have tended to view military funding of new technologies in the USA as a highly successful industrial policy. However, debates over military funding tend to become bogged down in the question "Is military funding good for industry?" at rather too simple a level. The examples of the Strategic Computer Programme (SCP – concerned with artificial intelligence) and the Very High Speed Integrated Circuit Program (VHSIC – concerned to reorient US microelectronics and systems houses towards military needs for electronic components, now that civilian needs form the greater part of demand) relate to rather different industrial situations and to very different points in the "life cycle" of, respectively, the artificial intelligence and the microelectronics industries. In principle, the SCP is analogous to the Minuteman and Apollo interventions in the nascent semiconductor industry of the 1960s than to VHSIC, which attempts intervention in a mature industry. European military interventions tend to cluster later in the product cycle than those of the USA.

Early in the life of a technology, a substantial intervention like SCP or the Minuteman programme dominates the pattern of development. It swamps other research and forces technology along particular paths of development. (For example, Noble in 1979, claims that USAF funding of computer numerically controlled machine-tool technology promoted digital program control, rather than the alternative "record-playback" technology where a skilled worker's actions are recorded and used to control production.) Later in the life cycle, technological paradigms have become entrenched. Tradition, practice, established market characteristics, user behaviour and the combination of research paths which have been chosen or ignored in the past conspire to impede intervention. Thus, while the Very High Speed Integrated Circuit Programme (VHSIC) represents only a minor diversion, it is not clear that the $1 billion entailed (about five times the originally planned expenditure) has had much effect. It may be a better bet that it has somewhat speeded the industry along its existing course.

Table 24 indicates the stage of the relevant life cycle at which IT policy interventions are focused. (For the purpose of the table, the life-cycle stages are described as: 1 – innovation; 2 – imitation; 3 – maturity and stabilisation; 4 – decline and new product substitution.) Some US military programmes (such as VHSIC) have tried to influence the latter stages – arguably with limited success. New, AI-related interventions stress the early stages. Japanese "catch-up" programmes have not needed to involve measures on both the supply and the demand sides. Demand demonstrably existed already because Japanese policy and industry were operating within *existing* markets. There were successful firms and countries with which Japan strove to catch up. Selective intervention to favour Japanese over other suppliers was, on the other hand, very much a feature of Japanese policies ranging from computer procurement to trade policy and establishing corporations such as JECC, whose role was to offer Japanese-made computers on a leased basis. Actions on the demand side are beginning to become more important as Japan moves from imitation to innovation. Several projects are underway which explore the opportunities for new telecommunications products and try to measure characteristics of demand.

The medium and small countries' interventions are harder to classify. Most operate at a mixture of stages, reflecting both uncertainty about whether the proper national role is catch-up or innovation and the difficulties of reaching the technological frontier. UK and EEC policies are firmly in the "technology push" mould. Neither Alvey nor ESPRIT addresses the conditions on the demand side which would be necessary if they were concerned with trying to take technological leadership. In so far as they actually relate to "catch-up" activities in existing markets, this poses no problems beyond the need to find ways to manipulate the rules of competition in the favour of the assisted firms, but to the extent that parts of these programmes attempt radical innovations the absence of demand-side actions could be problematic.

The point in the industry life cycle at which intervention is attempted affects the likelihood of success and the types of intervention which are appropriate. Intervention is more expensive late in the cycle, because the character of an established industrial and technological structure has to be altered. Intervention to *create* a technology and an industry is cheaper, but requires coupling between supply and demand sides. It is inherently risky because of the need for an eventual transition between policy-created and market-led demand. "Catch-up" is the easiest form of intervention in the sense that the coupling with the demand side is automatic and policy can operate within an existing technological paradigm which is known to be successful.

4. Conclusions

The economic importance of electronics in the present stage of economic development has made it a central concern for policymakers promoting industrial restructuring from the declining sectors to new "high-technology" branches. The perceived policy challenge of the Japanese Fifth Generation project has led to a broad range of responses, most of which have not shared that project's focus on AI. The creation of "meta-firms" for basic or "pre-competitive" R&D has been a significant innovation which may alter the characteristics of industrial competition and structure, just as the invention of the industrial R&D laboratory did a century ago.

Policymakers' ability to promote industrial restructuring, and the policy tools at their disposal, vary – partly as a function of the perceived *legitimacy* of government intervention. Their strategies need to *couple* interventions and events on the supply and demand sides and to involve a realistic view of the opportunities for intervention at different stages of industry life cycles. Close liaison between relatively stable groups of policy makers and industrialists over a period of time helps to allow state intervention to *develop* industrial capability and leadership. The relative lack of success of IT policies in some countries is associated with less stable industry-government relations and less comprehensive policy analysis.

The major policy opportunity provided by the present stage of convergence within the information technologies is to break the bandwidth bottleneck of existing telecommunications networks, so as to enable a new spurt of IT-based growth. Recent policy efforts focusing on supply- and demand-side actions have provided many important ingredients for this next growth stage, not the least of which is growing technological capability on both sides. Those countries moving swiftly to IBM appear likely to attain significant competitive advantages within the IT industries and in that major part of the IT-using economy for which telecommunications plays a significant part in competitiveness. The need to go beyond the abilities of most markets to cope – the level of investment required is very high, and the pay-off will not be immediate. This provides an almost classical case for intervention, where government takes on the role of *enabling* economic growth to occur.

BIBLIOGRAPHY

Abernathy, W.J. and Utterback, J.M., "Patterns of Industrial Innovation", *Technology Review*, Vol. 80, 1978.

Arnold, E. and Senker, P., *Designing the Future - The Implications and Skills in the British Engineering Industry*, Occasional Paper No. 9, Watford, Engineering Industry Training Board, 1982.

Arnold, E., *Computer-Aided Design in Europe*, Sussex European Papers No. 14, Brighton, Sussex European Research Centre, 1984.

Arnold, E. and Guy, K., *Parallel Convergence: National Strategies in Information Technology*, London, Frances Pinter, 1986.

Arnold, E., "Some lessons from government information technology policies", Technovation, Vol. 5, 1987, pp. 247-268.

Arnold, E., *A Review of the Alvey Intelligent Knowledge-Based Systems Programme*, 1987.

Barrow, I. and Curnow, R., *The Future with Microelectronics*, London, Frances Pinter, 1978.

Borrus, M., Bar, F., Cogez, P., Thoresen, A.B., Warde, I. and Yoshikawa, A., *Telecommunications Development in Comparative Perspective: The New Telecommunications In Europe, Japan and the US*, (mimeo), Berkeley Roundtable on the International Economy, University of California at Berkeley, May 1985.

Brady, T. and Senker, P., *Maintenance Skills in the Engineering Industry: The Influence of Technological Change*, Occasional Paper No. 8, Watford, Engineering Industry Training Board, 1982.

Braverman, H., *Labour and Monopoly Capital*, New York, Monthly Review Press, 1974.

Braun, E. and Senker, P., *New Technology and Employment*, London, Manpower Services Commission, 1982.

Committee on Assessment of the DoD Very High Speed Integrated Circuits Program, *An Assessment of the Impact of the Department of Defense Very High Speed Integrated Circuits Program*, Washington DC, National Materials Advisory Board, Commission on Sociotechnical Systems, National Research Council, Publication NMAB-382, National Academy Press, 1982.

Coombs, R.W., "Innovation, automation and the long-wave theory", *Futures*, Vol. 13, No 4, pp. 308-322.

English, M. and Watson-Brown, A., "National Policies in Information Technology: Challenges and Responses", *Oxford Surveys in Information Technology*, Vol. 1, 1984, pp. 55-128.

Freeman, C. and Soete, L., *Information Technology and Employment: An Assessment*, Science Policy Research Unit, University of Sussex, 1985.

Freeman, C., Clark, J. and Soete, L., *Unemployment and Technical Innovation: A Study of Long Waves and Economic Development*, London, Frances Pinter, 1982.

Gershuny, J., *Special Innovation and the Division of Labour*, Oxford University Press, 1983.

Guy, K. and Arnold, E., *An Overview of Policy Initiatives in the United States' Information Technology Sector*, paper prepared for the Science, Technology and Industry Directorate of the Organisation for Economic Co-operation and Development, Brighton, Science Policy Research Unit, University of Sussex, March 1987.

Illinois Institute of Technology, *Technology in Retrospect and Critical Events in Science (Project TRACES)*, NSF-0535, Washington DC, 1968.

Kaplinsky, R., *Automation: The Technology and Society*, Harlow, Essex, Longman, 1984.

Kraft, P., *Programmers and Managers: The Routinisation of Computer Programming in the United States*, New York, Springer Verlag, 1977.

McLean, J.M. and Rush, H.J., *The Impact of Microelectronics on the UK: A Suggested Classification and Illustrative Case Studies*, Occasional Paper No. 7, Brighton: Science Policy Research Unit, 1978.

Mensch, G., *Stalemate in Technology*, Cambridge, Mass., Ballinger, 1979.

Miles, I., *Work in Information Society*, (A Report to the Joseph Rowntree Memorial Trust), Brighton, Science Policy Research Unit, University of Sussex, 1987.

Mowery, D. and Rosenberg, N., "The Influence of Market Demand Upon Innovation: A Critical Review of Some Recent Empirical Studies", *Research Policy*, 8, 1979.

National Economic Development Office, Information Technology Economic Development Committee, Long-Term Perspectives Group, *IT Futures...IT Can Work: An Optimistic View of the Long-term potential of Information Technology for Britain*, London, Nedo Books, 1987.

Nobel, D., "Social Choice in Machine Design: The Case of Automatically Programmed Machine Tools", in Andrew Zimbalist (ed.), *Case Studies on the Labour Process*, New York, Monthly Review Press, 1979.

Organisation for Economic Cooperation and Development, Committee for Information, Computer and Communications Policy, "Information and Communications Technologies for Economic Development", (Note by the Secretariat), ICCP/HLM(87)3, Paris, 12 March 1987.

Okimoto, D.I. and Hayase, H.K., "Organisation for Innovation: NTT Central Research Laboratories and NTT Family Firms", (mimeo), Stanford University, 1985.

OTA (Office of Technology Assessment), *Information Technology R&D: Critical Trends and Issues*, Washington DC, US Congress, Office of Technology Assessment, OTA-CIT-268, 1985.

Pavitt, K. (ed), *Technological Innovation and British Economic Performance*, London, Macmillan, 1980.

Rothwell, R., Freeman, C., Jervis, P., Horsley, A., Robertson, A.B., Townsend, J., "SAPPHO Updated: Project SAPPHO Phase II", *Research Policy*, Vol. 13, No. 3, 1974.

Rothwell, R. and Zegveld, W., *Innovation and the Small and Medium-sized Firm*, London, Frances Pinter, 1982.

Rothwell, R. and Zegveld, W., *Reindustrialisation and Technology*, London, Longman, 1985.

Schumpeter, J. A., "The instability of capitalism", *Economic Journal*, Vol. 32, 1928, pp. 361-386.

Schumpeter, J.A., *Capitalism, Socialism and Democracy*, (2nd edn.), New York, Harper and Row, 1947.

Schumpeter, J.A., *The Theory of Economic Development: An Inquiry into Profits, Capital, Credit, Interest and the Business Cycle*, transl. Rivers Opie, London, Oxford University Press, 1961.

Sigurdson, J., *Industry and State Partnership in Japan: The Very Large Scale Integrated Circuits (VLSI) Project*, Discussion Paper No 168, Lund, Sweden, Research Policy Institute, 1986.

Skolka, J., "Long-term effects of unbalanced labour productivity growth", in Solari and Pasquier (eds), *Private and Enlarged Consumption*, Amsterdam, North-Holland, 1976.

Soete, L., *Technological Trends and Employment Vol 3: Electronics and Communication*, Aldershot, Gower, 1985.

SPRU-IRG (Science Policy Research Unit, University of Sussex – Innovation Research Group, Brighton Polytechnic: Ian Miles, Howard Rush, Ken Guy, John Bessant), *New IT Products and Services – Technological Potential and "Push"*, Report to the Long-term Perspectives Group, Information Technology Economic Development Committee, National Economic Development Office (mimeo), Brighton, University of Sussex/Brighton Polytechnic, 1985.

SPRU Women and Technology Studies, *Microelectronics and Women's Employment in Britain*, Occasional Paper No. 17, Brighton, Science Policy Research Unit, University of Sussex, 1982.

SPRU, (forthcoming), *Interim Report on the Evaluation of the Alvey Programme*(title to be determined).

Stankiewitz, R., "The Place of Basic Technologies in the R&D Policies of the Small Industrialised Countries", in (eds) P.H. Kristensen and R. Stankiewitz, *Technology Policy and Industrial Development in Scandinavia*, Proceedings of a workshop held in Copenhagen, May 1981, Lund, Sweden, Research Policy Institute, 1982.

Stewart, T., "How to design a workable system", *Word Processing Now*, Business Systems and Equipment/McLean Hunter Ltd, London, July 1979.

Stonier, T., *The Wealth of Information: A Profile of the Post-Industrial Economy*, London, Thames Methuen, 1983.

Swords-Isherwood, N. and Senker, P. (eds), *Microelectronics and the Engineering Industry: The Need for Skills*, London, Frances Pinter, 1980.

von Hippel, E., "Users as Innovators", *Technology Review*, Vol. 80, No. 3, 1978.

Wasson, C. L., "How predictable are fashion and other life cycles?", *Journal of Marketing*, Vol. 32, 1968, pp. 36-43.

Weizenbaum, J., *Computer Power and Human Reason: From Judgement to Calculation*, (Freeman, 1976), Middlesex, Harmondsworth, Penguin, 1984.

WHERE TO OBTAIN OECD PUBLICATIONS
OÙ OBTENIR LES PUBLICATIONS DE L'OCDE

ARGENTINA - ARGENTINE
Carlos Hirsch S.R.L.,
Florida 165, 4° Piso,
(Galeria Guemes) 1333 Buenos Aires
Tel. 33.1787.2391 y 30.7122

AUSTRALIA - AUSTRALIE
D.A. Book (Aust.) Pty. Ltd.
11-13 Station Street (P.O. Box 163)
Mitcham, Vic. 3132   Tel. (03) 873 4411

AUSTRIA - AUTRICHE
OECD Publications and Information Centre,
4 Simrockstrasse,
5300 Bonn (Germany)   Tel. (0228) 21.60.45
Gerold & Co., Graben 31, Wien 1 Tel. 52.22.35

BELGIUM - BELGIQUE
Jean de Lannoy,
Avenue du Roi 202
B-1060 Bruxelles   Tel. (02) 538.51.69

CANADA
Renouf Publishing Company Ltd
1294 Algoma Road, Ottawa, Ont. K1B 3W8
Tel: (613) 741-4333
Stores:
61 rue Sparks St., Ottawa, Ont. K1P 5R1
Tel: (613) 238-8985
211 rue Yonge St., Toronto, Ont. M5B 1M4
Tel: (416) 363-3171
Federal Publications Inc.,
301-303 King St. W.,
Toronto, Ont. M5V 1J5   Tel. (416)581-1552
Les Éditions la Liberté inc.,
3020 Chemin Sainte-Foy,
Sainte-Foy, P.Q. G1X 3V6,   Tel. (418)658-3763

DENMARK - DANEMARK
Munksgaard Export and Subscription Service
35, Nørre Søgade, DK-1370 København K
Tel. +45.1.12.85.70

FINLAND - FINLANDE
Akateeminen Kirjakauppa,
Keskuskatu 1, 00100 Helsinki 10   Tel. 0.12141

FRANCE
OCDE/OECD
Mail Orders/Commandes par correspondance :
2, rue André-Pascal,
75775 Paris Cedex 16   Tel. (1) 45.24.82.00
Bookshop/Librairie : 33, rue Octave-Feuillet
75016 Paris
Tel. (1) 45.24.81.67 or/ou (1) 45.24.81.81
Librairie de l'Université,
12a, rue Nazareth,
13602 Aix-en-Provence   Tel. 42.26.18.08

GERMANY - ALLEMAGNE
OECD Publications and Information Centre,
4 Simrockstrasse,
5300 Bonn   Tel. (0228) 21.60.45

GREECE - GRÈCE
Librairie Kauffmann,
28, rue du Stade, 105 64 Athens Tel. 322.21.60

HONG KONG
Government Information Services,
Publications (Sales) Office,
Information Services Department
No. 1, Battery Path, Central

ICELAND - ISLANDE
Snæbjörn Jónsson & Co., h.f.,
Hafnarstræti 4 & 9,
P.O.B. 1131 – Reykjavik
Tel. 13133/14281/11936

INDIA - INDE
Oxford Book and Stationery Co.,
Scindia House, New Delhi 110001
Tel. 331.5896/5308
17 Park St., Calcutta 700016   Tel. 240832

INDONESIA - INDONÉSIE
Pdii-Lipi, P.O. Box 3065/JKT.Jakarta
Tel. 583467

IRELAND - IRLANDE
TDC Publishers - Library Suppliers,
12 North Frederick Street, Dublin 1
Tel. 744835-749677

ITALY - ITALIE
Libreria Commissionaria Sansoni,
Via Benedetto Fortini 120/10,
Casella Post. 552
50125 Firenze   Tel. 055/645415
Via Bartolini 29, 20155 Milano   Tel. 365083
La diffusione delle pubblicazioni OCSE viene
assicurata dalle principali librerie ed anche da :
Editrice e Libreria Herder,
Piazza Montecitorio 120, 00186 Roma
Tel. 6794628
Libreria Hœpli,
Via Hœpli 5, 20121 Milano   Tel. 865446
Libreria Scientifica
Dott. Lucio de Biasio "Aeiou"
Via Meravigli 16, 20123 Milano   Tel. 807679

JAPAN - JAPON
OECD Publications and Information Centre,
Landic Akasaka Bldg., 2-3-4 Akasaka,
Minato-ku, Tokyo 107   Tel. 586.2016

KOREA - CORÉE
Kyobo Book Centre Co. Ltd.
P.O.Box: Kwang Hwa Moon 1658,
Seoul   Tel. (REP) 730.78.91

LEBANON - LIBAN
Documenta Scientifica/Redico,
Edison Building, Bliss St.,
P.O.B. 5641, Beirut   Tel. 354429-344425

MALAYSIA/SINGAPORE -
MALAISIE/SINGAPOUR
University of Malaya Co-operative Bookshop
Ltd.,
7 Lrg 51A/227A, Petaling Jaya
Malaysia   Tel. 7565000/7565425
Information Publications Pte Ltd
Pei-Fu Industrial Building,
24 New Industrial Road No. 02-06
Singapore 1953   Tel. 2831786, 2831798

NETHERLANDS - PAYS-BAS
SDU Uitgeverij
Christoffel Plantijnstraat 2
Postbus 20014
2500 EA's-Gravenhage   Tel. 070-789911
Voor bestellingen: Tel. 070-789880

NEW ZEALAND - NOUVELLE-ZÉLANDE
Government Printing Office Bookshops:
Auckland: Retail Bookshop, 25 Rutland Stseet,
Mail Orders, 85 Beach Road
Private Bag C.P.O.
Hamilton: Retail: Ward Street,
Mail Orders, P.O. Box 857
Wellington: Retail, Mulgrave Street, (Head
Office)
Cubacade World Trade Centre,
Mail Orders, Private Bag
Christchurch: Retail, 159 Hereford Street,
Mail Orders, Private Bag
Dunedin: Retail, Princes Street,
Mail Orders, P.O. Box 1104

NORWAY - NORVÈGE
Narvesen Info Center – NIC,
Bertrand Narvesens vei 2,
P.O.B. 6125 Etterstad, 0602 Oslo 6
Tel. (02) 67.83.10, (02) 68.40.20

PAKISTAN
Mirza Book Agency
65 Shahrah Quaid-E-Azam, Lahore 3 Tel. 66839

PHILIPPINES
I.J. Sagun Enterprises, Inc.
P.O. Box 4322 CPO Manila
Tel. 695-1946, 922-9495

PORTUGAL
Livraria Portugal, Rua do Carmo 70-74,
1117 Lisboa Codex   Tel. 360582/3

SINGAPORE/MALAYSIA -
SINGAPOUR/MALAISIE
See "Malaysia/Singapor". Voir
« Malaisie/Singapour »

SPAIN - ESPAGNE
Mundi-Prensa Libros, S.A.,
Castelló 37, Apartado 1223, Madrid-28001
Tel. 431.33.99
Libreria Bosch, Ronda Universidad 11,
Barcelona 7   Tel. 317.53.08/317.53.58

SWEDEN - SUÈDE
AB CE Fritzes Kungl. Hovbokhandel,
Box 16356, S 103 27 STH,
Regeringsgatan 12,
DS Stockholm   Tel. (08) 23.89.00
Subscription Agency/Abonnements:
Wennergren-Williams AB,
Box 30004, S104 25 Stockholm Tel. (08)54.12.00

SWITZERLAND - SUISSE
OECD Publications and Information Centre,
4 Simrockstrasse,
5300 Bonn (Germany)   Tel. (0228) 21.60.45
Librairie Payot,
6 rue Grenus, 1211 Genève 11
Tel. (022) 31.89.50
Maditec S.A.
Ch. des Palettes 4
1020 – Renens/Lausanne   Tel. (021) 635.08.65
United Nations Bookshop/Librairie des Nations-
Unies
Palais des Nations, 1211 – Geneva 10
Tel. 022-34-60-11 (ext. 48 72)

TAIWAN - FORMOSE
Good Faith Worldwide Int'l Co., Ltd.
9th floor, No. 118, Sec.2, Chung Hsiao E. Road
Taipei   Tel. 391.7396/391.7397

THAILAND - THAILANDE
Suksit Siam Co., Ltd., 1715 Rama IV Rd.,
Samyam Bangkok 5   Tel. 2511630

INDEX Book Promotion & Service Ltd.
59/6 Soi Lang Suan, Ploenchit Road
Patjumamwan, Bangkok 10500
Tel. 250-1919, 252-1066

TURKEY - TURQUIE
Kültur Yayinlari Is-Türk Ltd. Sti.
Atatürk Bulvari No: 191/Kat. 21
Kavaklidere/Ankara   Tel. 25.07.60
Dolmabahce Cad. No: 29
Besiktas/Istanbul   Tel. 160.71.88

UNITED KINGDOM - ROYAUME-UNI
H.M. Stationery Office,
Postal orders only: (01)873-8483
P.O.B. 276, London SW8 5DT
Telephone orders: (01) 873-9090, or
Personal callers:
49 High Holborn, London WC1V 6HB
Branches at: Belfast, Birmingham,
Bristol, Edinburgh, Manchester

UNITED STATES - ÉTATS-UNIS
OECD Publications and Information Centre,
2001 L Street, N.W., Suite 700,
Washington, D.C. 20036 - 4095
Tel. (202) 785.6323

VENEZUELA
Libreria del Este,
Avda F. Miranda 52, Aptdo. 60337,
Edificio Galipan, Caracas 106
Tel. 951.17.05/951.23.07/951.12.97

YUGOSLAVIA - YOUGOSLAVIE
Jugoslovenska Knjiga, Knez Mihajlova 2,
P.O.B. 36, Beograd   Tel. 621.992

Orders and inquiries from countries where
Distributors have not yet been appointed should be
sent to:
OECD, Publications Service, 2, rue André-Pascal,
75775 PARIS CEDEX 16.

Les commandes provenant de pays où l'OCDE n'a
pas encore désigné de distributeur doivent être
adressées à :
OCDE, Service des Publications. 2, rue André-
Pascal, 75775 PARIS CEDEX 16.

72380-1-1989

OECD PUBLICATIONS, 2, rue André-Pascal, 75775 PARIS CEDEX 16 - No. 44417 1988
PRINTED IN FRANCE
(93 88 05 1) ISBN 92-64-13102-7